FAITH, FEMINISM,
and the FORUM OF SCRIPTURE

FAITH, FEMINISM, *and the* FORUM OF SCRIPTURE

Essays on Biblical Theology and Hermeneutics

Phyllis A. Bird

CASCADE *Books* • Eugene, Oregon

FATH, FEMINISM, AND THE FORUM OF SCRIPTURE
Essays on Biblical Theology and Hermeneutics

Copyright © 2015 Phyllis A. Bird. All rights reserved. Except for brief quotations in critical publications or reviews, no part of this book may be reproduced in any manner without prior written permission from the publisher. Write: Permissions, Wipf and Stock Publishers, 199 W. 8th Ave., Suite 3, Eugene, OR 97401.

Cascade Books
An imprint of Wipf and Stock Publishers
199 W. 8th Ave., Suite 3
Eugene, OR 97401

www.wipfandstock.com

ISBN: 978-1-4982-2149-8

Cataloging-in-Publication data:

Bird, Phyllis A. (Phyllis Ann), 1934–

Faith, feminism, and the forum of scripture : essays on biblical theology and hermeneutics / Phyllis A. Bird.

xvi + 174 p. ; 23 cm. Includes bibliographical references.

ISBN: 978-1-4982-2149-8

1. Bible. O.T.—Criticism, interpretation, etc. 2. Bible. O.T.—Feminist criticism. 3. Bible—Theology. 4. Bible—Hermeneutics. I. Title.

BS1199 W7 B57 2015

Manufactured in the U.S.A.

Author Bible translations are based on the New Revised Standard Version (NRSV), © 1989, Division of Christian Education of the National Council of Churches of Christ in the United States of America, with minor modifications by the author to emphasize features of the Hebrew text. Translations from the New Revised Standard Version are marked (NRSV).

Contents

Preface / vii

Acknowledgments / xiii

Abbreviations / xiv

1. Old Testament Theology and the God of the Fathers: Reflections on Biblical Theology from a North American Feminist Perspective / 1

2. Theological Anthropology in the Hebrew Bible / 45

3. The Authority of the Bible / 67

4. The Bible in Christian Ethical Deliberation Concerning Homosexuality: Old Testament Contributions / 127

Bibliography / 163

Preface

The essays in this volume were written at different times for different audiences on different topics, but all share a common interest in the theology of the Hebrew Bible—as articulated by its ancient authors and redactors, and as apprehended by contemporary readers. Three themes in this collection are highlighted in the title: faith, feminism, and the forum of Scripture. "Faith" and "feminism" represent perspectives and commitments that I bring to the subjects of the individual essays.[1] "Forum" describes a feature of the biblical text as I understand it. It identifies the Bible as a site of debate, where readers overhear the conversations of an ancient community and are drawn into its debate to continue it in their own time and place. This understanding involves an historical-critical approach to the text that sets the biblical writings in the social and religious contexts of their origins, enabling dialogue with the text that honors the integrity of the ancient writers and the "cross-cultural" nature of the encounter. It also rests on literary criticism, which reveals the distinct voices in the text.

The features accented here play a role in all of my work,[2] but they receive focused attention in these essays—in relation to questions of Biblical Theology (as a discipline), theological anthropology, the authority of the Bible, and sexual ethics. Each essay is independent and may be read in

---

1. All the essays resulted from invitations to contribute to colloquia or publications on assigned subjects.

2. They are rooted in my history, where faith came first, formed in a Christian family of deep social consciousness and fed by a love of the Bible awakened by encounter with the Old Testament prophets. Historical criticism came next, opening the biblical texts to the world of their origins and refocusing my first academic love (sociology and anthropology) on ancient Israel. Feminism came last, as a movement that breached my consciousness only as I assumed my first teaching position. In feminism, a heritage of social consciousness, galvanized by the civil rights movement, found new expression.

any order, but the first two as presently arranged are concerned primarily with issues of historical theology and the last two with hermeneutics.

Chapter 1, "Old Testament Theology and the God of the Fathers," gives specific attention to feminist interests and historical criticism in considering the future of Biblical Theology in OT/HB[3] studies. It also focuses on North America as the context in which these relationships are explored, inquiring about the aims and audience of Biblical Theology today in a context whose academic and ecclesial configuration is radically different from that in which it originated. The genesis of this essay was an invitation to contribute to the colloquium "Biblische Theologie" in the symposium commemorating the 100th birthday of the German Old Testament scholar Gerhard von Rad.[4] The assignment to this colloquium surprised me, since I had written nothing on biblical theology, at least not as generally recognized. I accepted it as an incentive to explore a field of OT/HB scholarship that had been largely neglected in my studies. My attempts to understand that neglect, and assess the role of the subject in the milieu in which I had been trained and in which I taught, led me to focus on the needs and constraints of America's dual system of biblical education (secular universities and schools of theology), and on feminist views of biblical theology and Hebrew Bible more generally.

The result is a reassessment of the aims and audience of Old Testament Theology and a proposal for a theology informed by feminist sensibility, but not a "Feminist Old Testament Theology." My approach in this essay is heavily indebted to the work of Phyllis Trible, the sole female author included in the two anthologies of Old Testament Theology published by Ben Ollenburger in 1985 and 2004.[5] In attempting to formulate an alternative approach, I maintain the necessity of an historical dimen-

---

3. Throughout this volume the terms *Old Testament* (*OT*) and *Hebrew Bible* (*HB*) are used in various combinations and concentrations to refer to the Hebrew (and Aramaic) writings traditionally known by Christians as the Old Testament. Usage depends largely on context and the conventions of publishers and editors. *OT* is generally employed in theological contexts and references to historical Christian usage, while *HB* has become the dominant ecumenical and academic usage and is generally employed in these essays in historical references to the writings of ancient Israel. On the problems of *Hebrew Bible* as used in many churches, see chapter 3, n. 16.

4. The symposium under the title Das Alte Testament und die Kultur der Moderne was held at the University of Heidelberg, 18–21 October 2001. This essay, with the subtitle "Reflections on Biblical Theology from a North American Feminist Perspective," was published in the proceedings of the colloquium in Hanson et al., eds., *Biblische Theologie*, 69–107.

5. Ollenburger, *Old Testament Theology*; and Ollenburger, *Flowering*, respectively.

sion and consider ways of incorporating gender sensitivity into a wider range of texts and topics than commonly considered.

Chapter 2, "Theological Anthropology in the Hebrew Bible," is an example of historical theology that aims to describe the theological understanding of the human and humankind presented in the Hebrew Scriptures—without consideration of contemporary implications or judgment concerning the "truth" of its views.[6] But the language in which the subject is formulated is that of Christian theology, and the editor's request for a focus on the *imago dei* of Genesis 1:26–27 reflects the dominant role of this text and term in Christian theology and anthropology, beginning with the New Testament. As all historical writing, this essay reflects my own standpoint and interests, as well as the editor's, even as it attempts to represent the views of the biblical writers. My interests are registered particularly in attention to the role of gender in the understanding of the human, and in an attempt to broaden the textual basis on which a theological anthropology is based.

Thus the *imago* text of Gen 1:26–27 is set in its OT context, literarily and historically, compared with the narrative of Gen 2:4b—3:24, and connected to the reappearance, and variation, of its distinctive formula in Gen 5:1–3 and 9:1. Attention is given to the account of disobedience in the Garden, the question of mortality and sin, and the significance of gender distinction in both creation accounts. All of these questions are considered against the ancient Near Eastern sources that supplied key ingredients in the biblical formulations and transformations. In addition to the creation texts of Genesis, the witness of historical narrative, laws, exhortations, psalms, and wisdom literature is invoked as essential to the biblical understanding of the human, in relation to God and to the rest of creation. As a work of descriptive historical theology this essay provides a biblical source and stimulus for reflection on the same questions today in the light of contemporary experience.

Chapter 3, "The Authority of the Bible," is concerned with theological speculation and doctrine *about* the Bible as a source of knowledge about God and a vehicle for communication from, and to, God. It is written from a standpoint within the Christian community, as the work of a biblical scholar concerned with the use of the Bible in the church's preaching and teaching, addressed to an audience of pastors and

---

6. The article was written for *The Blackwell Companion to the Hebrew Bible*, Leo Purdue, ed., a volume designed for a broad audience of students, scholars, and the general public.

theology students.[7] It is also written with a specifically feminist motive. False, or inadequate, notions of biblical authority have led many, if not most, feminist theologians and biblical scholars to reject the concept of authority altogether, as inherently coercive and oppressive, particularly as applied to the Hebrew Bible with its patriarchal norms. This article responds to the feminist challenge, as well as challenges from other quarters, by tracing the development of modern theories of biblical authority to show how claims of divine origin, infallibility, and inerrancy arose as attempts to defend the Bible against perceived threats from new sources of knowledge about the world and its inhabitants.

More fundamentally, however, it examines the concept of authority, and its application to the Bible. It emphasizes the relational nature of authority, which is not effected by assertion alone, but requires acknowledgment. It recognizes that authority is contextual, relative to particular situations, and argues that it must be conceived in terms appropriate to the nature of its subject and of the relationship. The authority of a book is different from that of a person, and different kinds of writings exercise authority in different ways. The challenge of constructing an understanding of biblical authority that encompasses the Scriptures as a whole, in all of their diversity, is the primary subject of this essay.

Chapter 4, "The Bible in Christian Ethical Deliberation Concerning Homosexuality[8]: Old Testament Contributions," addresses a subject of current debate in American churches, from the perspective of a biblical scholar and a member of a denomination torn by conflict over the issue.[9] The occasion for this essay was a Consultation on Homosexuality and Ethics, organized to engage in debate over the "interpretation of the Bible in relation to the morality of homosexual acts and relationships."[10] It was

7. It was written for the introductory volume of the *NIB* (1:33–64).

8. The inadequacy of this term, which was the language of the time, is discussed in the essay (chapter 4).

9. Although the original occasion for this essay was almost two decades ago and many American churches have welcomed homosexual members, debate continues in many congregations and national religious bodies, including in my own United Methodist denomination, where the Bible is understood to be the key obstacle to full acceptance.

10. The consultation, organized by David Balch under a grant from the Louisville Institute, was held at Brite Divinity School, Texas Christian University, 26–29 September, 1996. This article was originally published in the proceedings of the consultation, edited by Balch under the title *Homosexuality, Science, and the "Plain Sense" of Scripture*, 142–76. The quotation is from ibid., 1.

intended to serve pastors and other church leaders through discussion in which "persons who represent both poles of the discussion presented their interpretations of evangelical and mainline church understandings of science, Old and New Testaments, and theology."[11]

The article begins with a full and fresh analysis of all of the Old Testament texts commonly cited as evidence for views of homosexual practice in ancient Israel and its canonical texts, treating narrative as well as prescriptive texts and augmenting this corpus with comparative evidence from Egypt and Mesopotamia. Although my intentions in this article were pastoral, aiming to address a broad spectrum of church leaders, the need for a full historical-linguistic analysis of the biblical, and extra-biblical, texts required the introduction of technical arguments and terminology not usually found in articles for a general audience. Nevertheless, the article lays out an argument that a general reader can follow and provides an extended section of "conclusions and implications for contemporary use."

This article, as every other article in this volume, led me on a path of exploration and discovery that I would not have undertaken without it. It led me to consider how well-known texts, viewed in their ancient contexts, might point in new directions, and to ask what neglected texts might contribute to an understanding of the issues raised by contemporary experience—which does not fit the categories of the biblical texts cited as examples. The complete absence of any apparent interest in same-sex relationships between women and the language and contexts in which male-male sexual relations are presented in the Hebrew Bible, and records of surrounding cultures, make it clear that the activity is viewed in terms of a patriarchal society's concern for male honor.

The essays are presented here as originally published, with minor stylistic revisions and corrections of errors, but without attempts to update bibliography or engage subsequent arguments. Only where I have changed my mind on a subject have I revised the text to reflect my current understanding, with a note explaining the revision. Despite changing circumstances and subsequent publications on the issues treated

---

11. Ibid. I dislike the "polar" distinction and do not think that the terms "evangelical" and "mainline" adequately characterize the positions represented by the participants. My United Methodist identification places me in the "mainline church" camp, but my forty-year affiliation with Hispanic congregations of that denomination puts me in an "evangelical" environment, and a United Methodist colleague presented an opposing view at the consultation.

here, these essays continue to express my views on the subjects and to invite response.

Acknowledgments

The author and publisher gratefully acknowledge permission to reprint the following articles in this volume:

"Old Testament Theology and the God of the Fathers: Reflections on Biblical Theology from a North American Feminist Perspective" was originally published in *Biblische Theologie: Beiträge des Symposiums "Das Alte Testament und die Kultur der Moderne" anlässlich des 100. Geburtstags Gerhard von Rads (1901-1971) Heidelberg, 18.-21. Oktober 2001*, edited by Bernd Janowski, Michael Welker, and Paul D. Hanson, Altes Testament und Moderne 14 (Münster: Lit, 2005), 69-107, and is used with permission of Lit Verlag.

"Theological Anthropology in the Hebrew Bible" was originally published in *The Blackwell Companion to the Hebrew Bible*, edited by Leo G. Perdue, Blackwell Companions to Religion (Oxford: Blackwell, 2001), 258-75, and is used with permission of Wiley Global Publishers.

"The Authority of the Bible" was originally published in *The New Interpreters Bible*, edited by Leander E. Keck (Nashville: Abingdon Press, 1994), vol. 1, 33-64, and is used by permission of Abingdon Press; all rights reserved.

"The Bible in Christian Ethical Deliberation concerning Homosexuality: Old Testament Contributions" was originally published in *Homosexuality, Science, and the "Plain Sense" of Scripture*, edited by David L. Balch (Grand Rapids: Eerdmans, 2000; reprinted, Eugene, OR: Wipf & Stock, 2007), 142-76, and is used by permission of Wipf and Stock Publishers.

Abbreviations

ABD	*The Anchor Bible Dictionary*. 6 vols. Edited by David Noel Freedman. New York: Doubleday, 1992
ANET	*Ancient Near Eastern Texts Relating to the Old Testament*. 3rd ed. Edited by James B. Pritchard. Princeton: Princeton University Press, 1969
AOAT	Alter Orient und Altes Testament
BDB	Brown, F., S. R. Driver, and C. A. Briggs. *A Hebrew and English Lexicon of the Old Testament*. Oxford: Clarendon, 1907
BN	*Biblische Notizen*
BRev	*Bible Review*
BRM	Babylonian Records in the Library of J. Pierpont Morgan. New Haven 1917–
BWL	*Babylonian Wisdom Literature*. Edited and translated by W. G. Lambert. Oxford: Oxford University Press, 1960
BZAW	Beihefte zur Zeitschrift für die alttestamentliche Wissenschaft
CBQ	*Catholic Biblical Quarterly*
CC	Continental Commentaries
ConBOT	Coniectanea biblica: Old Testament Series

CT	Cuneiform Texts from Babylonian Tablets in the British Museum. London: Trustees of the British Museum, 1896–
HBT	*Horizons in Biblical Theology*
HSM	Harvard Semitic Monographs
HSS	Harvard Semitic Studies
Int	*Interpretation*
JAAR	*Journal of the American Academy of Religion*
JBL	*Journal of Biblical Literature*
JSOT	*Journal for the Study of the Old Testament*
JSOTSup	Journal for the Study of the Old Testament Supplement Series
KAI	*Kanaanäische und aramäische Inschriften.* Herbert Donner and Wolfgang Röllig. Wiesbaden: Harrassowitz, 1964
KAV	O. Schroeder, *Keilschrifttexte aus Assur verschiedenen Inhalts.* Wissenschaftliche Veröffentlichung der deutschen Orient-Gesellschaft 35. Osnabrück: Zeller, 1970
NIB	*The New Interpreters Bible.* Edited by Leander E. Keck. Nashville: Abingdon, 1994–2004
NPNF	*Nicene and Post-Nicene Fathers. First series.* Edited by Philip Schaff. Peabody, MA: Hendrickson, 1944
OBO	Orbis Biblicus et Orientalis
OBT	Overtures to Biblical Theology
OTL	Old Testament Library
PSB	*Princeton Seminary Bulletin*
PTMS	Princeton Theological Monograph Series
QD	Quaestiones Disputatae
RB	*Revue biblique*

RGG	*Religion in Geschichte und Gegenwart*. 4th ed. 9 vols. Edited by Hans Dieter Betz. Tübingen: Mohr/Siebeck, 1998–2007
RLA	*Reallexikon der Assyriology*. Edited by Erich Ebeling et al. Berlin: de Gruyter, 1928–
RSN	*Religious Studies News*
SAA	State Archives of Assyria. Helsinki 1987–
SBL	Society of Biblical Literature
SBLBSNA	Society of Biblical Literature: Biblical Scholarship in North America
SBLSymS	Society of Biblical Literature: Symposium Series
SJT	*Scottish Journal of Theology*
THAT	*Theologisches Handwörterbuch zum Alten Testament*. 2 vols. Edited by Ernst Jenni and Claus Westermann. Munich: Kaiser, 1979
ThTo	*Theology Today*
TS	*Theological Studies*
UF	*Ugarit-Forschungen*
USQR	Union Seminary Quarterly Review
VT	*Vetus Testamentum*
VTSup	Vetus Testamentum Supplements
WBC	Westminster Bible Companion
ZAW	*Zeitschrift für die alttestamentliche Wissenschaft*

1

Old Testament Theology and the God of the Fathers

Reflections on Biblical Theology from a North American Feminist Perspective

INTRODUCTION

The title I provided long before this colloquium[1] was intended to indicate the area of my interest, without binding me unduly—because I had scarcely begun to think about the subject of biblical theology. With the coordinated terms I intended to signal two approaches to the study of the Hebrew Bible whose relationship I wished to explore. In the course of my work, however, I found it necessary to give focused attention to distinctive features of the context from which I approach the subject and hence to questions concerning the nature and function of the discipline and its genre(s) in that context. As a result, my essay has acquired a different shape and emphasis than originally foreseen. Nevertheless, the original title still expresses what for me is the central issue: the Bible's dual identity

---

1. This essay was composed for the colloquium called Biblische Theologie, which took place in Heidelberg on 20 October 2001 as part of the Symposium "Das Alte Testament und die Kultur der Moderne" on the occasion of the one-hundredth birthday of Gerhard von Rad.

as ancient and contemporary word and the theological demand to honor the claims of both.

I understand *theology* to describe reflection on the meaning of religious experience and efforts to articulate systems of religious belief. It seeks patterns of coherence and is concerned with norms and truth claims. The qualifier *Old Testament* orients this activity to the Hebrew Scriptures—and places it within a tradition of Christian theological reflection. I use the traditional Christian terminology to identify the avenue by which I approach the subject of biblical theology, as well as the focus of my attention.[2] Biblical theology cannot be Christian, and Christian theology cannot be biblical, without the witness of the Hebrew Scriptures. And although that witness, for the Christian interpreter, is necessarily bound to the canonical witness of the early church and read through the lens of Christian faith, I believe it is compromised and distorted when it is not first received as Israel's witness.[3] The responsibility of the OT scholar is to ensure that that witness is heard as accurately and empathetically as possible.[4] My desire to guard the integrity of the OT witness as well as my limited competence in NT studies make it impossible for me to do justice to the larger topic of this colloquium (biblical theology) without first clarifying my understanding of the theology of the Old Testament as a source for Christian theology.[5]

Old Testament theology, conceived either in descriptive or normative terms, points to a constructive enterprise concerned with formulations of faith that invite, if not compel, connections and comparisons with contemporary belief. In contrast, *the God of the fathers* suggests an approach

---

2. I make explicit acknowledgment of my Christian identity, because I do not think that biblical theology must be a Christian enterprise, despite its origins and history. In referring to the subject as an academic discipline within the field of biblical studies, I use the nonconfessional qualifier *Hebrew Bible* (*HB*) or, to acknowledge multiple perspectives and uses, the dual form *OT/HB*. There is no common term or conception for the body of literature shared by Christians and Jews when the literature is considered from the perspective of its religious meaning and use.

3. The meaning and grounding of this assertion cannot be laid out here. Cf. Rendtorff, "Approaches," 26; and Janowski, "One God," 301–6.

4. Empathic hearing does not preclude criticism. On OT theology as descriptive historical theology, see below.

5. My defense of a focus on the OT alone was prompted by an initial understanding of the colloquium topic as "pan-biblical theology," to use James Barr's terminology (*Concept*, 1). I have subsequently adopted his usage, in which "OT theology" is understood as a particular species of the genus "biblical theology." I therefore use the terms interchangeably when referring to the discipline, or activity, in generic terms.

to the texts that accents the historical particularity of the witness and the cultural framing, and content, of its theological affirmations. While this particular formulation highlights gender, and more particularly patriarchy, as an aspect of the conception—an aspect seen by many today as one of the most problematic features of the biblical legacy—it points to a more general problem. A fundamental problem for all theology, but particularly for theologies with a scriptural base, is the question of how the faith of the ancestors can become the faith of the present generation in a manner that does justice both to the tradition and to the intellectual and spiritual demands of the present.[6] Patriarchy and gendered images of the divine are simply two particularly visible features of the biblical legacy that have become morally and intellectually problematic for contemporary faith and theology.

My original intention was to take up the debate on the nature of the discipline and the organization and content of an OT theology associated with the names of Walther Eichrodt and Gerhard von Rad. I was drawn in this direction not only by my appreciation for the work of von Rad, whom we honor in this symposium, but also by the fact that these were the names and the issues that dominated the discussion during my seminary days and early teaching—the last time that I have had occasion to think in any sustained manner about the question of "biblical theology." So I must begin with the confession that I have been an outsider to the subject and the debate surrounding it for most of the past thirty years. What I have discovered in my attempts to reenter the discussion and survey what I have missed is that I have not been alone in my place outside the camp. And it is the particular profile of the outsiders that has given me pause and required me to reorient my contribution to this colloquium. While I still want to deal with the issues I flagged in my title, I must approach them now by a different route.

A QUESTION OF CONTEXT

My reading over the past year has made me acutely aware of the role of context in shaping approaches to the subject of biblical theology. And

---

6. When do transformations of traditional formulations represent continuing affirmations of the essential tenets of the faith, and when do they signal a fundamental departure from them? Or when do traditional formulations of the faith betray the truth they originally communicated? This problem is shared by Judaism and Islam but is not confined to heirs of Abraham and Moses.

the context from which I approach the question makes me very much an outsider to the debate that has flourished in German-speaking circles. As a North American and as a feminist, I feel compelled to ask how the subject relates to the contemporary study and teaching of Bible and theology in North America, and more particularly how it relates to the interests of feminist theologians and biblical scholars. What has become glaringly evident in my review of the literature on biblical theology is that feminist voices, or simply women's voices,[7] have been almost totally absent from the discussion. This absence is all the more noteworthy in the United States, where women and feminism have achieved a substantial representation within the academic study of religion and the Bible, and where renewed interest in the theology of the Hebrew Scriptures has been marked by a widening of the circle of discussion to include significant Jewish participation. Thus it seems imperative to ask why women/feminists are apparently not interested in biblical theology—or why they have rejected it as a form of feminist biblical scholarship.

I initially thought I could deal with this "side issue" in a separate paper, so as not to detract from the "central" issues I had planned to address. But my work on that paper[8] and my subsequent reading have convinced me that the silence of feminist voices points to critical problems in the conception and practice of biblical theology today. What has emerged from that study is a recognition that the fundamental terms need to be rethought: Whom does this enterprise serve? Who needs it? How is it to be conceived? Where is it to be situated—in relation to biblical and theological scholarship, the teaching of Bible and theology, and the needs of the church? What form or forms should it take? The same questions arise from attention to the distinctive features of teaching Bible and theology in the United States, which reflect a relationship of church and religion to state and university quite different from that in Germany.[9] The recitation of the history of the discipline that typically prefaces each new treatment of the subject traces a tradition that remains essentially unbroken in German-speaking Europe, despite major shifts and vigorous

---

7. I do not equate women's and feminist perspectives, nor do I think that men are incapable of feminist interests or advocacy. Generally speaking, however, feminist perspectives will not be articulated where women are not present.

8. Bird, "Feminist."

9. I use this as shorthand for "German-speaking Europe," which, while not uniform, shares substantial features of theological education and biblical scholarship.

internal debate. The latest debate, initiated by Rainer Albertz,[10] is firmly situated within that tradition. It makes assumptions about the relationship of biblical studies to theology and the place of both in the academic curriculum that are alien to the American scene.[11]

The North American Context

Biblical theology arose as a response to a particular set of needs, and major shifts in the conception of the discipline reflect changes in the conditions and needs. The one point in the history of the discipline where significant American involvement is evident is in the Biblical Theology Movement of the post–World War II era, when, under the influence of Karl Barth, interest in theological interpretation of the Bible enjoyed a brief renaissance in some academic settings (chiefly in seminaries).[12] Without further analysis of the movement or its demise, I would simply emphasize that it too was a child of its day—and related to particular features of biblical study in America. When Brevard Childs proclaimed the failure of the movement and began to articulate his canonical approach to interpretation, it was with the intention of restoring an explicitly theological perspective to the study of Scripture in a time and place where biblical studies, not only had declared its independence from ecclesiasti-

---

10. Albertz, "Religionsgeschichte." The entire issue of *Jahrbuch für biblische Theologie* 10 (1995) is devoted to discussion of Albertz's proposal.

11. The most recent overview of the subject, by Henning Graf Reventlow ("Modern Approaches" [2001]) recognizes a "widened sense" of the term "Biblical Theology," which it traces to the United States (221). Cf. Long, "Rival Gods," who speaks of a "shift toward contestatory diversity played out on leveled fields, at least in North America" (233). For an Australian view of the discipline as inherently pluralistic, see Brett, "Future," especially 481–83. See further discussion below.

12. Whether the recent work of Walter Brueggemann (*Theology of the Old Testament: Testimony, Dispute, Advocacy*) represents a significant new direction in biblical/OT theology in the United States is difficult to assess at this point, but there does seem to be new interest and activity in the field. See below. The following sketch of biblical studies in North America is based on Ernest Saunders, *Searching the Scriptures: A History of the Society of Biblical Literature, 1880–1980*, supplemented by personal records and recollections, and by memos from several program-unit chairs. Special thanks are due the SBL archivist, Andrew Scrimgeour, who searched through the program books of the annual meetings to provide me with data on the history of various program units. Unless otherwise acknowledged, all the references to specific units, programs, and chairs come from information he supplied to me in telephone conversations of 11 and 12 March 2002.

cal and dogmatic constraints, but was also claiming the status of a secular discipline. While Childs's debt to Barth is considerable, his program was shaped by features unique to the North American religious and academic situation.

This is characterized by religious pluralism; separation of church and state (accompanied at times by strong suspicion of religion);[13] increasing secularization of culture—with significant resistance from various quarters;[14] and the establishment of departments of religious studies, including biblical studies, in secular universities. German biblical scholars may define their work in purely historical terms, but the context in which they operate and in which their work is employed is the theological faculties of universities. Biblical studies is a theological discipline in German-speaking Europe.[15] Only in such a context does Albertz's proposal to replace OT theology with study of the history of Israelite religion—as an introduction to Old Testament study—make sense. The idea of OT theology as the "summarizing (*zusammenfassende*) discipline"[16] is inconceivable in most places where OT/HB is taught in the United States. That is why new proposals concerning the nature and content of biblical theology must ask whom such a work is intended to serve and with what aim.

---

13. The separation increased throughout the middle decades of the twentieth century but had begun to be challenged on a number of fronts during the final decades of the century.

14. Exhibited in battles over, e.g., prayer in public schools, displays of Christian symbols on public buildings, the teaching of evolution (understood as an assault on Christian belief and freedom of religion), and debates about provisions for distinctive dress and observances of Jews, Muslims, and members of other religious groups.

15. Biblical scholars in the United States are not normally identified as "theologians" even when they teach in theological seminaries—and many would find the epithet demeaning. The ThD (Doctor of Theology) has been replaced in most institutions by the PhD as the degree for academic study of the Bible, and religion; and biblical scholars who teach in theological schools related to universities (such as Harvard Divinity School) prefer to be identified in scholarly meetings by the university name alone. The stigma that attaches to theology in academic circles reflects a widely held view that religious belief is incompatible with scientific rigor, a view fed by a strong element of anti-intellectualism in American religion, reinforced by popular media preachers who lack academic training but use honorary degree titles to claim authority. The derogation of theology is also sustained by academics who have sought freedom in the university from an oppressive or constricting religious past.

16. Albertz, "Religionsgeschichte," 3–4.

History of Biblical Studies in the United States

Prior to the mid-twentieth century, biblical studies in the United States was also a theological discipline, at least for most scholars and institutions. Academic study of the Bible was confined to theological seminaries and religiously affiliated colleges and universities.[17] Religious instruction was, and is, excluded from public education at the primary and secondary levels. In 1948 and 1952, however, the Supreme Court issued decisions interpreting the constitutional prohibition of the establishment of religion in a manner that allowed for the inclusion of nonsectarian study of religion as a part of a liberal arts program in state-supported higher education.[18] As state colleges and universities moved to establish departments of religious studies, church-founded institutions were severing or weakening their church ties in an effort to compete with state-funded institutions for students, faculty, and funds. Religious pluralism and a nonsectarian approach to the study of religion and the Bible increasingly characterized both private and public institutions of higher education. Only in theological schools training religious professionals,[19] and in colleges or universities with a strong religious identity (mostly Catholic or conservative Protestant), is Bible taught with an explicit theological or confessional orientation.[20]

The changes in the study and teaching of the Bible sketched above are part of a larger and more complex development in which study of the Bible as the foundational theological subject gave way to two broad multidisciplinary fields: biblical studies and religious studies.[21] Theol-

---

17. Some public colleges and universities had courses on the Bible as literature, such as the one offered in the English department at the University of California at Berkeley when I was a student. That course, together with an anthropology course on primitive religion, constituted the total offerings in religion. To study theology (in the broadest sense of the word) I had to go to a seminary—a postgraduate institution.

18. Saunders, *Searching*, 41–42.

19. Also called (theological) seminaries or divinity schools, these institutions have a variety of programs and religious affiliations. They may be independent institutions or allied with a college or university. Doctoral programs may be found in any of these types of institutions but are not a normal part of education for professional ministry.

20. The developments chronicled here are unique in their particular manifestations and in the degree of separation or alienation between biblical studies and theology, but the move toward independence of biblical studies from theology is not unique. Cf. Barr, *Does Biblical Study?*

21. This development may be illustrated by two signal moments in the history of the two professional societies representing the two fields. In 1962 the Society of

ogy found a place in the latter, as a discipline in its own right, but kept only a tenuous hold in the former—as an aspect of other studies and as a marginalized special interest (biblical theology). As theology developed its own array of subdisciplines, it became increasingly cut off from biblical scholarship, which was proliferating specialties of its own. Conversation between specialists in the two fields was made difficult by the distinct methods, aims, and norms developed by each,[22] with the result that biblical scholars and theologians no longer speak the same language.[23]

Educational Institutions

The traditional locus for the study and teaching of the Bible as an academic discipline was the theological seminary or school of theology, and the majority of those engaged in teaching and research on the Bible today still operate within this context. But the nature of the current student body and the interests and needs of the churches and society have affected the way that Bible is taught, as well as research and writing on the OT/HB.[24] While conservative seminaries typically stress biblical study as foundational for theology and ministry under doctrines of scriptural inspiration and authority that encourage biblical theology and close textual study in

---

Biblical Literature and Exegesis, meeting in the classrooms of Union Theological Seminary in New York (a site reflecting the society's origins as an association of seminary professors, and the occasion of my first attendance, as a student at the seminary), voted to drop "exegesis" from its name, presaging the more radical changes ahead. The following year an earlier offshoot, the National Association of Bible Instructors (NABI), changed its name to the American Academy of Religion (AAR), reflecting the expanding horizons of the Bible departments found in most colleges and universities established before the advent of state- and community-supported higher education (Saunders, *Searching*, 53). See further discussion below.

22. Biblical studies is a text-centered field with no unifying subject, method, or point of view, in contrast to theology with its common subject (the nature of God and speech about God). Thus, theology draws on a variety of fields and disciplines (including literature, linguistics, history, sociology, archaeology, and history of religion) for its questions as well as its methods.

23. See below. The problem is not simply one-way. If theology has become problematic in the study of Bible, the place of the Bible, as understood by current biblical scholarship, seems equally problematic in much contemporary theology.

24. Religious pluralism within the Christian sector of society presents the dual faces of sectarianism and ecumenism. Increasing cooperation and dialogue across denominational and even religious lines is accompanied by renewed emphasis on denominational identity, resurgent fundamentalism, and bitter internal debates construed as conflicts over biblical interpretation and authority.

original languages, liberal seminaries tend to place greater emphasis on pastoral skills, spiritual life, and moral and ethical concerns. Experiential approaches to theology may be stressed over (or against) historical and systematic studies, and religious, as well as cultural, diversity is celebrated and defended. Many seminaries and denominations (including my own) require no biblical languages for graduation or ordination, and students in the introductory course in OT/HB often have had no previous instruction in Bible. The basic theological curriculum in most liberal seminaries today has no place for the traditional OT theology in its required courses in Bible, except perhaps as an adjunct text. While elite seminaries and schools with doctoral programs offer more opportunities for specialized study and teaching, it is only in recent years that new interest in biblical/OT theology has given it a place as an advanced course or special offering.[25]

A second site of biblical scholarship and teaching in the United States today is the religious studies department of a university or liberal arts college. Some universities also have Jewish studies programs or departments of (ancient) Near Eastern studies, which may offer courses in HB and/or the history and religion of ancient Israel. Study of the HB may also be found in departments of English or literature. Biblical scholars who teach in such contexts may bring a theological interest to the subject—which may or may not find expression in their teaching—but they may also reject any religious claims of the text. They may treat the Bible as a religious document, with attention to its meaning for particular communities of faith (ancient, modern, or both), or they may treat it simply for its literary, historical, or cultural interest. OT/HB theology might still find a place in such a setting—as a form of intellectual history—but this would be rare and confined to advanced and specialized courses. Undergraduate introductory courses in Bible for students of differing faiths and none would have even less need than seminary introductions for such a specialized work as an OT/HB theology.

---

25. In my seminary a ten-week course must introduce content, history, and methods of study for the entire OT; ten-week English exegesis course completes the OT requirement for graduation. In such a curriculum there is no place for specialized studies of either the theology of the OT or the history of Israelite religion. Even in a seminary like Princeton, however, where the introductory course spans a full academic year and heavy emphasis is placed on Bible, an OT theology is too specialized for use in beginning OT study.

The Society of Biblical Literature

In addition to the teaching contexts in which most biblical scholars in North America work, publishers and professional societies create contexts for scholarly research and debate that play a significant role in shaping scholarly interests and emphases. Religiously affiliated publishing houses and periodicals have provided primary stimulus and support for theological interpretation during a period when scholarly agendas were being shaped by a professional association that was generally suspicious, and at times openly hostile, toward theological interests. The Society of Biblical Literature (SBL) requires particular attention because of the critical role it has played in defining the ethos of North American biblical scholarship—an ethos that has given little visibility or support to theological interests.

From origins as a small group of senior scholars based in New York, the Society was transformed in the late '60s and early '70s into a truly national society of several thousand members, organized into dozens of seminars and working groups, with regional associations, a multifaceted publication program, and links to other scholarly associations. It redefined its mission to emphasize the creation and dissemination of new knowledge and sought to enlist the energies of younger scholars, whose numbers had increased dramatically with the proliferation of religious studies departments in public institutions. This transformation had the effect of shifting the balance of power and orientation within the Society from the seminary to the secular university, and from theological interpretation to interpretation of a purely historical, linguistic, or social-scientific nature.[26]

By the late '60s scholarly interpretation without theological presuppositions or aims had become the accepted norm in the Society, at least at the rhetorical and organizational level, and suspicion or rejection of theological interests continued to define the general ethos of the Society

---

26. Saunders, *Searching*, 53–55. This shift had antecedents in the '40s and '50s, when opposition to the Biblical Theology Movement led some within the Society to declare theological interpretation illegitimate. Morton Smith sounded the alarm in his presidential address of 1945, calling for a biblical research solely devoted to discovery of "the facts," and Robert Pfeiffer, in his 1950 address titled "Facts and Faith in Biblical History," insisted that "the descriptive method in the history of religion . . . and the normative method of theology are mutually exclusive." Others, however, expressed concern over the secular drift of the '50s and the idolizing of the natural sciences, arguing that scholars must be conscious of the social and spiritual consequences of their work (ibid., 54–55).

during most of the following decades.[27] Resistance to this trend may be seen in the establishment of an Old Testament Theology Section in 1971.[28] And new developments in the '80s and '90s brought a widening of interest in theology under the banner of hermeneutics,[29] as well as renewed vigor in the "classical" field of OT theology.[30] Increasing numbers

27. Despite the triumph of "historical" over "homiletical" approaches during the '60s and '70s, unresolved tensions remained. Robert Funk, first executive secretary of the reorganized Society (1968–74), acknowledged this state in his presidential address of 1975 when he characterized the SBL as "a fraternity of scientifically trained biblical scholars with the soul of a church," noting the "anomalies" of "publicly pledg[ing] allegiance to so-called scientific study of the Scriptures while being covertly deferential to an unexamined presupposition of the authority of Scripture." These dual allegiances, he argued, created "certain incongruities for biblical studies in the humanities wing of the secular university." Reporting these remarks, Saunders (*Searching*, 69) adds his own pointed comment: "whether or not the biblical text has any discoverable meaning for the interpreter and the interpreter's life . . . is the basic issue raised in German research but deliberately evaded in the American scene."

28. The fact that no such group had existed previously in the Society suggests that OT theology, as a distinct discipline or specialization, had remained an essentially German interest after the demise of the biblical-theology movement. It may also suggest a continuing covert theological interest (see previous note) that did not seek formal recognition until it could no longer find expression in other forums. Interest in biblical theology, broadly understood, was never completely dead, as Bernhard Anderson demonstrated in his presidential address at the 1980 centennial session (Saunders, *Searching*, 69). It should be noted that no comparable group existed on the NT side, where theology appears to have remained far more integrally related to the discourse of the field, and where hermeneutical theory had a prominent place. Conversation between NT scholars and systematic theologians seems to have been maintained at a significant level. Thus OT theology had a special role to play in maintaining conversation with theology—and in claiming the OT for the church, an apologetic aim that has required rethinking of the subject in conversation with Jewish scholars (see below). No unit on biblical theology existed in the SBL prior to the Consultation formed in 2000.

29. A Process Hermeneutics Group existed from 1975 to 1983, revealing the influence of current interests in the field of theology on the field of biblical studies. The new hermeneutical interests of the '80s and '90s have a different origin, arising from the concerns of particular "identity groups" (see below), although they also had originating impulses in new theological movements, such as liberation theology, feminist theology, and Black theology (see below).

30. The Old Testament Theology Section seems to have experienced a low point in the late '70s and early '80s, with the result that Bruce Birch, who assumed the chair in 1982, was advised that his term might be the last (Birch, private communication). A panel that year on "The Future of Old Testament Theology" seems to have stimulated, or caught, an awakening interest in the subject, and it was followed in 1983 by a program on "The Task of Old Testament Theology." (The papers from the two sessions, by Walter Brueggemann, Paul D. Hanson, Walter Harrelson, Rolf Knierim, Roland E. Murphy, and W. Sibley Towner were published in *HBT* 6/1–2 [1983–84]). See below.

of women in the Society and a small African American presence led in the '70s and '80s to the formation of program units concerned with the particular hermeneutical interests of these groups.[31] These units gave recognition to the role of experience and religious tradition as well as culture in interpretation of the Bible. The growing force of postmodernism, with its rejection of the ideals of "objectivity" and distance associated with historical criticism, fostered interest in the subjectivity and social location of the interpreter, while increasing "globalization" encouraged efforts of "contextual interpretation." Religious identity could resurface in this pluralistic milieu at the same time that the theological imperialism of supposedly neutral historical scholarship was denounced. The question, whose Bible is it anyway? was being raised from a number of different directions, including that of Jewish interpretation.[32]

Women's interests first found expression in the Women's Caucus in Religious Studies, a nonofficial organization of women in the American Academy of Religion (AAR) and SBL, founded in 1971 under the leadership of Carol Christ (AAR) and Elisabeth Schüssler Fiorenza (SBL).[33] Only in 1980 did women's interests find a place in a program of the SBL—in a panel on "The Effects of Women's Studies on Biblical Studies," organized for the 1980 centennial under the general rubric of "The History and Sociology of Biblical Scholarship."[34] The following

31. In the case of women, hermeneutical discussion was confined at first to the AAR, with attention in the SBL being directed to women in the text and in the social world of the Bible. See below.

32. Cf. Davies, *Whose Bible Is It Anyway?* Davies's question had a narrower intent: to assert the fundamental distinction of confessional from nonconfessional approaches to the study of the biblical literature—as implying separate disciplines (ibid., 13)—and to lay out a nonconfessional discourse concerning the characterization of the deity *YHWH* and the way in which ancient writers made use of the notion of this deity (ibid., 16).

33. See Schüssler Fiorenza, *Rhetoric*, 20. Women had constituted close to 10 percent of the membership of the SBL at the height of the first wave of feminism in 1920 but had declined steadily in relative numbers until 1970 when they reached a low of 3.5 percent. It was only with the second wave of feminism, however, that women's issues began to impact the Society, spurred by the Women's Caucus (ibid., 19-20).

34. See Collins, *Feminist Perspectives*, 1. The panel presentations, by Mary K. Wakeman, Katherine Doob Sakenfeld, Elisabeth Schüssler Fiorenza, and Collins, with responses by Letty Russell and Rosemary Radford Ruether, were published in *JSOT* 22 (1982) 3-71, with an introduction by Phyllis Trible, who had chaired the panel. In identifying this as "the first program unit of any SBL Annual Meeting to be devoted specifically to women," Collins observes that it "only made more apparent that women are a minority in the SBL and that feminism had made little impact on the guild."

year a Consultation on Women in Scripture was held, resulting in the formation in 1983 of the Women in the Biblical World Section—a unit that continues to the present (2002). It was not until 1989, however, that feminist hermeneutics appeared as the subject of an SBL program unit, although a Feminist Hermeneutics Project existed in the AAR as early as 1981, drawing contributions from many feminist biblical scholars over a number of years.[35] A 1985 AAR Consultation on Women in the Church included a segment on "Word and Women," consisting of a panel on Letty Russell's book *Feminist Interpretation of the Bible* and chaired by Katharine Doob Sakenfeld. Thus feminist biblical hermeneutics was cultivated first in the AAR, in association with liberation theology. The SBL Consultation on Feminist Theological Hermeneutics held in 1989 became a Group in 1991. In 1999 it became a Section, changing its name to "Feminist Hermeneutics of the Bible"—dropping the original reference to "theology."[36]

African American interests found their first expression in the SBL in a Consultation on Black Biblical Studies in 1985. In 1987 it became the African-American Theology and Biblical Hermeneutics Group, changing its name and status in 1999 to become the African-American Biblical Hermeneutics Section. As in the case of feminist hermeneutics, the impetus for the formation of the unit and the initial formulation of the focus seems to have come from theology or the AAR, reflecting the development of Black theology. And as in the case of feminist hermeneutics, any reference to theology is finally eliminated from the name.

A Consultation on the Bible in Africa, Asia, and Latin America was held in 1989, becoming a Group in 1991 and continuing through 2001. In 1995 concern for the specific cultural and religious features of the Caribbean led to a Consultation on The Bible in Caribbean Culture and Tradition. After the normal two years as a Consultation, it was decided to merge with the broader Group, and the name of the latter was changed in 1997 to The Bible in Africa, Asia, Latin America, and the Caribbean. From 1995 to 1997 the distinct perspectives and interests of biblical scholars of Asian origin were explored in a Consultation on Asian and Asian-American Biblical Studies. In 1999 a Group was formed, changing its name in 2000 to Asian and Asian-American Hermeneutics Group. In

---

35. Organized by Letty Russell, it was inaugurated as a "Joint Symposium" and appears as a special program during the first two years, coming under the wing of the AAR Liberation Theology Group in 1983.

36. See further discussion below on feminist heremeneutics.

all the program units focusing on contexts and traditions of biblical interpretation outside North American academic tradition, theological interests and church practice have played a significant role in the discourse. The perception that these units brought inappropriate confessional interests into the SBL has led some members of the Society to protest that they did not belong in a scholarly society.

Despite the broadened hermeneutical activity detailed above, it was in relation to Jewish-Christian dialogue that the discipline of biblical theology began to break out of its inherited tradition and engage a wider constituency. The conversations initiated in the aftermath of the Shoah and the increasing Jewish presence in departments of biblical studies (and even seminaries) brought new sensitivity to Jewish perspectives within the SBL, with corresponding changes in nomenclature. Thus the OT Theology Section became the Theology of the Hebrew Scriptures Section in 1985 and determined to encourage Jewish participation.[37] The question of Jewish OT/HB theology was being raised in the late '80s by a number of authors as part of a broader discussion of Jewish and Christian approaches to biblical interpretation.[38] In 1996 the section featured a panel discussion with two Jewish and two Christian speakers,[39] and in 1998 it added a Jewish cochair.[40]

---

37. Matityahu Tsevat had been invited to address the 1985 meeting on the question "whether 'Old Testament Theology' had any interest or counterpart in Jewish scholarship or whether it was a solely Christian enterprise." His affirmation that it did have a place, or ought to, led to the reported changes, according to the recollections of the chair at the time (Bruce Birch, e-mail, 27 November 2001). The replacement of "Old Testament" by "Hebrew Bible" seems, however, to have taken place throughout the Society between 1984 and 1985 (Scrimgeour, personal communication, based on the Program book of 1985).

38. Jon Levenson's provocatively titled essay, "Why Jews Are not Interested in Biblical Theology" (1987), seems to have served as a catalyst for the subsequent discussion, although other Jewish contributions to the subject appeared at the same time or earlier. See Tsevat, "Theology." Further contributions to the continuing Jewish-Christian discussion on biblical theology include Rendtorff, "'Biblical Theology'"; and Sweeney, "Tanak versus Old Testament."

39. The papers, by Tikva Frymer-Kensky, Sweeney, Brueggemann, and Jorge Pixley, were subsequently published, together with additional essays, in Bellis and Kaminsky, *Jews, Christians, and Theology*.

40. Joel Kaminsky, who subsequently shared the leadership with a Korean-American, Wonil Kim.

Feminism as Context[41]

What is not yet visible in this broadened constituency and debate on biblical theology is significant female presence and feminist perspectives, either in the SBL or in the broader arena of publication. The underrepresentation of women in the Theology of the Hebrew Bible Section during most of the '90s occurred despite the efforts of a female chair, Alice Ogden Bellis, to encourage women's participation. Why did her seven-year effort find so little response?[42] And what does this mean for the discipline? I have focused on the organization of North American biblical scholars in the SBL as a way of identifying trends and interests within the field of biblical studies, and because the SBL unites biblical scholars of diverse backgrounds and commitments working in a variety of settings, both secular and religious.[43] My primary interest has been the place of theology in the study of the Bible, because I believe that the future of OT/HB theology in the American context is closely related to this broader issue. But it is also critical for understanding feminist responses, because the theological claims made by or for the Hebrew Bible have been particularly problematic for feminists. Some feminists, responding to the theological legacy of biblical patriarchy, want to cut theology free from the (Hebrew) Bible, while others want to cut the Bible free from theology.

41. Although assigning this a separate section, I am treating feminism as a part of the North American context, because that is where I want to analyze its impact on attitudes toward biblical theology. I recognize feminism as a global movement, but with distinct features in different cultural, religious, and political contexts. And although feminist biblical scholars in German-language areas have contributed specifically to the discussion on biblical theology, they are often concerned with different issues than those at the forefront of discussion in the United States, and their work is, unfortunately, little known among most American-born feminist biblical scholars.

42. Bellis was recruited for the Steering Committee as its first woman in 1993 and became chair in 1995. She continued in the position until 2000, recruiting Kaminsky as co-chair in 1998 in order to have both a Jew and a Christian in the leadership of the section. Although her efforts to increase women's participation produced some dramatic changes in the last several years (three women served on the Steering Committee in 2001, and additional women's voices were included in the publication of the 1996 panel), she acknowledges resistance on the part of women to present papers in the section, as well as failure of the section to address feminist concerns (e-mail, 23 July 2001).

43. An increasingly large membership from outside North America must qualify any effort to identify the SBL with North American interests. Nevertheless, I think it is still representative of biblical scholarship in North America—which is increasingly characterized by a "globalization" that breaks the older pattern of dependence on German scholarship.

Before I attempt further analysis, I must extend my documentation of women's silence beyond the SBL section on the Theology of the Hebrew Scriptures. The fact that none of the more than sixty OT theologies produced during the past century[44] were authored by women is easily explained by the relatively recent entry of women into the field of OT scholarship, as well as by the nature of the task. Few, if any, feminist OT/HB scholars have the range and depth of exegetical experience to attempt a comprehensive treatment of the type required, or traditionally assumed, by the genre. Less obvious are the reasons for their absence from other forms and forums of discussion involving less comprehensive demands.

My attention was first drawn to the problem by the panel discussion of James Barr's important work, *The Concept of Biblical Theology*, at the SBL meeting of 2000. The audience in the large auditorium virtually mirrored the all-male panel on the platform. This pattern replicates the gender profile of most anthologies and collected essays bearing titles relating to biblical theology. Of the twenty-five authors chosen to represent Old Testament theology in the twentieth century in an anthology published in 1992,[45] Phyllis Trible is the lone female. Twelve years later, in the "revised and augmented" second edition,[46] Trible is still the only woman, although the revised list of contributors includes five additional men. The 1993 Festschrift for Norbert Lohfink titled *Biblische Theologie und gesellschaftlicher Wandel*, a title that would seem to invite feminist contributions, contains twenty-two essays, all by males.[47] The twenty-five articles in the Festschrift for Rolf Knierim under the title *Problems in Biblical Theology* (1997)[48] are likewise all by males. Even the recent Festschrift for James Crenshaw, described by its subtitle as *Studies on the Nature of God*,[49] contains but one essay (of sixteen) by a woman.[50]

---

44. Rendtorff ("Approaches," 19) estimated "some sixty," admitting, however, that he did not count them.

45. Ollenburger, et al., *Flowering*.

46. Ollenburger, *Old Testament Theology*.

47. Braulik et al., *Biblische Theologie*. Two of the titles contain references to women: Clifford, "Woman Wisdom in the Book of Proverbs"; and Miller, "Things Too Wonderful."

48. Sun and Eades, *Problems in Biblical Theology*.

49. Penchansky and Redditt, *Shall Not the Judge?*

50. A word of qualification is in order concerning Festschriften, although I think it does not invalidate the general pattern. Because contributors are often drawn largely from former students and colleagues, a priest, such as Lohfink, who has taught in a predominantly male environment, may be expected to have a relatively small pool of

The pattern of women's silence in the field identified as biblical/OT theology is clear, but what does it mean? First, I think it does not mean that feminists are not interested in the theology of the Hebrew Scriptures, or that they have not been engaged in theological interpretation, despite the rejection of theology by some feminist biblical scholars. Nor does it mean that feminist scholarship is inconsequential for biblical theology. Feminists are in fact engaged in doing biblical theology in a variety of forms and contexts, and their studies of individual texts, images, and themes, of the language and forms of the writings, and of the world in which they arose, have greatly enriched, and challenged, our understanding of the theology of the OT/HB.[51] But these contributions have yet to be registered in any significant degree in comprehensive and synthetic works on the subject.

One of the reasons, I think, that so few women were involved in the SBL Theology of the Hebrew Scriptures Section is that other demands, from inside and outside the academy laid prior claims on our energies,[52] and other subjects or sections had greater urgency or offered a more inviting forum for feminist ideas. For women trying to gain a foothold in the profession, and sharing the perceptions and concerns of

---

potential female contributors. Cf. the Festschrift for J. Christiaan Beker: Kraftchick et al., *Biblical Theology: Problems and Perspectives*, whose seventeen essays include three by women. Two are by Princeton colleagues (Kathleen E. McVey and Sakenfeld), and one is a contribution from a former student (Kathleen M. O'Connor). More difficult to assess is the role of personal relationships with teachers and mentors in shaping women's professional interests and activities.

51. To lift out individual names and works from a body of writings that is now too large and diverse to survey under a single heading is a risky undertaking. It risks identification of feminist theological contributions with particular scholars and particular approaches, and it must necessarily leave unnamed a host of important contributors, especially younger scholars. But there is a further risk related to the nature of feminism itself: Given that feminism involves a new way of looking at the world that encompasses all realms of knowledge and experience, the insights and critique that arise in one field or discipline often have implications for another. Thus feminist biblical theology draws upon the work of feminist scholars who have no theological interests, and of scholars who reject the theology they find in the texts. Consequently, the pool of contributors is substantially larger than the number of feminist authors who engage directly in theological reflection on the OT/HB. For a broad sample of feminist commentary, see Schottroff and Wacker, *Kompendium* and, for a more general audience, Newsom and Ringe, *Women's Bible Commentary*.

52. I include myself in this category of women who were not involved in this section.

sisters outside the academy,[53] programs on feminist hermeneutics and women in Scripture and the biblical world offered needed contexts in which to explore the interface of those concerns with the traditions of the discipline and to forge new directions in biblical interpretation. The Consultations, Groups, and Symposia on issues relating directly to women, and the formal and informal associations between women and program units of the SBL and the AAR,[54] served to energize and support feminist scholars and scholarship. But these same structures and dynamics also served to isolate feminist discussion from the larger debate, especially in the "traditional" or "classic" subjects, such as OT theology.[55] In light of this pattern, one must ask, what will it take for feminist contributions to move from the ghetto of feminist studies into the "mainstream"—or for the "mainstream" to realize that it is only a current in the turbulent waters of the discipline?

I have argued that women, and feminists, have in fact been engaged in biblical theology. But the form that this has taken has been largely hermeneutical, and limited to the interpretation of selected texts or corpora, or analysis of particular themes, concepts, and images.[56] It has also

53. Feminism is not simply a way of looking at the world but is first and foremost a movement for change that combines critique with advocacy. Feminism in the academy cannot divorce itself from its prophetic roots and from the ongoing struggle of women everywhere to claim their full humanity and free themselves from every form of cultural bondage associated with their sex. Because of these circumstances, feminist scholarship has struggled with the ideals of "objectivity" associated with historical-critical methods—with different outcomes, from insistence on "committed" scholarship as definitive of feminist approaches to defense of various forms and uses of historical criticism. See Collins, *Feminist Perspectives*, 3–5, and below.

54. Feminist interests in theology and hermeneutics found a more welcome reception, at an earlier period, in the AAR (see above), where women constituted a considerably larger proportion of the general membership—and leadership—than in the SBL. In this connection it is worth noting that the one feminist biblical scholar who has been most closely identified with biblical theology, Phyllis Trible, published her path-breaking article, "Depatriarchalizing in Biblical Interpretation," in the journal of the AAR (*JAAR*), rather than the SBL journal (*JBL*). On the difficulty of bringing women's perspectives and interests into the SBL, see Collins, *Feminist Perspectives*, 2–3.

55. Newer subjects and methods such as literary, rhetorical, and ideological criticism, and social-scientific studies appear to have greater appeal for women/feminists. On the tensions in women's scholarly commitments and agendas, see Collins, *Feminist Perspectives*, 3–5, who highlights the findings of Dorothy C. Bass ("Women's Studies") on the separate processes underlying the development of feminist hermeneutics and the rise of women in biblical scholarship.

56. Despite the risks noted above (n. 51), it seems essential to identify some examples of feminist interpretation that is engaged more or less directly with issues of

involved forms of reading "against the text" and has dared to accuse the God of the tradition on behalf of the victims of patriarchy.[57] In contrast to these piecemeal approaches, "salvage operations," and counterreadings, OT theology as a summarizing and synthesizing discipline, and genre, aimed at articulating the essential theological content of the whole OT/HB, seems to require a different kind of engagement—and investment—an engagement with the Bible/OT as a whole, which accords authority to the whole. Here, I think, is the fundamental problem for feminists. The presupposition or demand that the whole of the OT/HB be understood as authoritative is deeply problematic for many women. For many, this means accepting the claims of normativity made on behalf of Israel's patriarchal God in his role as author and defender of Israel's patriarchal social and religious order. Feminists who reject this androcentric construct of divinity and humanity have little incentive to articulate a theology of the OT/HB or to engage in discussion of the subject. That is why I suggested in my earlier paper that a "feminist Old Testament theology" might be viewed as an oxymoron. The fundamental issue, of course, is the question of normativity, or the nature of the truth claims made by and for the portrait offered by the Hebrew Scriptures—more broadly, the nature of biblical authority.[58]

---

biblical theology. Best known, perhaps, are the exegetical studies of Trible collected in *God and the Rhetoric of Sexuality* and *Texts of Terror*. See also Sakenfeld, "Problem"; Newsom, "Moral Sense"; and studies of Genesis 1–3 in Bird, *Missing Persons*, 123–93. Other types of feminist contributions include studies of the figure of Wisdom in Proverbs (Camp, *Wisdom*; Newsom, "Woman"; O'Connor, "Wisdom Literature"); literary and archaeological studies of goddesses and cult in Israel and the HB (Ackerman, "'And the Women Knead Dough'"; Jost, *Frauen*; Schroer, "Göttin"; Hadley, *Cult of Asherah*); monographs and essays on theological terms and concepts (Sakenfeld, *Meaning of Ḥesed*; Wacker, "Feministisch-theologische Blicke"; Bird, "Theological Anthropology" [chap. 2 in this volume]); and commentaries (Nielsen, *Ruth*; Pressler, *Joshua, Judges, and Ruth*; see also n. 51 above).

57. See, e.g., Trible, *Texts of Terror*; and Weems, *Battered Love*—both published in the series Overtures to Biblical Theology.

58. See Bird, "Authority of the Bible" (included in this volume as chap. 3); and Bird, "Biblical Authority." On feminist hermeneutics, with attention to differing attitudes and approaches to biblical patriarchy and androcentrism, see Tolbert, *Bible and Feminist Hermeneutics*, especially Tolbert, "Defining the Problem"; Osiek, "Feminist and the Bible"; Sakenfeld, "Feminist Perspectives"; Sakenfeld, "Feminist Biblical Interpretation"; and Camp, "Feminist Theological Hermeneutics." For the German-speaking context, see Schottroff, et al., *Feministische Exegese*. The complexity of current feminist approaches to the Bible is illustrated by the two-volume work edited by Schüssler Fiorenza, *Searching the Scriptures*, which is still not comprehensive.

I will return to this issue as I lay out my own thinking on the subject, but first I must add one further word concerning the silence of women in OT theology. It is to stress the fundamental ambivalence that characterizes most women's approach to the HB/OT in general. No woman who claims a feminist consciousness can read these texts without experiencing some sense of pain and alienation—unlike most male readers and scholars. The kind of deep, unproblematized love of the Bible revealed in the homage to von Rad that opened this symposium is impossible for most women biblical scholars and conscienticized readers. Women who love these texts also know them as toxic—as dangerous to women's physical and mental health. They know that women's lives have been constricted, warped, and violated by these texts and their interpreters. Some have experienced denial of their vocation on the basis of these texts, others have met roadblocks to personal and professional fulfillment, while still others simply feel the weight of the absence or silence of women in the text. So even if they believe that the poison is in the interpretation rather than the text itself, or that the text supplies an antidote, they cannot approach the Scriptures unaware of their potential to harm. That is what distinguishes feminist approaches, however varied. And until all readers acknowledge this dangerous legacy and share the pain of exclusion or estrangement, there can be no gender-inclusive reading or theology.

OVERTURE FOR A FEMINIST BIBLICAL THEOLOGY

In 1989 Phyllis Trible published an article titled "Five Loaves and Two Fishes: Feminist Hermeneutics and Biblical Theology,"[59] the sole work by a woman included in the anthology of twentieth-century contributions to Old Testament theology noted above. Because it addresses the subject of this colloquium and does so in explicitly feminist terms, I find it necessary to set my own views in relation to Trible's. While I share many of her values and concerns, I differ in my understanding of the task and aims of biblical theology and the nature of biblical authority—or the way in which the Bible functions as a source for contemporary theology.

In her 1989 essay, Trible declared that although it was not yet the season to write a feminist biblical theology, it was time to make

---

59. *TS* 50 (1989) 279–95; it is reprinted as "Feminist Hermeneutics and Biblical Theology" in Ollenburger, *Flowering*. Major sections are incorporated into Trible, "Treasures."

overtures—a position she reiterated in 1993.⁶⁰ She begins with a history of the discipline, whose climax she finds in the period 1933–1960, a period framed by the works of Eichrodt and von Rad.⁶¹ With the fall of the "great consensus" in the early '60s, she sees the discipline in a period of decline—extending to the time of her writing—with few new biblical theologies and none dominating the field.⁶² Yet she maintains that the subject had "grown through experimentation," and identifies "conversation between sociology and theology, discussion of canon, and development of bipolar categories for encompassing scriptural diversity" as elements of this growth. "More broadly," she concluded, "biblical theology [had] begun to converse with the world."⁶³

It is in this expanded conversation with the world that she situates her feminist approach to the subject, setting it over against a two-hundred-year history whose characteristics she summarizes as follows:

> First, biblical theology (more often OT theology) has sought identity, but with no resolution. Over time the discussion has acquired the status of *déjà dit*; proposals and counterproposals only repeat themselves. Second, guardians of the discipline have fit a standard profile. They have been white Christian males of European or North American extraction, educated in seminaries, divinity schools, or theological faculties. Third, overall, their interpretations have skewed or neglected matters not congenial to a patriarchal point of view. Fourth, they have fashioned the discipline in a past separated from the present. *Biblical theology has been kept apart from biblical hermeneutics.*"⁶⁴

Trible's emphasis is on the final point. It is the separation of biblical theology from hermeneutics that she wishes to challenge as a feminist, joining feminist critique to challenges coming from many other directions. Among these she identifies "liberation theologies [which] foster redefinition and application," "issues such as ecology, medical ethics, creationism, and spirituality [which] press for dialogue," "racial, religious,

---

60. Trible, "Treasures," 41.

61. Ibid., 34. During this period, she observes, male European Protestant scholars controlled the subject—wherever it was taught. In the United States she names James Muilenburg, James D. Smart, Bernhard W. Anderson, and especially George Ernest Wright.

62. Ibid., 34–35.

63. Trible, "Feminist Hermeneutics," 453; cf. Trible, "Treasures," 35.

64. Trible, "Feminist Hermeneutics," 454 (italics added); cf. Trible, "Treasures," 35.

and sexual perspectives," and "African-Americans, Asians, and Jews[, who] shape the discipline differently from traditional proponents."[65]

I think Trible is right in insisting that the circle of debate on the subject must be widened to include voices not previously heard or even raised; and I think she is right in asserting that this is already taking place. But as she also notes, it is not taking place in the circles perpetuating the "great tradition," symbolized by the production of volumes titled "OT/Biblical Theology" or examining the concept of biblical theology.[66] I share Trible's concern for hermeneutics, as well as her identification of the issues pressing for dialogue, but I do not want to abolish the separation of biblical theology from hermeneutics. I want to preserve the dialogical character of the encounter between ancient text and modern context(s) by maintaining the distinction between historical statements of belief and contemporary affirmations of faith. I believe there is need for a biblical theology understood as a historical discipline—without thereby rejecting the legitimacy or value of a biblical theology understood primarily as a constructive enterprise oriented by contemporary issues of faith.[67] Thus I want to argue for an alternative to Trible's understanding—as a feminist

---

65. Trible, "Feminist Hermeneutics," 454. Six years earlier, Bruce Birch also saw new vitality in a field widely held to be in a state of crisis. Introducing a collection of essays on the theme "Old Testament Theology: Its Task and Future" (see n. 30 above) he noted "a remarkable flurry of new publication in Old Testament theology" beginning already in the late '70s, citing "new works of significant importance" from Samuel Terrien, Paul Hanson, Phyllis Trible, Walter Brueggemann, Brevard Childs, and Claus Westermann, along with "numerous periodical articles" (Birch, "Old Testament Theology," iii; see also iv–viii). Despite evidence of new forms (only two of the works cited by author are styled "OT theologies"—both by Europeans) and increased emphasis on hermeneutics, the horizons of the discipline suggested by Birch are considerably narrower than those envisioned by Trible.

66. Though not itself a biblical theology, Barr's *Concept of Biblical Theology* stands in the tradition of those theologies, while opening the way to a rethinking of the discipline and its relations to (on the one hand) theology and (on the other hand) biblical studies. It offers what in my view is a much-needed and insightful analysis of the problems and prospects of the subject or discipline, which should be of use to scholars of diverse persuasions. Yet its provocative, and at times caustic, tone, as well as its lack of sympathy for (or even acknowledgment of) new voices pressing for inclusion will likely limit its use by those who wish to see a larger place for contextual theologies of various types. See Bellis, "Walter Brueggemann and James Barr."

67. With Trible ("Feminist Hermeneutics," 464), I use "constructive" as a term of contrast to "historical," recognizing, however, that historical theology, as every work of historical writing, is also a constructive effort. See further discussion below.

alternative, that will also serve the interests and needs of others in the North American context.

A Question of Identity

I have begun with the question of the identity and aims of the discipline, because I believe this is the fundamental question, and because this is where I part company with Trible. Trible emphasizes the unresolved nature of the debate over the identity of biblical theology as a problem that has characterized the history of the discipline, suggesting that it signals the need for a new approach.[68] I am not troubled by the lack of consensus. It belongs to the nature of the subject or discipline as uniting subject matter and interests belonging to two fields of specialization with distinct, and in part incompatible, methods and aims.[69] And it is dictated by the Bible's dual identity as both ancient writings and contemporary book: historical testimony to the faith of ancient Israel and early Judaism and contemporary guide to belief and practice. How is the integrity of this dual nature to be maintained and honored within the field of OT/HB

---

68. Trible, "Feminist Hermeneutics," 451, 454. She begins her sketch of the history by observing that "biblical theologians, though coming from a circumscribed community, have never agreed on the definition, method, organization, subject matter, point of view, or purpose of their enterprise" (451). Her review highlights conflict and contention: "the discipline flourished in disputation"; "interpretive approaches began to contend with descriptive"; "searches for unifying themes brought disunity"; "concepts . . . vied for supremacy"; "chronologies of biblical content clashed with categories of systematic theology" (451-52). Yet in considering the ferment introduced by feminism, she affirms the necessity of "the perennial rethinking of biblical theology" (458). Cf. Albertz, "Religionsgeschichte," 7-14, who would abandon the enterprise altogether.

69. The problem is illustrated by the need for a two-part article on the subject in the new *RGG*. See Janowski, "Biblische Theologie: I. Exegetisch"; Welker, "II. Fundamentaltheologisch" for a helpful overview and typologies of different construals of the subject. The lack of consensus, accented by Trible and Albertz, is recognized by all who have treated the subject, but with differing assessments and responses. Some have attempted to limit its legitimate task, form, or method in quite different ways. See, e.g., Knierim, "Task of Old Testament Theology," with responses by Walter Harrelson, W. Sibley Towner, and Roland E. Murphy, and rejoinder by Knierim (reprinted with some changes in Knierim, *Task*, 1-56); John Collins, "Critical Biblical Theology?"; Ollenburger, "Biblical Theology"; and Barr, *Concept*. Others show an openness to multiple approaches — either because these belong to the nature of the subject, or because no single definition has succeeded in dominating the field. See, e.g., Rendtorff, "Approaches," 19; Long, "Rival Gods"; Brett, "Future"; and Brueggemann, "Futures," 1.

studies? How does one do justice to these differing perceptions of text and canon? Whose theology does the biblical scholar seek to articulate? For whom? What is the relationship between the descriptive-historical and the normative-constructive tasks of theology? I am convinced that debate about the nature of biblical theology needs to continue, and feminists need to be a part of it. Trible's proposal for a feminist biblical theology elaborates one answer to these questions, but it does not close the debate concerning either the nature of biblical theology or the form of feminist engagement with it.

Trible positions herself on the constructive side (or toward the constructive pole) of biblical theology by her definition of the subject and by her explicit disavowal of the historical tradition whose demise she correlates with the new movements in theology that began in the '60s. Asking whether feminism and biblical theology can meet, she elaborates: "after all, feminists do not move in the world of Gabler, Eichrodt, von Rad, and their heirs." "Yet," she continues, "feminists who love the Bible insist that the text and its interpreters provide more excellent ways."[70] These remarks call for further analysis, but here it must suffice to say that they do not represent the views of all feminists, or even "feminists who love the Bible"—although I believe they do reflect a widely shared sense of alienation or distance from a tradition of OT scholarship that dominated most of the past century.[71] Trible's disavowal of the heritage of Gabler is evidenced in her definition of biblical theology, which removes it from any historical (or ecclesial/religious) context or constraint. For Trible, biblical theology is simply "an articulation of faith as disclosed in Scripture." This "open" definition corresponds to her understanding of the Bible as a "pilgrim, wandering through history, engaging in new settings, and ever refusing to be locked in the past."[72] Trible accents the power of the reader to alter the meaning and force of the text,[73] describing the task of a feminist biblical theology as that of "redeem[ing] the past

70. Trible, "Feminist Hermeneutics," 458.

71. Trible's claim to speak for feminists in this declaration implicitly denies the legitimacy of feminists who work within the historical tradition of OT scholarship. I find it no more problematic to claim the inheritance of Gabler, Eichrodt, and von Rad than to acknowledge that I am an heir of Abraham, Moses, and Ezra. I chose therefore to place my interpretive work, including my critique, within the tradition that Trible rejects, while engaging at the same time in the "conversations with the world" (cf. ibid., 453) that she highlights.

72. Ibid., 458.

73. Trible, "Treasures," 49.

(an ancient treasure called the Bible) and the present (its continuing use) from the confines of patriarchy."[74] While she accords an essential role to descriptive and historical study (in the initial exegetical work), she views the primary task as constructive and hermeneutical, aiming to "wrestle from the text a theology that subverts patriarchy."[75]

I would welcome the theology Trible envisions in her "overtures," which would focus on the "phenomenon of gender and sex in the articulation of faith" as the key to its content and contours.[76] A theology of the Hebrew Scriptures systematically informed by feminist concerns and focused on texts and ideas of importance to feminists would call attention to the inadequacies and biases of existing theologies and suggest alternative paradigms and readings. I think there is need for such a work—both by those who have experienced biblical patriarchy as an obstacle to faith, and by those who have not yet recognized the distorting effects of patriarchal androcentrism in biblical theology. Nevertheless, I remain ambivalent about the concept of a feminist biblical theology and find Trible's proposal problematic in a number of ways.

I am ambivalent about the concept because it suggests a special theology for a special audience, which would seem to reinforce the present separation of feminist voices within the discipline. On the other hand, such a targeted work may be what is needed to open conversation and lead to the integration of feminist insights into "general" OT/HB theologies.[77] Trible herself clearly envisions a broader audience, and her aim is nothing less than the articulation of a "constructive theology for female and male . . . for the redemption of humankind."[78] I share her view of the goal and horizons of feminist theology—as a constructive enterprise—but I cannot follow the moves she makes from the OT/HB to normative theological statements, and my own view of the theology of the OT/HB,

---

74. Ibid., 38; cf. 49.

75. Trible, "Feminist Hermeneutics," 464.

76. Ibid., 461–62. The work would be grounded in exegesis, highlighting neglected texts and reinterpreting familiar ones to recover forgotten women and to accent female depictions of God; it would expose and denounce patriarchal bias and memorialize its victims. It would begin, as the Bible itself, with Genesis 1–3 and find its base in creation theology. And it would expose and denounce idolatry in the Scriptures, from within the Scriptures (ibid., 461–63).

77. On the issues relating to "general" and "special," or targeted, works, see below.

78. Trible, "Treasures," 49.

both in its historical context and as a source for contemporary theology, is substantially different from hers.

A Question of Norms

Trible's rejection of historical theology as a vehicle for feminist theological interpretation and her proposal for a constructive feminist biblical theology raise a number of questions for me concerning the criteria of assessment[79] and the relationship of historical to constructive theology. Although I shall argue for a historical approach, I recognize a range of options between the strictly historical (which always has a contemporary orientation and involves value judgments) and the normative-constructive (which always involves historical judgments). But I am uncertain how to judge Trible's proposal. How does the theology she envisions relate to other forms of theology on the one hand, and to the Bible's full theological witness on the other? And by what criteria of adequacy or truth is it to be assessed? At times Trible seems to suggest that feminist biblical theology is simply feminist theology that takes the Bible (actually only the HB) as its primary source. But the theology she proposes is inadequate as an articulation of Christian faith. It offers no hint of how the NT—or any other source of faith besides feminism—might relate to this "articulation of faith as disclosed in Scripture." At the same time, it appears to neglect much of the theological content of the Hebrew Bible[80] and, in my view, distorts some of its witness.

Such limitations and "failings" seem, however, to be inherent in the genre. Any theology (historical or constructive) that attempts to treat the OT/HB as a whole will have to be highly selective, both with respect to the biblical sources, and with respect to the range of contemporary issues engaged.[81] One might argue that the use of gender and sex as an organiz-

---

79. The more fundamental question concerns the place of normative judgments in biblical theology, which is blurred by the field-bridging character of the subject.

80. This judgment is necessarily premature, given the nature of her essay; it is based on the themes and issues she has identified.

81. While a constructive theology will forefront contemporary issues, they are not excluded from a descriptive, historical work. E.g., a treatment of "holy war," which must necessarily have a place in a descriptive historical theology, must also either include some acknowledgment of similar ideas or appeal to biblical models, or both, in postbiblical history and in the world of contemporary readers. It must also attempt to clarify the truth claims involved in the concept (see Collins, "Is a Critical Biblical Theology?" 9; cf. Barr, *Concept*, 492–94). The historian must come to the past with critical

ing theme is comparable to the use of such concepts as *covenant, reign of God*, or *divine presence*—with the same drawbacks. Unlike the notions of covenant, however, or the reign of God, gender introduces a distinctly modern concept and awareness; and despite the fact that the choice of such concepts as covenant undoubtedly reflects theological interests of the scholars' own times, these concepts are thematized in the Hebrew Scriptures in a way that gender is not.[82] To make gender the focus of an OT theology is to give it a status it does not have in the biblical writings.[83] While I believe this is a justifiable move in a theology concerned to address the primary stumbling block of many contemporary readers and a source of distortion in traditional OT theologies, my preference is to treat the subject of gender historically, as part of the cultural world of the biblical writings. I see it as a more pervasive influence than Trible's analysis suggests, but as a distorting element that should not be allowed to obscure the fundamental theological ideas of the OT/HB.[84] So while I would not make gender the focus of a theology of the OT/HB, I believe that no theology today (historical or constructive) can be considered adequate if it fails to incorporate a gender analysis.[85]

This brings me again to the question of evaluation or judgment, the area in which I feel the greatest uncertainty in considering Trible's proposal—or any other conception of biblical theology that subordinates the historical to the normative-constructive task. What canons of assessment apply to such a work? For me, biblical interpretation that is oriented toward contemporary issues falls into the same general category as the exegetical sermon and the hermeneutical essay, both of which I would judge by the dual criteria of fidelity to the biblical sources and theological adequacy (judged by the canons of my theological tradition)

---

awareness of the world in and for which that past is to be interpreted. See below.

82. Trible, *God and the Rhetoric*, 12-23, attempts to find a thematizing statement in Gen 1:27 by constructing the phrase "image of God male and female" as a "topical clue" that authorizes a focus on gender and female images of God.

83. This is a distinct issue from that concerning the use of modern analytical concepts—a usage I would defend. A theology is a translation that must use the language and concepts of its readers, expanding or modifying them as needed to accommodate the meanings in the text.

84. This may appear very similar to Trible's aim of "liberating the Bible from the confines of patriarchy," but it differs in its emphasis on historical meaning as distinct from contemporary belief, and on the manner of assessing and responding to gender bias.

85. See below.

as a response to the particular contemporary problem(s) or situation(s) it addresses.[86] My training as a biblical scholar makes me more secure in the former task, but as a Christian believer I accept responsibility for the latter—despite the inadequacies of my theological training. Yet even my ability to judge fidelity to the biblical text, which for me requires historical contextualization, is challenged by Trible's view of reader-determined meaning.[87] Thus the problem of assessment that confronts me in her conception of the subject is not simply a matter of the relative weight of the normative-constructive component in relation to the descriptive-historical, but the dissolution of the historical by the constructive.

ALTERNATIVES

I have lifted up Trible's proposal because it offers a clear articulation of a feminist approach to biblical theology and because it differs from my own. Critique of her proposal has helped me to clarify my own understanding of the problems and issues. What I want to do now is sketch out an alternative, or alternatives, admitting that I am still uncertain about the form or forms of biblical theology that will meet the demands of the text (as I understand them) and the needs of readers[88] in the several religious and cultural contexts in which I find myself and exercise my vocation as a biblical scholar. By way of transition, I want to characterize my view of the biblical text and the task of interpretation in relation to Trible's.[89] I begin with her statement of aims, cited above.

---

86. This is a complex judgment, involving not only conformity to theological norms but also appropriateness to the given situation.

87. Trible, "Feminist Hermeneutics," 463; specific critique, 462 n. 57 and 463 n. 61.

88. There is a third point of accountability, viz. the tradition that has mediated the text to the reader. But this represents the default meaning, which is normally privileged and is heavily shaped by the theological interests of the community that transmits it. It is in attention to the text apart from the tradition, and to the reader in the reader's particular location, that the discipline of biblical studies makes its special contribution, while always engaged in some form of interaction with the received tradition. In privileging the biblical text apart from the tradition, I stand within a Protestant Christian tradition that clearly contrasts with Jewish approaches to biblical interpretation. See, e.g., Frymer-Kensky, "Emergence," 111, 113, 121.

89. I understand my work as a biblical scholar to involve a variety of roles and responsibilities relating to the academy, the church, and the "world"—some overlapping, others distinct. Thus, e.g., the OT theology that I would write for biblical scholars would be different from the theology I would write for a church audience—though I would regard the former as a service to the church as well as the academy (see

Trible's aim to "redeem" the Bible (as an "ancient treasure" and in its continuing use) from the "confines of patriarchy" suggests a cultural captivity that must be broken in order for the Bible to be restored or reclaimed as a theological source. The idea of "redemption" is appealing, but also problematic, because patriarchy is an integral aspect of the language and world of the text. It is only through this distorted medium that we encounter (in Scripture) the God who transcends and judges the conditions of this historical witness. The Bible cannot escape the confines of history. Whether the God to which it testifies is so bound is another matter—which cannot be tested or confirmed by literary or historical means. Shifting metaphors, Trible speaks of "wrestling" from the text a theology that will subvert patriarchy. Although I find this metaphor more apt as a description of the hermeneutical process, it also suggests that the Bible contains all that is needed for contemporary belief, requiring only the effort of the reader to release it. I find similar problems with Trible's metaphors of treasure house (from which to seek out treasures that will serve feminist theological needs) and remnant (a theology to be recovered by lifting up neglected or suppressed traditions).[90] Such scripturally charged metaphors command rhetorical authority but suggest a recovery operation that minimizes or denies the radical disjunction between the biblical world and our own.

In contrast to this treasure hunt, I want to hold on to the whole theological testimony of the OT/HB, in its patriarchal form, as a source for a contemporary feminist theology. Instead of seeking a remnant, I want to explore the ancient conversations in which the biblical texts participate—within the religiocultural world of the ancient Near East and within the canon of Scripture—in order to apprehend the theological issues at stake therein and extend and transform those conversations into contemporary speech in encounter with contemporary problems and questions. I see a more complex interaction with the biblical texts, in which the

---

discussion below on the intended audience and function of biblical theology). In this essay, I am concerned with the role of theological interpretation in the academic field of OT/HB studies and the function of OT theology in that context. It is unclear to me from Trible's essay on biblical theology (published in a journal of theology) who her intended audience is.

90. Trible, "Feminist Hermeneutics," 458, 464; cf. Trible, "Treasures," 32, 49. These metaphors are found throughout Trible's writings.

ancient context and the religiocultural dynamics operative there play a more critical role in shaping contemporary theological responses.[91]

"Special" and "General" Theologies in the North American Context

A defining feature of the North American context—as well as the global context—is an irreducible pluralism that makes "special" theologies both necessary and problematic. If emphasis in biblical theology is placed on meaning for today, then it would appear that there can only be "special," or particular, theologies, shaped by the traditions and needs of particular groups of readers. But this creates a new set of challenges for the discipline—as well as the church.[92] Although none of us today can do justice to the full range of experience and perspectives represented in our field of study, all of us, especially in North America, now work in situations that require us to reach beyond the group or culture in which we were socialized. "Special" theologies expose the hidden boundaries and biases of "general" theologies, revealing them to be likewise governed by special interests—albeit of the dominant group(s). But by targeting distinct groups and interests outside the old area of consensus they leave open the question concerning the ground and impetus for conversation across these boundaries of religious, cultural, and class identity.[93] This makes

---

91. There is an underlying question here of the nature of biblical authority, which I flagged earlier as critical for feminist attitudes to biblical theology. For Trible it seems to reside in the text itself as it wanders through history, generating new meanings and correcting false constructions of itself. Trible appears to view Scripture as self-sufficient, leading her to seek grounding principles for her methodology and her critique in the Bible itself. Thus she does not consider outside sources of evaluation and authority, such as the Christian community, the rule of faith, or the Christian conscience but views the Bible as standing over the individuals and communities it encounters on its journey. In contrast to Trible, who holds a text-immanent view of biblical authority, I understand the Bible as a site of revelation past and present, whose authority has a historical dimension and a necessary relationship to the communities of faith that transmit and interpret it (see n. 58 above). It has proved impossible in this essay to treat the issue of feminist understandings of biblical authority more generally, as I had earlier intended. There is now a large and varied literature on feminist hermeneutics, with implied notions of authority, though the issue of authority itself is often not addressed in these works. See, e.g., Camp, "Feminist Theological Hermeneutics" and the subject index of Schüssler Fiorenza, *Searching the Scriptures*.

92. A distinct but related set of issues arises in relation to contextual theologies, which cannot be pursued here.

93. I am grateful for the degree to which differing perspectives and experiences were programmed into this colloquium, but the voices are far from equal, and we must

the question of "center" or essential content all the more urgent—and historical inquiry essential, in my view. Fresh attempts to formulate the fundamental theological content of shared texts as a historical task in an ecumenical context should serve to enhance interreligious dialog and invite critical appraisal of traditional understandings, as well as new readings.[94]

Historical Theology as a Feminist Option

In view of the limits of this essay, I will begin with a brief summary statement of my approach and the rationale for it, following this with more detailed arguments and further considerations of the nature and aims of the discipline as space allows. I affirm the concept of biblical theology as a historical and descriptive discipline[95] within the field of biblical studies,[96] understanding it as a complement to the history of the religion

---

all learn how to carry on this new conversation. Sustained efforts and intentionality will be needed to assure that conversation continues, that it includes the widest range of experience possible, and that weak voices are not submerged.

94. On historical criticism as providing a framework for debate among scholars of differing prejudices and commitments, see Collins, "Is a Critical Biblical Theology?" 7–8. Adjudicating—or contesting—the truth claims of constructive theologies cannot be done in the sphere of historical study, but historical study can help to clarify where and how the constructive effort has moved beyond the historical base.

95. Or activity—a characterization favored by Ollenburger ("Biblical Theology," 37, 54). The language of "discipline" is used quite freely in the literature, and it is often unclear to me what claims are entailed in this designation. Collins ("Is a Critical Biblical Theology," 14; cf. 9) argues that biblical theology is not a "self-sufficient discipline" but rather a "subdiscipline" [of historical theology], whose contribution is to the "broader subject of theology." My understanding of it as a historical and descriptive activity is close to that of Barr (*Concept*, 1–17), and I find his analysis of its similarities and contrasts to other modes of studying the Bible generally instructive and congenial (ibid., 62–84, 100–139, etc.).

96. The location of the subject is critical for determining appropriate methods and aims. Thus Collins ("Is a Critical Biblical Theology," 8–9), who places it within the field of historical theology (see previous note), is concerned with the kind of theological statements that are compatible with its historical character and the critical methodology that history demands. Although he places it within the field of theology, he recognizes areas of overlap with the history of religion (ibid., 9). By placing it in the field of biblical studies, I want to assert the legitimacy, and necessity, of theological interpretation in a field that no longer understands itself (at least in the United States) as a subfield of theology but continues to be essential to theology, in both its critical and confessional forms. On the relationship, and distinctions, between biblical theology and doctrinal theology, see Barr, *Concept*, 62–76. Barr characterizes biblical theology

of Israel and early Judaism, focusing on religious ideas, with attention to how they cohere, change, and interact with other ideas in response to new experience.[97] As descriptive, historical study, it invites participation by scholars of different faiths, or none, and it demands no assent to the beliefs described. It does demand willingness to enter the belief-world of the text, and disciplined effort to comprehend the testimonies of faith encountered there without imposition of personal values and judgments—an ideal that is never fully realized but is nonetheless essential.[98] Because such a theology is determined first of all by the contours and confessions of the historical text, it cannot be feminist or liberationist or Christian or Jewish. But every version (and there can only be versions, never definitive statements) will be a distinctly individual creation, shaped by the peculiar sensitivities and biases of the author—including feminist sensitivities and biases.

The effort to comprehend the faith of the biblical authors and editors in their world(s)—and articulate it for modern readers in their world(s)—does not require the scholar to suspend faith or judgment any more than any other form of historical scholarship or effort of cross-cultural understanding and interpretation. It does require respect for the otherness of the testimony, which allows ancient views and values to be heard as potential critique of the reader's, but also demands evaluative judgment. How that judgment is registered in the interpretive work of presenting the theology of the Hebrew Scriptures will depend on the author, as will the criteria that guide the judgment.[99]

---

as having a "mediating function between critical biblical study and theology in the stricter sense" (ibid., 83) but locates it as an "aspect of exegesis" (ibid., 251).

97. There are areas of overlap with history of religion and with literary studies as attention is directed to how the ideas find expression in certain literary and cultural forms and in certain social and historical contexts. See Barr, *Concept*, 100–139; cf. Collins, "Is a Critical Biblical Theology," 9.

98. The ideal is not a caricatured "objectivity" but a sympathetic hearing that attempts to assume the text's point of view before assessing the message. It does not preclude judgment (see below), and it recognizes the subjectivity of the reader as a tool of understanding. But it attempts to avoid imposition of alien values, by enlisting the aid of other readers as well as other ancient texts. Thus comparative literary and sociohistorical analysis is essential to the effort. Cf. Barr, *Concept*, 15–16, 205–8.

99. Although I emphasize the descriptive historical task of biblical theology, I believe this is compatible with John Collins's view of the theological task as "the critical evaluation of biblical speech about God," which does not simply report what biblical authors believed but attempts to "clarify the meaning and truth-claims of what was thought and believed from a modern critical perspective" (Collins, "Is a Critical

My advocacy of a historical approach is not a retreat from hermeneutics. As a Christian and a feminist, I am committed to a theology that will meet the moral and intellectual demands of the world in which I live—a world of poverty, violence, and oppression; of unimaginable wealth and technological miracles; of sterile earth and polluted seas and mass extinction of species; of racial-ethnic, sexual, and ideological conflicts rending the human family. I believe that the Hebrew Scriptures are an indispensable source for such a theology. But the means by which I would appropriate those resources are dialogical in nature and context-specific. And the theology that would meet the contemporary demands of faith, including feminist demands, will not be a biblical theology, but a theology in which the biblical witness is joined to the testimonies of history, experience, and reason in a fresh articulation of faith.[100] If the Bible is the indispensable source of all Christian theology, it is not the only source, and its own testimony presses readers to look beyond it for signs of divine presence and activity.

I have argued that a historical approach to biblical theology does not involve an abdication of judgment or rejection of ethical demands upon the interpreter. But the genre of the OT theology, as a summarizing work, necessarily limits the type and amount of interaction between the text and the reader's context. That is why I prefer to locate the primary work of theological interpretation and judgment of Scripture elsewhere—in the encounter with specific problems and needs of contemporary faith and life: in sermons (always with a particular congregation and occasion in mind), in lectures (to particular audiences), in essays addressing particular problems or issues (arising in the text and its history of interpretation or arising in the world of the reader[101]), and in teaching and counseling. My choice of historical method as the primary mode of encounter with the text is dictated by personal experience, desire to converse with a wider audience, and ethical considerations. I believe in according an ancient author the same respect due a contemporary writer, or a student or colleague in face-to-face communication, which means that I seek to discern the intention of the other as expressed in and through the words

---

Biblical Theology," 9).

100. I reveal my Wesleyan heritage with this "quadrilateral."

101. E.g., Bird, "Genesis 1-3 as a Source for a Contemporary Theology of Sexuality"; Bird, "Genesis 3 in Modern Biblical Scholarship"; and Bird, "Bible in Christian Ethical Deliberation concerning Homosexuality" (chap. 4 in this volume)—written for a conference on pastoral responses to an issue of current debate in the church.

and gestures and tone of the utterance. The fact that many of the needed clues are lacking in ancient texts does not alter the goal or process in any fundamental way, except to place greater emphasis on contextual clues and analogy. I recognize that texts, released from their author's control, are multivalent, having as many meanings as readers. And I also recognize that meanings are shaped by communities of interpreters. But I chose to honor the author (and redactor and collectors, insofar as they have left discernible imprints on the text) over the reader precisely because the author's intention has traditionally been subordinated to that of interpreters who would use the words for their own purposes. For me, this is a feminist issue. As women's words have been suppressed or made to serve men's interests, so the words of biblical authors have been made to serve the religious and political agendas of church and synagogue, state and society. So I remain convinced that a historical approach to the theology of the Hebrew Scriptures best serves feminist interests—as well as the needs of other biblical scholars and theologians—while protecting the text from arbitrary use.

Rethinking the Discipline and the Genre

With this confession I return to the question of whose interests an OT/HB theology is intended to serve. Who needs it? For what purpose? Or, why is it necessary, or desirable, at all? It is no longer sufficient simply to carry on the tradition descended from Gabler because it has established itself as an academic specialty (here I share Trible's concern, though not her solution). In particular, the genre of the OT theology needs to be rethought[102] in relation to contemporary needs and audiences, which are now multiple and varied. Albertz's proposal was an effort to address this question, but in a decidedly German context. Although his presupposition that OT theology has functioned as an introduction to OT studies does not speak to the North American context, I think he is right in suggesting that the primary audience is students of the OT/HB, or pastors and biblical scholars, rather than (systematic) theologians. While a traditionally stated goal of biblical theology has been to serve the theological

---

102. It is often unclear in discussions of "OT/HB theology" whether the subject is a field of inquiry, a type of activity, or the product of such efforts—viewed as their goal. Reviews of the history of the discipline typically focus on signal works, which are usually comprehensive in aim, or which seek to identify the central or distinctive ideas of the OT.

needs of the church as a foundation for dogmatics, or as an alternative, it is not clear to me that it has actually functioned in this way,[103] nor is it clear how it might best serve church theology or theologians today.[104] The Protestant principle of the primacy of Scripture requires any theology claiming the name Christian to be "biblical." What then is the need for a distinct biblical theology, and how do the two relate to each other? The fact that few contemporary theologians can command the full theological resources of the canon, and especially the Hebrew Scriptures, points to the need for some sort of interpretive filter or bridge between exegesis and confessional theology, but it is not clear to me that a comprehensive and synthetic work—with its own distinctive theological stamp—is the logical or best form for such mediation.[105]

I am inclined to think that targeted studies are the most useful form of biblical theology for those outside the field. The most productive interchanges between theology and biblical studies may be those that take place in consideration of particular problems, texts, or themes, or that build on personal relationships between individual theologians and biblical scholars. An advantage of limited and focused studies is that they allow for closer interaction with particular audiences and their particular interests and needs.

Evidence of renewed interest—and continuing difficulty—in conversation between biblical scholars and theologians was exhibited in two sessions of the 2001 Annual Meeting of the SBL. The Biblical Theology Consultation (a new program in its second year) presented a panel on the theme "The Wrath of God," with papers by Jewish and Christian OT/

---

103. In practice, the direction of influence has seemed to be from dogmatics to biblical theology, with categories of the former imposing themselves on the latter—a threat that von Rad attempted to counter with his concept of OT theology as "Nacherzählung [re-telling]" (von Rad, *Old Testament Theology*, 1:121). See Janowski, "Biblische Theologie," 1545–46.

104. Although Collins criticizes various attempts to make biblical theology serve doctrinal ends, he sees the discipline as a form of historical theology, and as such "one source among others for contemporary theology" ("Is a Critical Biblical Theology," 9). Cf. Barr (*Concept*, 67; cf. ibid., 62–76, 240–52), who speaks of biblical theology as a "participant" in the considerations of doctrinal theology. While arguing that biblical theology will have to be regarded as an "essential component in the total structure of theology" (ibid., 242), Barr insists that the source of doctrinal theology is not the Bible (ibid., 74).

105. Cf. Ollenburger's critique ("Biblical Theology," 48–54) of the notion that biblical theology should be understood as a "point of mediation between the particularities of the texts and the generalities of dogmatics" (ibid., 54).

HB scholars and "responses" by Jewish and Christian theologians.[106] The "respondents" both gave papers of their own that seemed scarcely to acknowledge, much less dialogue with, the biblical papers. It would appear from the program's design that the planners understood "biblical theology" to involve interchange between biblical scholars and theologians—in contrast to the Theology of the Hebrew Scriptures Section, where the participants have been primarily, if not exclusively, biblical scholars. Another panel concerned with the relationship between Bible and theology was presented by the Christian Theology and Bible Group, on the theme "Scripture and Truth." The audience seemed to consist primarily of theologians (members of AAR), and the language of theology dominated the presentations, apart from one paper by an OT/HB scholar, whose exegetical approach contextualized the question of "truth" in particular literary-historical situations-in-life.[107] Thus different modes of analysis—and a different vocabulary—characterized the two disciplines as they engaged in theological reflection. Again, conversation between the disciplines, seemed to be minimal.

THEOLOGY OF THE OT/HB AS A COMPREHENSIVE AND SYNTHETIC WORK

I have argued that much of the work of biblical theology might be carried out in limited studies, but I have come to believe that there is also a need for comprehensive and synthetic works of OT/HB theology, not primarily as a service to theologians, but to biblical scholars, teachers, students, and pastors. In fact, I would argue that it is necessary for every student of the HB, including those with no theological interest or religious commitment. OT/HB theology is necessary because of the nature of the texts as theological literature—whether or not they make explicit theological statements. It is needed first to make sense of the intellectual world of

---

106. Strictly speaking, "theologian" describes only the Christian respondent but is extended here to include the Jewish philosopher who served as a counterpart. The presenters were Benjamin Sommer ("Anthropopathism and Divine Wrath in Hosea 11 and Interpretive Tradition") and Terrance Fretheim ("Wrath of God in the Old Testament"), with Peter Ochs and Miroslav Volf as the respondents.

107. The presentations included papers by Katherine Grieb ("Lead Me in Your Truth and Teach Me: Some Reflections on Scripture and Truth"), Dennis Olson ("God, Truth, and the Torah: Reflections on Human Knowing in the Pentateuch"), Michael Welker ("Theology, Truth, and Scripture"), and Nicholas Wolterstorff ("Scripture and Truth"), with a response by B. Marshall.

the texts, and hence of the texts themselves, and second to draw out and clarify the truth claims made or implied by those texts. A descriptive historical theology that renounces efforts to formulate meaning for today is still theology, concerned with the question of ultimate meaning and truth, and not a mere reporting and cataloging of beliefs. It should enable modern readers to understand what is at stake in the OT/HB's portraits of God and statements of divine nature and will, so that they are not dismissed prematurely as anthropomorphic caricature or superficial "biography."

My argument here is that OT/HB theology can no longer be tied to the confessional needs of a particular religious community.[108] It must now engage the wider world to which the Bible belongs. Theology is too fundamental to the biblical writings to be claimed—or dismissed—as the exclusive province of believers. And theology is too important to be left to theologians. On September 11, 2001, we saw the devastating consequences of theology in the service of demonic aims, and the roots of that theology—as well as evidence of similar perversions—are in the OT/HB itself. I think it is both necessary and desirable to envision an OT theology designed for a multireligious and secular audience, one that might be used as a part of an introductory course, or as a separate study.[109] Moreover, I believe that a work that enables the reader to enter as fully as possible into the thought world of the text and engage in the battles of belief fought out there will serve the needs of Christian believers as well as the needs of others. The form that such a theology will take will depend on the particular audience and author.

I have argued for a form of OT/HB theology that does not tie it to a particular trajectory of faith. At the same time, I think there is also a need within the communities of faith that read these texts as Scripture to trace the lines between biblical faith and contemporary belief more explicitly. This may take a variety of forms, proceeding either from a biblical or a contemporary starting point; but the effort will need to come primarily from biblical scholars, who have the requisite knowledge of the texts. As

---

108. In fact, there are inherent contradictions between that traditional function and the method employed by the discipline. See below.

109. Such a theology would not advocate a particular trajectory to contemporary faith but would make differing trajectories intelligible—and would identify features suppressed or discarded by later traditions. As every historical work does, however, it will betray the standpoint and interests of its author. But the usefulness of the work will be judged by the credibility of the account it offers, not by the beliefs of the author.

an activity of biblical scholars, dependent on their primary competence with the biblical text, it requires recognition in the field of biblical studies, but the activity must be understood as a constructive theological activity and a contribution to the field of theology—and thus requires recognition as a legitimate form of theology. The risks are considerable: on the one hand, the risk of compromising the literary-historical analysis with confessional demands or theological agendas; on the other, the risk of theological naivete or "biblicism" that isolates the Bible as a source and fails to integrate its results into a larger theological system. Despite the risks of violating the canons of both fields in their present academic autonomy—and the attendant risks of being disowned by both fields—I am not willing to declare this activity illegitimate.[110] But I do think that this form of biblical theology needs a descriptive historical theology as a foundation and guard against unwarranted construals. And it is to this historical task that I prefer to devote my energies—as a theologian.[111] I am not prepared to propose a particular form or emphasis for such a theology, but I do want to sketch some features that I think are essential to reflect our present knowledge of the OT/HB and its world and the needs of contemporary readers attempting to understand the theology of this canonical corpus.

Features of an Historical and Descriptive Theology of the OT/HB

A historical and descriptive theology of the OT/HB would be limited to the data of the HB itself—read in the context of extrabiblical evidence for religious belief and practice of the time.[112] It would be both historical and canonical, giving attention to the religiocultural contexts of individual

---

110. While I agree with Collins's analysis of the inherent conflict between confessional faith as a dogmatic system and historical critical method ("Is a Critical Biblical Theology," 7–9), I think there is a practical need for combining confessional and historical modes of knowing, which must open the "assured results" of both to reformulation. Thus I am willing to grant legitimacy to a wide range of mediating forms of biblical theology, including Trible's.

111. Theological sensitivity is just as essential to historical as to constructive theology. I should add a further motive for both the descriptive and the constructive efforts, namely, the need of the biblical scholar to make sense of the theological testimony of the OT/HB for her- or himself.

112. For an effort to integrate the "external evidence" for the theology of ancient Syria-Palestine and neighboring lands into a theology of the OT/HB, see Janowski, "Theologie."

traditions and larger literary complexes, from the earliest tradition units to the latest redactional levels. Thus, e.g., it would treat the God of the fathers as representing both a stage in the development of Israelite religion (relating to the clan, in which the patriarchal head held religious authority) and a continuing affirmation of God's special relationship to the community (notions of election, promise, and providence), an affirmation whose claim is both tested (by the exile) and contested (by notions of universalism and by skepticism).

Such a theology would attempt to comprehend the diverse testimony as parts of a whole, defined on the one hand by a canon that has channeled connections and conversations among the texts, but also by processes of theological reflection that stand behind the canon, determining the selection of canonical texts.[113] It will be, necessarily, systematic—whether the drive for coherence is understood to inhere in the scriptural testimony itself[114] or to derive from the needs of the modern theologian-historian.[115] Whatever the structure chosen to present the fundamental religious ideas, the theology must have a chronological dimension. Time/history in the Hebrew Scriptures is both a condition of the data and a subject of theological reflection. An attempt to give an integrated account of the whole theological testimony of the Hebrew Scriptures is not in fundamental conflict with the recognition of multiple and conflicting theologies within that corpus.[116] Conflicting views only make sense within a shared universe of thought and discourse.[117] To do justice to the diverse theological data of the HB, a theology of the

---

113. The canonical whole is not an arbitrary whole, despite the accidents of history and the religiopolitical forces operative in the selection.

114. So Knierim, "Task," 30–31, 47–48; and Knierim, "On the Task," 108–127.

115. It is clear in any case that the drive to comprehend ever-greater complexes of evidence is a feature of the redactional/canonical process itself and not simply a modern imposition.

116. I regret that I am unable to take account of Erhard Gerstenberger's *Theologies of the Old Testament*, as the German version was unavailable to me and the English translation not yet published. A key hermeneutical question, which cannot be treated here, is the question of how different confessional traditions and readers have assessed the authority of conflicting theologies within the Scriptures.

117. The attempt to articulate the underlying system of beliefs reveals the shifting boundaries of the area of shared belief, which expands and contracts—at times simultaneously. At times in Israel's history, the competing theologies lie within the realm of Israelite Yahwism; at other times they lie in a shared religious universe that links Israel or Yahwism, or both, with surrounding nations or religions.

Hebrew Scriptures must be both historically specific and systematic.[118] And it must deal with the relationship of theological ideas to social and political realia.

Feminist Contributions to a Descriptive Historical Theology of the OT/HB

What I have described has very close connections with a history of the religion of Israel, but it is not the same thing. Its primary data are the statements of the HB, understood as a limited corpus constituted by a process of composition and selection that has imposed certain value judgments on the data of religious experience and expression in ancient Israel. Here is where feminism has an essential contribution to make—to identify but one point of engagement.[119] Contemporary awareness of the social location and identity of all authors and literature requires attention to these same factors in the literature of ancient Israel. This means that the theological statements of the HB, which constitute the data for any OT theology, must be understood to be partial and skewed—not only by the elite status of the authors (a presupposition of all early writing), or by the particular historical and political factors that assured the survival and dominance of certain theological views, but because they represent the theological insights and experience of only half the population. To that extent they are a deficient, and distorted, testimony.[120] The silence of women is of a different order than the silence of particular social classes, ethnic groups, or political parties, because it runs through every class and social category. It is a matter of the most basic of all human distinctions— a distinction linked to biological markers and endowed with social meanings and consequences in every society. It is also a distinction that is given explicit recognition in the OT/HB and invested with religious

---

118. Different theologies will handle this dual demand in different ways. One might argue, for example, that creation is the fundamental concept of OT theology, giving this priority in structuring the work. But it is clear from the total evidence that while creation may be logically and canonically prior, it is not historically or experientially first, and this tension between historical and canonical priority has theological significance.

119. I do not mean to limit feminist interest or contributions to considerations of literary production and canon formation. See below.

120. The underlying assumption of this statement is that men cannot speak for women and that men's religious experience cannot provide a fully adequate description of the nature of God and God's relationship to humanity and the world.

significance and theological interpretation.[121] What then is the meaning—and what the truth value—of a theology that claims to speak about the ultimate nature and meaning of life but speaks only in a male voice? And how shall we respond to this fundamental distortion in our sources?

There is no single or simple answer to this question. We are only beginning to explore ways to move beyond a patriarchal past into a future shaped by the full participation of women with men—a future that would appear from the perspective of this colloquium to be well beyond our present horizons. In the meantime, however, I think it is at least reasonable to expect that gender analysis and recognition of the fundamentally skewed nature of our data find a place in every new effort to formulate a theology of the OT/HB. I do not think that any theology, descriptive or normative, can be said to present an accurate or adequate account if it fails to register the exclusive male orientation of the Bible's theological statements, and fails to reflect on the consequences of that fact. I also think that recognition of this skewing needs to be registered throughout the work, not simply in a prefatory statement or a chapter or section on female deities or attributes of deity. The whole of the Hebrew Scriptures is formulated in gendered language and concepts derived from gendered experience. Every theological idea or expression needs to be examined for implications of this gender bias. A theology today that universalizes concepts presented in the OT/HB in gender-specific language and contexts is not telling the truth about the OT/HB's theology.[122]

Consideration of gender bias might begin, by way of example, with the concept of *covenant*, a political metaphor derived from the realm of male experience and transformed into a theological construct in the realm of male religious activity. It is not a gender-neutral concept. And when marriage is presented as an alternative metaphor for the relationship between God and Israel, it is filled with specific gendered experience of marriage in which the male experience is projected onto God. The "pornographic" development of this metaphor, which has occasioned so much feminist rage, is simply one vivid example of the way the normally

---

121. This statement is not in conflict with my earlier insistence that gender is a modern concept. Gender is a modern analytical term that is used to interpret phenomena recognized under various terms and categories by all cultures.

122. A decision to universalize such language as a hermeneutical strategy is certainly an option that deserves consideration, but it needs to be intentional, and defended. On the related, but distinct, question of inclusive-language Bible translation, see Bird, "Translating Sexist Language."

hidden assumptions of male authors and audience determine the form and content of theological expression. But covenant is a relatively obvious example of a gendered category being treated as though it were a neutral and "natural" concept. Concepts such as *justice, righteousness, liberation,* and *love* need to be examined for gender implications as well. How are these terms actually used in the OT/HB? To what situations in life do they refer? From whose perspective are they formulated?[123]

I have chosen to highlight the androcentric bias that shapes and penetrates the OT/HB rather than to focus on the problem of the Bible's male God and the suppression of the goddess, because the latter problems are more widely recognized (although they have yet to receive adequate attention in biblical theologies) and tend to be viewed as the root problem and key issue for feminist theology. The question of female presence and representation *is* a key issue in conceptions of deity, but it is linked to a broad range of other gender-related issues that are rooted in the particular cultural context in which the biblical texts arose. That is why I believe that history of religion and cultural analysis are indispensable to OT theology, and why as a feminist I reject an approach to biblical theology that focuses simply on the women in the text and female images of God.

I do not want to understate the importance of the goddess (present and absent in the biblical text) for OT theology and the form of monotheism whose trajectory is traced through the Scriptures. Iconographic and epigraphic evidence now supplement biblical references and allusions to establish the presence of a female deity or deities as a significant element in Israelite religion during the period in which the canonical portrait of Israel's God was formed. If biblical monotheism was won at the cost of suppressing a female rival or representation of the divine, this has serious implications for any claims of universality—or authority—that may be made on behalf of the regnant Deity. Feminist readers who suggest that the cost has been too high deserve a fuller hearing and response than they have received in most OT theologies. But the historical circumstances and cultural context also require closer attention than they

---

123. For some initial efforts in this direction, see Ackerman, "Personal Is Political" (for evidence that the verb *to love* is identified exclusively with a male subject, or superior, in narrative use); and Bird, "Poor Man" (for evidence that "the poor," as the object of God's special concern, are always male). See also van Dijk-Hemmes and Brenner, *On Gendering Texts*; van Dijk-Hemmes and Brenner, *Reflections*; and Becking and Dijkstra, *On Reading.*

have been given in many views of the goddess and the Bible's patriarchal deity.[124] It is clear that the God of Israel and of the church has never fully overcome the defects or limits of origins as a male deity, posing a central problem for contemporary theology. But an OT theology that treats this problem in its historical context can help to show the religiopolitical and cultural factors involved in the theological construct we have inherited and can challenge abstracting and absolutizing claims.

As a feminist, what I seek in an OT theology is awareness of gender as a theological issue—an issue that pervades the whole of the Scriptures. I do not seek the elevation of biblical women, either in the text or behind the text, or the recovery of a suppressed goddess, but rather signs and directives that point toward a theological future that will be shaped by women's experience as well as men's and framed in the speech of both sexes.[125] Women from a patriarchal past can only speak out of the experience of patriarchy. While I would declare solidarity with them and insist that their memory be imprinted on the consciousness of every reader of Scripture, male as well as female, their lost voices will not produce a theology for today.[126] They can, of course, be given new voices—but that is a constructive task that does not belong to biblical theology as a historical discipline. I do not deny the power of the Bible's female images to serve present needs, but they need to be transformed, just as its male images require transformation. Awareness of the Bible's androcentric bias means that *none* of the language and images of the HB/OT may be appropriated uncritically for contemporary affirmations of faith. But that also means that explicitly patriarchal terms and concepts may be transformed to

---

124. Thus, e.g., distinctions need to be made between different female deities and the way they related to YHWH and the YHWH cult. E.g., only the Queen of Heaven (Jer 7:18; 44:17-19) appears as a rival to YHWH (whose contests were with Baal or other male deities), while Asherah appears as a consort, or merely a symbol embodying female attributes that could find only minimal and marginal representation in the God of the state and the clan. See Jost, *Frauen*; Hadley, *Cult of Asherah*; Binger, *Asherah*; M. S. Smith, *Early History*; M. S. Smith, *Origins*; and Keel and Uehlinger, *Gods*.

125. In these concluding remarks, I look beyond the descriptive historical theology that I have advocated toward the constructive theology that will incorporate feminist critique of a patriarchal past and feminist vision of a new creation—as a necessary expression of the Bible's own central theological affirmations.

126. There is a double issue here: the representation of women in the text—who appear and speak only as recorded or constructed by males—and the reconstruction of women behind the text, including their religious lives and beliefs. An understanding of both is essential to a proper understanding and appraisal of the OT texts as the product of a community of gendered religious experience and theological reflection.

serve a theology shaped by feminist sensitivities. A suffering servant and a crucified king have already provided precedent and paradigm for such transformations.

To return to the God of the fathers, symbol of a patriarchal religion and theology and symbol of the patriarchal tradition through which we have received this legacy, I believe we must retain this symbol within our repertoire of theological images—not only in a historical theology, where I have suggested it has multiple meanings, but also in a contemporary feminist theology. It is a necessary reminder of the cultural conditioning of all religious language and experience of the divine, and a reminder of the historical character of all theological constructions. It serves thereby to validate the search for new theological language appropriate to new religious experience and underscores the never-ending need to interpret the images of the past afresh, lest they become empty, or deceptive, idols.

2

Theological Anthropology in the Hebrew Bible

INTRODUCTION

Theological anthropology in both Jewish and Christian tradition has looked to Gen 1:26–27 as a foundational text. Here, in the Bible's first reference to humankind, humans are described in their "original" or "essential" nature as created "in the image of God." This striking correlation of the human with the divine is unique, and isolated, within the Hebrew Scriptures, but it generated a history of speculation that has continued unabated since the first centuries BCE.[1] A critical factor in this history is the distinctive interpretation given to the text in early Christian writings, which combined it with Genesis 2–3 in speculation on the problem of sin and the effect of the "fall" on the image. In New Testament writings of the Pauline school, Christ is identified with the image (Rom 8:29; 1 Cor 11:7; 15:49; 2 Cor 3:18; 4:4; Col 1:15; 3:10; Heb 1:3), and cast as a "second Adam" (Rom 5:12–21). Continuing speculation in the early church produced a doctrine of the *imago Dei* in which the Genesis text was read through the eyes of Paul—as interpreted by Augustine and other church "fathers."[2] As a consequence of this Christian dogmatic appropriation of the text, the theological anthropology of the Hebrew Bible has long been

---

1. For a survey of interpretations, see Westermann, *Genesis 1–11*, 147–55.

2. For a brief history of interpretation in Christian theology, see Hall, *Imaging God*, 76–112. More detailed treatments may be found in Cairns, *Image of God in Man*; and Berkouwer, *Man*.

subordinated to a biblical anthropology in which the Old Testament[3] witness was selected, and distorted, to fit the needs of a Pauline trajectory.

Although the concept of the divine image had an important place in Jewish theology—and ethics—it did not dominate Jewish anthropology in the same way as the *imago* symbol in Christian theology.[4] And while modern biblical scholarship attempted to free itself from dogmatic constraints, it has nevertheless been shaped in large measure by Christian (and post-Christian) agendas. The legacy of Christian theological speculation still weighs heavily on contemporary biblical interpretation—in the disproportionate attention devoted to the *imago* text and in the focus of the exegesis, which has been directed especially to questions of gender and dominion, and debate concerning the content of the "image." It has also penetrated deeply into Western culture, fueling contemporary debates over such issues as evolution, the role of women, environmental ethics, population control, and sexual orientation.

This essay is shaped by awareness of these contemporary debates, but its primary aim is to present the testimony of the Hebrew Bible as the testimony of ancient Israel and explore the meaning of its statements in and for their own time(s). As a work of descriptive theology, it adopts the perspective and tools of historical criticism. In attempting to articulate the theology of the ancient authors in their own historical settings, it recognizes multiple and conflicting voices and perspectives. But it also recognizes a canonical context, or canonical contexts, in which these voices are brought into dialogue with one another and with external traditions. Different canonical boundaries establish different arenas of discourse, and different reading communities give differing weight to the various sources. Thus Christian interpreters will set the theological anthropology of the Old Testament in relation to that of the New Testament, while Jewish interpreters will relate the same textual evidence to the ongoing tradition of rabbinic interpretation.

---

3. The term *Hebrew Bible* is adopted in this chapter as a nonconfessional designation for the Christian *Old Testament*. There is, however, no common term or conception for this literature when it is considered from the perspectives of the several religious communities that continue to regard it as sacred Scripture.

4. For an introduction to Jewish theological anthropology by a modern Jewish philosopher and biblical scholar, see Heschel, "Concept."

GENESIS 1:26-28 IN ITS HISTORICAL AND CANONICAL CONTEXT

Genesis 1:26–28, with its concept of the *ṣelem ʾĕlōhîm* ("image of God"), is too narrow a base upon which to construct a full theological anthropology of the Hebrew Bible, but it is a fitting starting point in its canonical position as the Bible's first word about the nature of humankind. It commands particular attention for its attempt to position humans within the created order, through explicit terms of relationship to other creatures and to the divine. But it is the claim of God-likeness, expressed in the language of divine image, that is most arresting. The history of interpretation of the passage has been dominated by attempts to specify the content of this "likeness" or "image." Proposals range from physical interpretations that equate the image with upright stature or some other aspect of bodily nature or appearance to psychosocial or spiritual interpretations that identify the image with such attributes as language, mental capacity, or ability to communicate with God. Attempts have also been made to understand the image in terms of the divine plurals of v. 26 or the gender dualism of v. 27. But the text, viewed in its larger literary context and according to the normal rules of Hebrew grammar, excludes all of these interpretations. To understand the meaning of its theological affirmations as an expression of Israelite theology, it must be considered in its primary exegetical context: the Priestly account of creation.[5]

Genesis 1:26–28 within the Priestly Account of Creation

The account of creation that opens the Hebrew Scriptures moves in a six-day progression from formless void to ordered universe, capped by a seventh day of rest for the Creator (Gen 1:1—2:4a). Through a series of solemn proclamations, God summons into being all of the elements of the ancient cosmos and all forms of life, both animal and vegetable. Compared to the creation myths known from the ancient Near East, it is an exceedingly spare account, and devoid of drama, resembling liturgy more than story. Modern scholarship has attributed it to a Priestly author or "school," whose distinctive style and theology can be traced through the first four books of the Bible. Thus it forms the first chapter of a distinct

---

5. The following analysis draws on more detailed studies in Bird, "'Male and Female He Created Them,'" 123-54; Bird, "Genesis 3," 174-93; and Børresen, *Image*, 5-28. Cf. Jónsson, *Image*; and commentaries.

literary work, or edition of the Pentateuch, as well as an introduction to the Scriptures as a whole. This same literary source or stratum continues in the genealogies that punctuate the book of Genesis and in the flood story, which contain the only other references to the divine image, or likeness, in the Hebrew Bible.[6]

Within this opening account of origins, the creation of humankind (ʾādām) is presented as the final and climactic act: ʾādām is the crown of creation.[7] This message of human exaltation is conveyed not only by the sequence of acts, which represents a hierarchy of being, but also by changes of diction, elaboration, and expansion of basic themes, and explicit statements of divine likeness and earthly dominion.

(26) And God said:
"Let us make ʾādām in our image, according to our likeness,
And let them have dominion over the fish of the sea and the birds of the air and the cattle and all the earth and everything that creeps upon the earth."

(27) And God created ʾādām in his image,
In the image of God he created him;
Male and female he created them.

(28) And God blessed them, and God said to them:
"Be fruitful and multiply and fill the earth and subdue it,
And have dominion over the fish of the sea and the birds of the air and every living creature that creeps upon the earth."

Despite the elaborations and distinctions in this account of the final act of creation, it shares a common literary structure with the other reported acts and incorporates themes belonging to the larger composition. The account as a whole is dominated by an interest in stability and order; each element or class has its place, and its nature and function

---

6. While the mid-twentieth-century consensus on pentateuchal history no longer holds, recognition of a distinct source, or strand of tradition, identified as P (for its "Priestly" characteristics) has remained largely intact and continues to serve my analysis.

7. Hebrew ʾādām is a collective noun (grammatically singular). It designates the species as a class, parallel to the other classes of life identified in Genesis 1—all collective nouns in Hebrew, generally translated as English plurals ("plants," "trees," "swarms," "birds," "beasts," etc.). See Bird, *Missing Persons*: Bird, "'Male and Female He Created Them,'" 141 n. 45; Bird, "Genesis 1–3," 161–62; 168–73. It is sometimes used for an individual in order to emphasize the species identification over every other distinguishing feature, such as gender or nationality.

are determined at creation. Thus the firmament is to separate the cosmic waters; the heavenly bodies are to mark times and seasons and govern day and night; and humans are to rule over the realm of living creatures. This ruling function of the human species is specified in the opening announcement that introduces the final act of creation. And it is in relation to this specification that the divine image must be understood, for it is the precondition of that rule. Humans are to be God's vicegerents on earth.

The Hebrew phrase ṣelem ʾĕlōhîm ("image of God") is the exact counterpart of the Akkadian expression (ṣalam-[god's name]: "image of Enlil [Marduk, etc.]"), which appears as an epithet of Mesopotamian kings. The king in ancient Babylonia and Assyria was understood to be a special representative of the god or gods, possessing a divine mandate to rule, and hence divine authority; but he was not himself divine. The epithet "image of the god" served to emphasize his divinely sanctioned authority and god-like dignity.

The Hebrew term ṣelem, like Akkadian ṣalmu, is used elsewhere to designate a statue or picture, a representation (of a god, animal, or other thing) that brings to mind, or stands in for, the thing it depicts or represents. Its biblical uses are mostly concrete, and mostly negative—describing foreign deities (Num 33:52; 2 Kgs 11:18; 2 Chr 23:17; Ezek 7:20, 16:17; Amos 5:26), golden images of mice and tumors (1 Sam 6:5, 11), and painted pictures of Babylonians (Ezek 23:14). It could also be used figuratively, to describe the insubstantial nature of life (Ps 39:6 [Heb. 39:7]) or a dream image (Ps 73:20). It is a term of holistic representation based on form. Thus when the expression "image of God," is applied to human beings, it suggests a notion of physical resemblance. Its meaning, however, is determined by its context of use, and its use here has no parallel within the Hebrew Bible. That is why the ancient Near Eastern parallels are critical; they evidence the identical phrase *and* similar associations.

"Image" and "Likeness"

The Priestly author has made use of a Mesopotamian royal epithet, but he has qualified or elaborated it in two ways. He has coupled it with the abstract noun děmût, meaning "likeness"[8] and employed both terms in

---

8. The noun, like the related verb *dmh* ("to liken"), emphasizes comparison, and hence similarity in difference.

adverbial constructions that describe the activity of the creator rather than the nature of the creature. Thus, according to Gen 1:26, 27, humans are not the image of God, nor do they possess it; rather they are created "in" or "according to"[9] the divine image and/or likeness.

Despite these qualifications, however, the basic sense of the characterization remains one of form or appearance; the one who is modeled on the divine must be understood as modeling the divine in the world of creatures. And although the noun *dĕmût* is used figuratively (Ezek 1:5, 26; 8:2; 10:1; cf. Isa 13:4), it is also used to describe a model of an altar (2 Kgs 16:10) and the "likeness" of oxen holding up the molten sea (2 Chr 4:3). Thus the two nouns are essentially synonymous, as suggested also by their interchange in Gen 5:1, 3. It would appear then that a God who elsewhere prohibits the making of any image as a representation of the divine (Exod 20:4) here accords this function and dignity to the whole of humankind; and a God to whom nothing can be likened (Isa 40:25; 46:5, 9) creates humankind in his own likeness. Such comparisons move outside the Priestly writer's own thought, as do the speculations about the meaning of the two terms that preoccupied Jewish and Christian interpreters through the ages. The latter require brief mention because of their influence in past exegesis.

Jewish interpretation generally recognized the two nouns as equivalent in meaning and accepted the corporeal nature of the image, resulting in speculation about the nature of the divine body and the "original" body of "Adam." In contrast, Christian interpretation associated both nouns with spiritual or mental faculties, or both,[10] making a further distinction between a "natural" and a "supernatural" likeness. According to Irenaeus, the "image" (Latin *imago*) represented the human nature that was unaffected by the fall—identified as rationality and freedom—while the "likeness" (Latin *similitudo*) represented the original relationship with God—which was lost in the fall and restored through Christ. Both Jewish and Christian interpretation focused on the distinguishing and enduring qualities of the original creation, and both assumed some degree of diminution or loss of the image as they sought, in different ways, to reconcile the claim of God-likeness with the realities of sin and death[11]

---

9. The two prepositions should be understood as having the same meaning, namely, "according to," "like" (or "as"). Cf. Gen 5:1, 3; 9:6 and the LXX.

10. Jónsson, *Image*, 12–13, 175–77; Cairns, *Image of God in Man*, 73–83. There were, to be sure, Jewish interpreters who found a spiritual meaning in the image.

11. See Heschel, "Concept," 154, 159–69. For Judaism, the cure for human

(see below). Both abstracted and absolutized the idea of the divine image, or likeness, removing it from its literary context.

It is context, however, that determines meaning in historical-critical interpretation. Thus while the notion of corporeal resemblance appears to stand behind the Priestly writer's use of the language of "image" and "likeness" in his account of origins (especially in Gen 5:1), it plays no role in the understanding of human nature or duty in the rest of the Priestly writings, and it has no echo or parallel elsewhere in the Hebrew Scriptures. Its theological significance is in the place it gives to humans within the created order, not in any physical or moral attribute of the species, either in its present or "original" state.

Ancient Near Eastern Context

According to Gen 1:26, humans are in some unspecified but essential way "like" God, and this is related to their position or function within the created order, as exercising dominion over their fellow creatures. In adopting this metaphor of ruler, couched in the language of ancient Near Eastern kingship, the author has constructed a portrait of human dignity and responsibility in creation that counters the picture presented by the creation myths of surrounding cultures. In those traditions, human beings were created to be slaves of the gods. They were to do the hard labor needed to maintain the functioning of the universe; they were to relieve the gods from their toil.[12]

The Priestly account of creation is a "countermyth" that redefines the nature of both God and humankind in its alternative view of the cosmos. God in the Priestly creation account is not only the sole actor and designer of the universe, who accomplishes everything that he proposes and recognizes it as good. The God of Genesis 1 has also designed a universe that does not require subsequent divine intervention or human petition to maintain its stability and course. It is not in danger of disintegrating or dying; it does not need to be revived or re-created in an annual New Years' ritual. Its orders are fixed and unchanging, and

---

corruption is Sinai and the covenant; for Christians, it is Christ. Both Christian and Jewish theologians encounter difficulties when they attempt to make the divine image *the* foundational concept for anthropology. As a nonmoral category it stands in inevitable tension with efforts to define the human in moral terms.

12. See, e.g., *Enuma Elish* 6.34-35 (*ANET*, 68); and *Atrahasis* 1.194-97 (Lambert and Millard, *Atra-ḫasīs*, 56-57).

each form of life, both plant and animal, is endowed with the means of reproducing its kind. Plants are constituted with seed-bearing organs for "automatic" reproduction, while living creatures are designed as sexual pairs (implied by the blessing) and enjoined to "be fruitful and multiply and fill the earth" (vv. 22, 28). This word of blessing and command applies to humans as well as other creatures. Like them, but unlike God, humans are sexual beings. That is the meaning of the statement that is added in v. 27 to the report of the final act of creation; *ʾādām* is created in the image of God, but *also* male and female.

Male and Female

Humans are understood as a distinct order of creature with a unique resemblance to God, but they are not divine. Like all other creatures they share the capacity and the duty to perpetuate their kind. But while sexual differentiation could be assumed of the other creatures and did not need to be specified, it could not be assumed of humans; for they have been defined only by their resemblance to God (v. 26)—and God for the Priestly author possessed no gender or sexuality.[13] The specification of creation as male and female is the necessary prerequisite to the blessing pronounced in v. 28.[14] The terms used here are identical to those used for the animal species in 6:19 and 7:9: *zākār* ("male") and *něqēbâ* ("female"). They are biological terms, not social terms—in contrast to the "man" and "woman" of Genesis 2–3.

Some interpreters have sought to explain the divine image through correlation of the "male-and-female" of v. 27 with the plural references to God in v. 26. Such correlation ignores the structure of the account, with its double theme of order and reproduction and its progressive articulation of the two. It also misinterprets the Priestly theology. The divine plurals of v. 26 ("Let us make *ʾādām* in our image") are no unreflective remnant of an earlier polytheism encompassing male and female deities, but a

---

13. Although the Priestly writer uses exclusively male terms to refer to God, they are to be understood metaphorically. Popular religion may have given YHWH a consort in ancient Israel, but the biblical writings consistently oppose any notion of sexuality for Israel's God.

14. A similar need to specify male and female lies behind the Priestly description of the animal pairs who enter the ark (Gen 6:19; 7:9). What may be assumed elsewhere must be spelled out there; the pairs that are to preserve their kind from the flood must be reproductive pairs.

rhetorical device of the author to emphasize the solemnity and deliberative nature of this final act of creation. The author draws on the mythic notion of the divine council, in which the voices of the heavenly court join that of the Deity without revealing their identity or compromising the authority of the sole God (cf. Isa 6:8). Analogous to the familiar "royal 'we,'" it claims universal authority and assent for its proclamation. But the word of Gen 1:26 does more. For the first time in the series of creation decrees, the form of the divine announcement shifts from indirect command ("Let there be X" or "Let Y bring forth X") to first-person speech. "Let us make" replaces the decrees of a distant monarch. The creature who will bear a divine resemblance cannot be conceived apart from divine self-involvement.

The divine plural indicates divine deliberation that sets this creature apart from all others, but it also serves to guard the boundary between ʾādām and God. For the image that likens the human to God is the image of ʾĕlōhîm, a plural noun. Israel distinguished its God from the gods of the nations, not only by the name Yahweh, but also by using the plural of the common noun for "god." As *the* God, ʾĕlōhîm incorporated the powers and attributes of all the gods of the nations, representing the entire pantheon in one. The image of such a God cannot be identified with any known representation. The plural guards the one within the many, so that the human representation cannot simply be "read back" to reveal the divine prototype.

The concept of the divine image is unique to the Priestly source in Genesis and finds no further theological elaboration within the Hebrew Scriptures. But it does appear in two other texts belonging to the Priestly account of origins. In Gen 5:1–3 and 9:6 allusions are made to the original creation account, in which attention is drawn to the continuing significance of the divine likeness as a mark of the species.

Image and Likeness of God in Genesis 5:1–3 and Genesis 9:6

Genesis 5 is a genealogical table, in which the species ʾādām is personified in an individual, "Adam." But the tension between the class term of Genesis 1 and the individual of Genesis 5 is preserved in the author's attempt to connect them. The chapter begins with an introductory title, "This is the book of the generations of ʾādām." Here ʾādām can be read either as a name or a collective noun (Hebrew writing does not distinguish names from common nouns). This is followed by a recapitulation of Gen 1:26–28 before the line of descent begins:

> On the day that God created ʾādām, he made him in the likeness (dĕmût) of God.
> Male and female he created them,
> And he blessed them and called their name ʾādām on the day when they were created. (Gen 5:1–2)

Here the idea of the divine likeness is conveyed through the single term *dĕmût* ("likeness"). The collective understanding of ʾādām is preserved by the plural pronouns and the explicit identification of the name with the plural representation: "and he called *their* name ʾādām." This passage leaves no doubt about the gender inclusiveness of the term in Genesis 1; both male and female are named ʾādām.

In the following sentence, however, the name describes an individual: "When ʾādām had lived a hundred and thirty years he became the father of a son in his own likeness (*dĕmût*), after his own image (*ṣelem*)" (v. 3). The compound expression for likeness reappears, with the terms in reversed order—not, however, with God as the point of reference, but Adam. The notion of physical resemblance seems unavoidable, but the meaning is to be found in the preceding words (vv. 1b–2). What this notice asserts is that the divine image identified with humankind at creation also characterizes successive generations. This distinguishing feature of the species is not lost or diminished, nor can it be won; it is a birthright. That it is immutable is brought out in Gen 9:1–7.

Here following the deluge, the blessing of procreation is repeated,[15] and the theme of human dominion is restated—now, however, with new provisions and new consequences. Dominion after the flood includes the use of animals for food, and hence killing, thereby altering the relationship between ruler and ruled. The language of holy war replaces the language of governance: "fear" and "dread" will fall upon all creatures, who are "delivered into the hand" of humans (vv. 2–3). But the new order that is announced to Noah and his sons is accompanied by restrictions: while humans may eat the flesh of other creatures, they may not eat the "life" (*nepeš*), identified here with the blood, which belongs to God (v. 4).

---

15. The command to be fruitful is addressed here to Noah and his sons (9:1), not Noah and his wife, revealing the author's focus on the male characters in narratives as well as genealogies.

Verse 5 shifts attention to the human as victim, and the divine speech shifts to first person as God declares that he will demand the life of any creature, beast or "brother," who takes a human life (v. 5). The principle of retribution is then stated in poetic form, and grounded in the notion of the divine image:

> Whoever sheds the blood of the human (*dam hāʾādām*),
> by the human (*bāʾādām*) shall his blood be shed,
> For in the image of God [God] made the human (*hāʾādām*). (v. 6)

Here is the basis for the notion of the sacred worth of every human being and the prohibition of taking a human life. If the Priestly writer envisioned circumstances in which God might permit or demand the taking of human life (as here in retribution), it is as a socially and historically conditioned response to a violation of the divine in the human. In this pronouncement, the terms of creation (ontology) are confronted by the circumstances of history, bringing anthropology into the realm of ethics and law.

Exaltation and Dominion in Psalm 8

The view that the human is creature yet elevated above all other creatures is associated in Genesis 1 (and 9) with the unique concept of the divine image, but the same idea is also found in Psalm 8. There the psalmist, contemplating the heavenly bodies as testimony to God's handiwork, asks,

> "What is the human (*ʾĕnôš*) that you mindful of him,
> A 'son of humanity (*ʾādām*)'[16] that you take note of him?"

His answer, like Gen 1:26, involves a comparison with God and employs a royal metaphor.

> You have made him little less than God (or divine beings, *ʾĕlōhîm*),
>   And crowned him with glory and honor.
> You have made him rule (*mšl hiphil*) over the works of your hands,
>   Put all [creatures] under his feet. (vv. 6–7)

---

16. Here the common Semitic *ʾĕnôš* ("a human" or "humanity") parallels the specifically Hebrew *ʾādām*. The expression "son/daughter of" is used to describe an individual member of a class.

Rule here is spelled out as subjugation through the image of the conquering suzerain placing his foot on the neck of the conquered (v. 7). The sense is close to that conveyed by the verb *rdh* ("have dominion") in Gen 1:26, 28—a verb that describes the exercise of authority or power over an individual, group, or territory, often in contexts that specify harsh or illegitimate rule. When used of kings, *rdh* usually describes their subjugation of other nations or peoples, or rule over their own people as though they were foreigners (Lev 25:43, 46, 53; 1 Kgs 4:24 [Heb. 5:4]; Ps 72:8; 110:2; Isa 14:2, 6; Ezek 34:4). Thus both Genesis 1 and Psalm 8 view humans within the created order primarily in terms of superiority and control over other creatures. In a hierarchy of being, humans stand next to God, to whom they are likened.

This exalted view of humans as the God-like among creatures and as rulers of the inhabited earth was, for its ancient author, a declaration of faith in the wisdom and power of God, not a claim of special entitlement or a theological justification for human exploitation of the environment. The commands given to humans at the conclusion of the Creator's work are initiating commands that envision a newly formed earth empty of human inhabitants and not yet brought under cultivation. Thus it must be filled ("be fruitful and multiply and fill the earth"), made livable ("subdue the earth"), and ordered ("have dominion over . . . every living creature"). The terms of the commands reflect Israel's world as a world of peasant farmers attempting to secure a precarious existence from a hostile land. For the earth to support life in this region of marginal rainfall it had to be "subdued," which entailed a constant battle. A recurring theme in the Hebrew Bible is the threat of land returning to "wilderness," where only thorns and briars grow, and inhabited only by wild animals (e.g., Isa 32:13).[17]

Genesis 1:26–28 in Canonical Context

The image of God that defines humans in Genesis 1 serves there as a royal metaphor, but the image itself has no content. Although it appears to originate in anthropomorphic conceptions of deity, it does not reveal the shape or character of the One it images. As a term for "likeness" it

---

17. The modern notion of dominion as stewardship (e.g., Hall, *Imaging God*) is a creative interpretation in a changed environment, but it introduces a sense of vocation that is lacking in the Priestly author's notion of image and dominion. See Hiebert, "Rethinking," 20–21.

is concrete, formal, wholistic—and empty; it cannot be identified with any organ, attribute, or capacity—however distinctive or desirable. But because it expresses a notion of correlation or correspondence, it is open to continued reinterpretation in relation to changing understandings of God and humankind.

One early line of interpretation combined elements of the Bible's two creation accounts, identifying the image of Genesis 1 with the man of Genesis 2–3. Emphasizing the secondary nature of the woman, as possessing the image only in a derived manner, it identified the "fall" of Genesis 3 with a loss of the image, for which it held the woman responsible. It is this interpretation that provided the background for NT and patristic speculation and underlies views of women's nature and place in the "orders of creation" that are still current today.[18] But this manner of combining the texts violates the terms of both OT accounts, in which the image is not lost or effaced and the man and the woman are held equally accountable for their disobedience to the divine command.

THE YAHWIST'S ACCOUNT OF CREATION (GENESIS 2:4b—3:24)

The account that begins in Gen 2:4b is the older of the Bible's two creation stories, known as the "Yahwist's" account for the author's use of the divine name YHWH (pronounced "Yahweh").[19] Like the Priestly account, it introduces a larger composition that spans the first four books of the Bible.[20] In its present form it is composite, presenting a story embedded within a larger story and moving in successive episodes from creation to "fall" and finally to "history." The frame story, which appears in 2:4b-8 and 3:23-24, tells of a human being (*hā'ādām*, "the human") who is formed from the dust of the ground (*'ădāmâ*) and placed in a garden; at the end he is driven from the garden to till the ground from which he was taken. The opening and closing scenes have only two actors: YHWH God and

---

18. See Bird, "Genesis 3," 175.

19. Also known as the J source or narrative, for the German spelling *Jahwist*.

20. See n. 6 above. The existence of a single source marked by the use of the divine name YHWH and continuing beyond the book of Genesis is questioned today. For the purposes of this essay it is sufficient to note the distinct literary style of this narrative that sets it apart from the preceding composition, and the fact that it appears to represent a new beginning of a composition that extends into the following chapter but is itself composite in nature.

"the human." This story is a story of a lost paradise and a lost opportunity for immortality (3:22), told as the story of the first human. It is a story that explains the terms of human existence at the point where "history" begins, that is, the conditions under which we (author and readers) live.

The author has personified humankind in a single representative, to whom he has given the name of the species; and as in Genesis 1, his model is male—here a peasant farmer. In place of the solemn declarations and liturgical cadences of the Priestly composition, the Yahwist's account exhibits the features and form of a folktale, describing a time "when the world was very young," when God walked the earth and animals could speak. It makes the same essential points about human nature as Genesis 1, but it does so through narrated actions rather than declarations. Here the human is formed from dust like the animals, enlivened by divine breath, given the plant world for food, and set over all other creatures, who are brought to him to name. The theme of sexual differentiation is here too, but the way in which it is introduced gives unique attention to the relationship between the sexes—in the "original" order and in the "fallen" state that describes life as we know it, "outside the garden."

The story begins with a solitary human, bearing the name of the species. But there is something defective about this representation; as YHWH God observes, "It is not good that the human should be alone." What he needs is a "help suitable (or 'fit') for him" (2:18).²¹ God then proceeds to create each of the animal species, from the same ground as his first creation, and to present them to "the human." But none proves to be a "suitable help." Only one of his own kind can meet that test. And so God extracts a rib from "the human," which he "builds up" (Heb. *bānâ*) into a woman. On seeing her, "the human" exclaims:

> This one at last is bone of my bone and flesh of my flesh;
> She shall be called *'iššâ* ("woman"),
> because she was taken from *'îš* ("man"). (2:23)

In his recognition of the woman as his own kind, he is revealed as "man." The woman who confronts him is a not a separate creation, formed from the ground like the animal species, but of the selfsame substance. The "help suitable for him" has been found, but in the moment of recognition she is no longer identified as a "help." Rather she is

---

21. The Hebrew expression *kĕnegdô* means "like his opposite (or 'counterpart'/'vis-à-vis')." See Bird, "Genesis 3," 181–83.

presented as one to whom the man is drawn, so that he leaves even father and mother to be united to her.

The author clearly intends to speak of the sexual drive and the institution of marriage (v. 24), as the means by which the species will be perpetuated. The message is essentially the same as Genesis 1. But the story has introduced new elements into the portrait of human existence that are not simply requirements of the story form; they belong to the essence of being human. Human life, in this account, is characterized by interactions—with other creatures, with others of the same species, and with God (elaborated as the story continues). Humans are relational beings in their fundamental nature. And these relationships have both social and psychological dimensions. Social institutions, represented here by the primary family unit, are essential to human survival and the fulfillment of human needs, and the relationship of the sexes is not simply physical but psychological. Being alone is "not good"; finding the one who will satisfy the need for a "suitable help" elicits an exclamation of recognition; a man will henceforth leave father and mother to "cleave" to his wife (2:24); and the woman's "desire" will be for her husband (3:16). Social terms ("man" and "woman") replace the biological terms ("male and female") of Genesis 1.

The story is told from the man's point of view, reflecting the male-centered society in which it arose; but the message is one of mutuality, of man and woman made for each other and bound together, in joy and (in the next episode) pain. There is no time in this account, unlike in the Priestly narrative, and sequence has no ontological meaning—either in creation or fall. Only when the man and woman appear onstage together is the creation complete, and the drama of life may begin. In the following episode the man and the woman are united in sin and bear equal shares of punishment. There, however, the woman has the lead role in the opening scene, speaking for the pair.

Sin and Its Consequences (Genesis 3)

The terms for the action in Genesis 3 have been set in the preceding chapter, in a prohibition announced when God placed "the human" in the garden (2:15–17). The prohibition carries the message that human life is limited; it has boundaries that may not be transgressed, and these are both physical and moral in nature. Although the boundaries change in chapter 3, the notion of limits does not. Humans are finite and bounded creatures, and the boundaries are set by God. In Genesis 2, the boundary is marked by a divine command: one tree of all the trees in the garden may not be eaten, on penalty of death. The prohibition assumes the freedom to disobey and the capacity for moral discrimination—to know right from wrong and to weigh the consequences of actions. Thus the "knowledge of good and bad (evil)[22]" represented by the forbidden tree is not the ability to distinguish *between* good and evil, but the ability to know all things, both good and bad—a divine attribute according to 3:22. The prohibition is presented as a test—and the outcome is known, for a prohibition in a story will always be violated. The story presented in Genesis 3 is an etiology; it seeks to explain why life as we know it is not as it was intended, or might have been.

Genesis 3 is a complex account, exhibiting internal tensions and interwoven with themes and characters from ancient Near Eastern myth and legend: a tree of life, a serpent, and a woman who imparts knowledge. But the Israelite author has used these traditions to create an entirely new story, with a new theological message. Israel's ancestors and neighbors had also speculated about the limits of human life and the qualities that distinguished humans from gods and other creatures. Their accounts focused on knowledge and death. The gods were characterized by superior wisdom and immortality; and while humans possessed a degree of knowledge that distinguished them from the animals, immortality eluded them. Ancient Near Eastern myth accounted for human mortality either as tragic loss or divine withholding.[23] Genesis 3:22–23 contains an echo of the latter tradition.[24] In the final form of the account, however, interest in immortality has been eclipsed by another concern, which focuses on the tree of knowledge, not the tree of life. For the Yahwist, the primary problem of human existence is not death but disobedience—here associated with the desire to obtain God-like wisdom.

Whence arises the impulse to disobey the divine command and question its motive? The author of Gen 3:1–7 is unwilling to lodge it within the human creation, and so he finds an instigator among the other creatures God has made: the snake, whom ancient lore endowed with quasi-divine powers. A symbol of immortality in its ability to rejuvenate

---

22. The Hebrew term (*raʿ*) describes aesthetic as well as moral judgments and also misfortune and displeasure.

23. See Bird, "Genesis 3," 184–86.

24. See Barr, *Garden of Eden*.

itself by shedding its skin, it was also ascribed special wisdom and associated with magic and the healing arts.[25] The Yahwist has tamed him; here he is only the "most crafty"[26] of the creatures God had made (3:1), and his power is only the power of suggestion. While this displacement of the impulse to disobedience does not absolve the human pair or solve the problem of the origins of sin within a divinely ordered creation, it does suggest that sin is not a defect of creation but arises in the exercise of God-given powers.[27] It arises in interactions involving external partners and internal conversations in which alternatives are envisioned and weighed. The snake plants the question that initiates the conversation and then claims to know God's mind: "God knows that when you eat of it your eyes will be opened, and you will be like God, knowing good and bad" (3:5).

The snake's words are addressed to the pair (the second-person verbs are plural in Hebrew), but it is the woman who weighs the arguments and the evidence. Observing that the fruit of the forbidden tree was good for food, pleasant to look at, and desirable to make one wise, and heeding the snake's assurance that they will not die, she eats—and gives to her husband, who also eats. Although the woman speaks and reasons, both man and woman eat, in knowing disobedience. And the divine sentences that follow draw no consequence from either the order of disobedience or the rationale offered. Neither reasoned reflection nor unreflective trust excuses the pair who have each chosen to heed the voice of another in place of the voice of God. That is the common crime addressed in the following judgment scene.

But divine judgment is not the first consequence of disobedience. Shame, not death, follows this act of human self-assertion, the pained recognition of altered conditions of life. It appears that the snake was right, at least on two counts: the violators of the prohibition do not die, and their eyes are opened. But their opened eyes do not give them the omniscience they desire, only acute self-consciousness of their own

---

25. Joines, *Serpent Symbolism*.

26. The Hebrew term (*ʿārûm*) is chosen for the wordplay it creates with the word for "naked" (*ʿărûmmîm*) in the preceding verse (Gen 2:25).

27. Terminology for sin is lacking in this passage, appearing for the first time in Gen 4:7, in relation to murder. What the garden story seeks to explain is the disposition toward sin, which is not "original" with creation but nevertheless characterizes every individual who goes forth from the garden or the womb. See Bird, "Genesis 3," 191–93 and Westermann, *Genesis 1–11*, 275–78.

vulnerability. Now they know themselves to be naked, before one another and God. The nakedness of their created state has become cause for shame; God's good gift of sexuality is transformed by human self-interest into a source of pain and exploitation. With this act of disobedience the "original" state of trusting relationships is broken; the couple now cover themselves and attempt to hide from God.

The judgment scene that concludes the story spells out the consequences of the broken relationship to God in every other relationship. As etiologies, the terms of the punishment are formulated in relation to the terms of creation—not the terms of the crime—and they are presented in close parallelism for the woman and the man. For the man, estrangement from God brings painful and incessant toil—in estrangement from the ground, from which he was taken; it no longer yields fruit freely but brings forth only thorns (3:17–19). For the woman, estrangement from God brings painful and repeated labor in childbirth—in estrangement from the man, from whom she was taken; he no longer yields freely to her desire, but instead rules over her (3:16).

One of the most remarkable features of this account is its view of the male domination that characterized the world of ancient Israel. For the Yahwist, this "given" order is the primary sign of disordered relationships in a creation estranged from God. Such was not the intended relationship of the sexes, he insists, but a tragic consequence of human rebellion. If he could envision no alternative under the prevailing social and economic conditions of his day, he could still identify this order as a distortion of the Creator's original design. In his story of origins it serves as the root expression of estrangement within the human community, which will soon extend to the relationship between brothers—and occupational groups (Genesis 4), father and son—and competing ethnic groups (Gen 9:20–27), and finally nations and peoples (Gen 11:1–9).

THE PRIESTLY AND YAHWISTIC ACCOUNTS COMBINED AND COMPARED

The Yahwist's story of creation complements the Priestly account by focusing on the social and psychological aspects of human nature and the human condition and by giving an essential role to the mind and the will. But it also stands in tension with the Priestly view, for it envisions a different world. The world of the Priestly writer is an ordered world in which history proceeds according to divine plan, and neither human ignorance nor arrogance can keep it from its intended course. In successive covenants with Noah and Abraham, God's purposes for the world are focused in a single people, who at Sinai are given the means in cult and law to maintain their identity and calling as a holy people.

The Yahwist's world is not so ordered. It is a world of human striving and failing, a world of violence that grieves the heart of its Maker (6:5–6). But it is also a world in which a righteous man can affect the Creator's decision to destroy (6:9; 18:16–33). And it is a world in which divine punishment is always followed by divine grace—beginning with the act of clothing the naked couple. For the Yahwist, a "fallen" human creation survives only through the grace of God—and by its wits. For the knowledge obtained from the forbidden fruit is essential to life outside the garden. The Yahwist, like the Priestly writer, knows that humans share some attribute of the divine, but he identifies this with the superior knowledge that sets humans apart from animals. The wisdom possessed by humankind is indeed a God-like quality (3:22), but under the conditions of human existence it is not an unmixed blessing. It is susceptible to distortion and manipulation, and it can hurt as well as heal.

THE PROBLEM OF GENDERED EXISTENCE

The creation accounts of Genesis 1–3 present two Israelite attempts to describe human beings in their essential nature. As accounts of origins, they attempt to look behind the features of history and culture and individual variation, while betraying these very particularities in their composition. Both accounts give pointed attention to sexual differentiation as an essential feature of human existence, but neither spells out the implications of this bifurcated nature for the common nature that both sexes share. In Genesis 1 this common nature is symbolized by the divine image. Although the model is male, the grammar makes clear that it characterizes the species as a whole. But gendered existence under historical conditions of life means gender-differentiated roles, values, and authority. In the male-oriented systems of authority and honor that characterized ancient Israel and the early church, the male was taken not only as the model of the human but as the norm. The female was legally and conceptually subordinate—or "other"—so that even in her most elevated image, as mother, she could not represent the species in the same way as the male.

Thus despite wider and more positive employment of female models and metaphors than is commonly recognized, the HB draws most of its generalizing statements about human nature and destiny from male experience. Tension between (on the one hand) attempts to discern the meaning of human existence common to all members of the species, and (on the other hand) recognition of biological and cultural differences (including age, race, gender, and class) as equally characteristic of the species, pervades the biblical writings and challenges contemporary theologians. But it went largely unrecognized until recent times. As a consequence, the theological anthropology in the HB and the theological anthropology derived from the HB both perpetuated a view of humans in the image of God as explicitly or implicitly male.

CREATION IN CONTEXT: THE WITNESS OF HISTORY, PROPHETS, WISDOM, AND PSALMS

The two creation accounts each served to introduce a history that placed Israel's origins in a global context. In their combined and augmented form (the Pentateuch) these sources offer a rich and varied portrait of life as divine-human interaction, in which human freedom and responsibility is always exercised within the guiding, chastening, and renewing providence of God. In this history, God not only acts but speaks. Thus large blocks of the Pentateuch consist of instructions, presented as divine speech, mediated by Moses (Deuteronomy, Leviticus, and portions of Exodus and Numbers). The corpus of prophetic writings further attests to Israel's belief in the continued speaking of God in its history and the need to attend to that word. To be human, according to the Hebrew Scriptures, is to know oneself addressed by God; to be a member of the covenant people is to know the name and history of that God and the meaning of the address.

The creation accounts do not exhaust Israel's theological reflection on the nature of the human being or on the meaning of human existence, but they do identify key elements that are assumed by other writings. The Yahwist's account of events in the garden assumes that humans are created with the capacity and freedom to make moral judgments. This capacity is also assumed by the Deuteronomist, who pleads with Israel to choose life and good—by obeying the commandments (Deut 30:15-19)—and by the prophets, who condemn evildoers and exhort to acts of justice and mercy. Although neither creation account spells out the content of the God-likeness shared by humans, both authors assume, with other biblical writers, that humans are capable of exhibiting God-like qualities and are most true to their own nature when they exercise these capacities. Thus Israel is exhorted to be holy as God is holy (Lev 19:2); to do justice and act mercifully, as God is just and merciful; to love God and neighbor, as God has loved them. It is in showing such divine qualities that humans reflect the nature of their maker and distinguish themselves from other orders of creation. Thus the limited focus of each creation text on a particular point of correlation between the human and the divine serves to alert readers to broader areas of correspondence assumed by other texts and writers.

If the creation texts point to a correspondence between the human and the divine, they also recognize an absolute distinction, emphasized in the Yahwist's account: "Dust you are and to dust you shall return" (Gen 3:19).[28] This too correlates with testimony found elsewhere in the Hebrew Bible (cf. Gen 18:27; Job 10:9; Ps 22:29 [Heb. 22:30]). Humans are frail as well as sinful. Their days are limited,[29] and full of sorrow. They strive for what they cannot attain. Their work finds no reward. These themes come to the fore in the Wisdom literature.[30]

The creation texts introduce us to normative, or at least dominant, currents of thought within ancient Israel, but there were dissenting voices and alternative views. Within the Wisdom writings (including the books of Proverbs, Ecclesiastes, Job, and certain psalms), we encounter skeptics who believed that the ways of God are unknowable and that humans are cut off from God, left to make their way unaided in a hostile or indifferent universe. Possessing both knowledge and moral instinct, they find no confirmation or reward in the exercise of these capacities; injustice prevails and ignorance is rewarded. Moral discernment reveals an unjust world. This skepticism confronts another view of the human cultivated

---

28. Notions of resurrection that find expression in later writings of the Hebrew Bible do not imply a more elevated view of human nature but derive from eschatological reflection that emphasizes God's continuing providence and creative power.

29. Ps 144:3-4 answers the question, what is ʾādām? with the statement: "They are like a breath (hebel); their days are like a passing shadow."

30. On the anthropology of the Wisdom traditions, see Perdue, *Wisdom*, 19-48, 333-36, etc.

in Wisdom circles, one that correlates right action with success and views wisdom as the key that unlocks the secrets of the divine.[31] Thus correlation between the human and the divine is exaggerated in this literature, both in its affirmations and in its denials.

Finally, there is the testimony of the heart, as it reveals the human condition in its ecstasy and its despair. The Psalms portray the human being in conversation with God—in every condition of life, and in individual and collective voice. Expectation of a hearing and a sense of absolute dependence on God are revealed here as fundamental to Israel's understanding of human existence. For the psalmist, divine silence only heightened the demand for a response. The thirst for God was implanted in the soul. The heart seeks refuge and rest in God—and finding it, rejoices. Humans are created for praise of their Creator. That is their primary vocation.

The Bible's first word about human beings sets forth the presupposition of all subsequent words by defining them in relation to God. But the content and consequences of that defining relationship are the subject of never-ending theological reflection and debate.

---

31. Skepticism becomes open revolt in Job as traditional theological affirmations are challenged and turned on their head. Thus Job parodies Psalm 8 with the complaint that God makes too much of lowly humankind. Humans are not the exalted rulers of creation but slaves, born to divine service (Job 7:1-2, 17-21). See Perdue, *Wisdom* 140-44, 335-36.

3

The Authority of the Bible

INTRODUCTION

The Bible has always had special authority for Christians, but the nature and consequences of that authority have been understood in different ways during the Bible's long history of formation and use. Fundamental to all views, however, has been the belief that the Bible constitutes a privileged source of knowledge about the nature and will of God. Traditionally this understanding was expressed in terms of divine authorship or agency. Thus the Bible was, or contained, the "word of God."

Throughout most of the church's history, the Bible's authority was simply assumed. It required no defense or theory of origin and operation. In modern times, however, beginning around 1700, traditional beliefs and sources of authority came under attack from several quarters. The church's attempts to defend the credibility and authority of the Bible against these assaults gave rise during the following centuries to the doctrines of authority and inspiration that have shaped current belief. Today these theories are being reevaluated and reformulated in the light of new questions raised by a "postmodern" age.

This essay considers the meaning of biblical authority for contemporary Christian faith. It adopts a historical approach but is oriented to American debate in the final decade of the twentieth century. Although it is informed by American Protestant experience, it seeks to place the question in a global and ecumenical context. In narrowing its focus to Christian understanding, it recognizes that other faith traditions view the Bible, in whole or in part, as sacred literature, according it varying types and degrees of authority. It also acknowledges a special indebtedness to Judaism, as a community of origin in which the earliest Christian Scriptures were formed, and as a continuing community of faith and scholarship. Nevertheless, the centrality of the witness to Christ in Christian understandings of Scripture gives distinctive shape and emphasis to Christian views of biblical authority.

Modern Debate

The subject of biblical authority has occupied a prominent place in the theological debates and church controversies of the twentieth century, especially in American Protestantism. During the latter half of the century in particular the question of authority has become the central theological issue relating to the Bible, especially within the evangelical or conservative wing of Protestantism.[1] As a result most recent literature on the subject has been shaped by the debate with and within evangelicalism. Discussion outside this orbit tends to be ignored or obscured, and issues of authority that are not framed in the dominant language of discourse tend to be neglected or misconstrued.[2]

Modern doctrines of biblical authority were formulated in response to the rise of new historical methods of interpretation (see below), and current debate among evangelicals and other conservatives remains focused on issues relating to historical criticism. But new challenges and

---

1. The term *evangelical* is used in this article to designate a broad segment of American Protestantism that understands itself as maintaining traditional or orthodox belief over against positions that are described variously as "liberal," "neo-orthodox," "modernist," or "progressive." In this broad usage it includes groups that may be defined by others as "fundamentalist," as well as those who prefer the label "neo-evangelical." Conservatives or traditionalists outside the Reformed tradition are less likely to adopt the evangelical label, although they often share closely related views concerning the Bible and biblical authority. For the function of scriptural hermeneutics, and views of scriptural authority, in defining positions within evangelicalism, see Sheppard, "Biblical Hermeneutics," 81–94.

2. See, e.g., the critique of Rogers and McKim, *Authority of the Bible*, by Avery Dulles ("Scholasticism," 339), who notes the omission of all Roman Catholic theologians since the Reformation.

new questions have arisen, outside and inside the old camps, and these are shifting the focus and terms of debate.

Within the old liberal wing of the church, a disposition to reject traditional authority, and to suspect authority per se, is giving way to a new quest for identity and norms. In a context characterized by religious and cultural pluralism and loss of common social values, the Bible is being rediscovered; and its primacy as a source for faith and life is being reaffirmed.[3] In the Roman Catholic Church, official acceptance of historical-critical methods has fostered a rebirth of biblical scholarship and contributed to a broad ecumenical consensus concerning methods of exegesis. At the same time, theological interpretation in all churches has remained heavily determined by confessional tradition, frustrating earlier hopes of achieving theological consensus by means of a common Bible interpreted by common exegetical methods.[4] Ecclesial tradition has been exposed as a far more dominant factor in biblical interpretation than Protestants have generally admitted, reopening older questions about both the nature and the locus of authority for interpretation, and the relationship of the Bible to tradition.

Academic study of the Bible is also undergoing major change. Once dominant historical-critical methods are being attacked or eclipsed by literary, structuralist, and reader-oriented criticism. Some of the new methods appear to invite or employ older, precritical ways of viewing the text, thus bypassing the controversies surrounding historical-critical interpretation. But they raise new questions about norms of interpretation and authority for faith that do not permit simple reaffirmation of traditional views. Often their assumptions about the nature of the text, and the reader, conflict with traditional understandings of the Bible as sacred Scripture.

Challenges to traditional conceptions and arguments concerning biblical authority are arising from other quarters as well, as voices excluded from earlier debate are heard. Those on the margins of the old centers of theological and ecclesiastical power remain suspicious of the relationship between the Bible and establishment theology (defined as "orthodoxy" or "traditional" faith). Many feminists, for example, find the

---

3. See, e.g., the new United Methodist statement on the primacy of Scripture in "Theological Guidelines: Sources and Criteria," contained in the 1988 and 1992 *Book of Discipline*, and the recent study document issued by the United Church of Canada, titled *Authority and Interpretation of Scripture*.

4. Flesseman-van Leer, *Bible*, 1–4.

concept as well as the claims of biblical authority problematic in light of their experience of the Bible as a weapon of patriarchy. African Americans bring another neglected perspective to the discussion, distinguished by a distinctive hermeneutic, shaped by experiences of slavery and racism and by a distinct cultural tradition. Different, but related, issues of authority are raised by other groups that have received the Bible from the hands of their oppressors or have experienced it as an instrument in the suppression of their cultural heritage (e.g., indigenous peoples of the Americas). The question of biblical authority is also being raised in a fresh and urgent way by encounters with nonbiblical religions, not only in distant lands, but also in America's cities and suburbs.

Doctrines and Definitions

Traditional understanding of the Bible's authority was closely associated with notions of divine communication. The Bible was described as God's "Word," although relatively few of its actual words are represented as divine speech. In attempting to explain how human language could represent divine thought, early Jewish and Christian theologians appealed to the concept of *inspiration*. The idea was derived from a prophetic model but was extended to writings and utterances of diverse origin and content. In its earliest use it was an inference from effect, a means of accounting for the acknowledged sacred character of certain writings, not a means of establishing their authority. And it described the (inspired) human agent, not the text. It soon developed into a means of asserting a variety of claims about the nature and content of the text itself, but it was not until the modern period that a fully articulated theory of inspiration was formulated or acquired the status of doctrine. In modern formulations, the doctrine of inspiration typically reverses the original order of reasoning; the inspiration imputed to the biblical texts is now seen as proof of their divine origin and authority, and guarantor of their truth.[5]

Because the authority of the Bible has been so closely identified with the doctrine of inspiration in modern discussion, efforts to analyze or reassert the Bible's claims to authority often focus on this concept.[6] Recent

---

5. Smith, "Inspiration and Inerrancy," 500–512; Achtemeier, *Inspiration and Authority*.

6. E.g., Gnuse, *Authority of the Bible*, 14–65; Johnston, *Evangelicals*, 15–47; Alonso Schökel, *Inspired Word*, 58–73.

attempts have been made to reformulate the notion of inspiration in a manner compatible with present knowledge of the origins of the canon and modern understandings of psychological and mental processes.[7] Nevertheless, the concept of inspiration remains a theory of agency that cannot in itself define or secure the authority of the Bible.[8]

Two other terms closely identified with claims of biblical authority are *inerrancy* and *infallibility*. Both represent modern attempts to spell out the implications of traditional belief in a new age confronted by new questions — in this case, questions about the veracity of biblical statements, occasioned by new knowledge and new canons of truth. Both seek to maintain ancient affirmations of the trustworthiness of Scripture as divine revelation, translating those affirmations into modern terms. Although the claims expressed by these two closely related concepts are considered by many as essential criteria of biblical authority, neither describes the full nature or scope of that authority, and both are second-order concepts, deriving their meaning from more fundamental affirmations (see below).

Debates over biblical authority tend to focus on particular attributes of the text and neglect the fundamentally relational character of all authority. Authority describes the power of one subject to influence another in such a way that a claim upon the other is established and acknowledged. The nature of the claim and the manner of its operation will vary with the subject and the relationship in which it is exercised, but it is not effected by assertion alone; it requires acknowledgment through appropriate response.[9] Authority is not a possession, nor can it be freely created. It is a quality of a relationship that develops over time and involves an element of trust and trustworthiness. And it is always exercised within a community.[10]

---

7. See esp. Gnuse, *Authority of the Bible*, 105-36.

8. See Flesseman-van Leer, *Bible*, 7.

9. Dictionary definitions are helpful in showing the wide variety of ways authority is exercised or expressed, e.g., through knowledge, prestige, and personal influence, as "weight of testimony" or "reliability of a source or witness" (Sykes, *Concise Oxford Dictionary*), but they tend to stress the power of the subject (e.g., Sykes, *Concise Oxford Dictionary* defines *authority* as "the power or right to make commands, enforce obedience, take actions, or make final decisions") and neglect the relationship in which it is exhibited. Authority is imputed to a subject from its effects on another subject, who obeys, follows, trusts, believes, and so forth.

10. Jodock, *Church's Bible*, 105-10.

Authority is contextual; it is always relative to particular situations and relationships. It is, therefore, highly varied, and variable, in its content, extent, and forms of expression. A given person, institution, or writing may exercise different types and degrees of authority in relation to different audiences, expectations, and needs. While some types of authority may be more generalized than others, such as the authority of a parent (in contrast, e.g., to that of a teacher), none is comprehensive—including the authority of the Bible. Although the authority of Scripture is understood to derive from God, the Bible itself has a particular and limited purpose in God's relationship to the church and the world, and its authority must be understood in relation to that purpose and those relationships. To equate the authority of the Bible with the authority of God is to fall into the sin of idolatry.

Much of the debate over the authority of the Bible concerns the nature of the authority, rather than the extent ("high" or "low"). What kind of book is this, and what kind of message, or communication, does it contain? To whom is it addressed, and under what conditions? Who or what determines appropriate expectations and responses?[11] Who may "rightly" interpret it, and according to what canons? How does it stand in relation to other sources of authority, and how are conflicting claims to be adjudicated?

Underlying many of these questions is the issue of meaning. The Bible's authority is one of communication; it depends on understanding. When its message is no longer comprehended, or when its word is heard as false or irrelevant, its authority is jeopardized or annulled. That is the reason for the crisis of biblical authority that has characterized much of the modern period; a radically changed world and worldview have rendered old ways of understanding the text unintelligible, objectionable, or simply inconsequential for many. Continued affirmation of the Bible's

---

11. The question of appropriate response or use is critical and often neglected, and it is the most difficult because it cannot be answered in purely formal terms. It concerns the way the Bible's authority functions in particular life situations, e.g., in ethical decisions (such as those relating to abortion, immigration, taxation, or the environment). In practice, the Bible as an authority for faith interacts with other authorities in complex ways that are not adequately represented by formal declarations or doctrines. See Kelsey, *Uses of Scripture* for one attempt to analyze how appeals to biblical authority function in the work of selected modern theologians. Cf. Johnston, *Evangelicals*, vii–viii, who laments the inability of evangelicals, all claiming a common belief in biblical authority, to agree on what this means in relation to many major issues of the day.

authority requires new ways of interpreting the text and appropriating its message. The question of biblical authority is inextricably bound up with the question of interpretation and hermeneutics. Thus some attention must be given in this article to key issues and episodes in the history of biblical interpretation that have particular bearing on the question of authority.

Two principles are crucial to assessing various interpretations and claims concerning the authority of the Bible, and to formulating a contemporary statement of its nature and consequences.

1. The Bible itself must be the primary source of any answer to the question of its nature and purpose, and any view of its message and authority must be consonant with its form—as an ordered collection of disparate writings.
2. The meaning and authority of the Bible cannot be determined apart from the community that created, transmitted, and interpreted it.

Both principles require that any understanding of biblical authority must have a recognizable historical dimension, even when the question is limited to contemporary authority. Scripture comes to us as a word from the past and exhibits in its language and content a continuing link with that past. It serves first of all as an indispensable memory of the church. But it must also be heard as a contemporary word, since it witnesses to a God who is not bound to the past but is active in the present, shaping the future. Thus the Bible's authority for the church also depends on its ability to speak an intelligible and credible word to the present generation.

These two functions of Scripture, as memory and present word, have corresponding forms of authority, which need not be formulated in identical terms and may change over time in relation to changing needs and worldviews. Any concept or claim of authority must be congruent, however, with the Bible's own internal witness to its nature and purposes. Theories of biblical authority that are to have credibility must honor the Bible's own word in its own world—which can never simply be equated with our own. The contribution of modern historical consciousness and modern historical study of the Bible is insistence that the integrity of the biblical witness not be compromised by denying or subordinating its historical character, hence its cultural particularity, to the demands of contemporary readers. The Bible's authority is intimately connected with its character as a bridge between the past and present activity of God.

SCRIPTURE IN ANCIENT ISRAEL

Scripture is the creation of a community[12] that recognizes certain writings as authoritative.[13] In the case of the Christian Bible, two communities were instrumental in shaping and defining the final corpus. What the church received from Israel and the synagogue had to be substantially reinterpreted in the light of the new revelation in Christ. Nevertheless, the Christian Bible remains in its most basic sense a Jewish Bible, in which the fundamental terms for the church's understanding of the divine presence that had broken into history and transformed its life were given to it by the community formed at Sinai. The people of the resurrection read their Bible as descendants and heirs of the people of the exodus.

The writings that the church describes as "Holy Scripture" and "Word of God" comprise a diverse collection of documents composed over a period of more than a thousand years and attributed to many different authors. Thus any notion of divine authorship must reckon with the Bible's own internal witness to its complex human origins. The fundamental issue in the history of debate over biblical authority is the question of how to acknowledge and relate the divine and the human nature of these writings.[14] Modern biblical and historical scholarship has enabled us to reconstruct much of the process by which our canon of Scriptures came into being, permitting us to see it as a historical product in a way that earlier generations could not. The Holy Book is seen once again as a collection (*ta biblia*, "the books," in its original Greek designation), but this time in a manner that relates individual writings more precisely to the situations in which they arose.

---

12. *Community* is used here as a flexible term for any communal entity with a sense of common identity. It may at times correspond to an entire people, nation, or religious group and at other times represent a particular party, church, or subgroup. Both of the two major faith communities with which we will be concerned were at all times internally diverse, so that the concept of community does not imply unanimity. The same qualifications pertain to such collective designations as "Israel," "the church," "the synagogue," and the like.

13. To say this is not to deny that it is also the product of inspired speakers and writers, or that it is ultimately the work of God. It is, however, to focus on the necessary communal act of recognition, without which there would be no Scripture.

14. The doctrine of inspiration has been particularly useful and appealing, despite its inadequacies, because it provides a means for affirming the divine origin of what are clearly human writings (Gnuse, *Authority of the Bible*, 4). Not until the modern period, however, was attention given to the question of how inspiration operated. See Smith, "Inspiration and Inerrancy," 505.

The books that make up our biblical canon did not originate as "Scripture" and, with notable exceptions, do not claim divine authorship or inspiration for themselves.[15] Within these books, however, are references to earlier writings for which divine authorship and authority are claimed. Thus New Testament (NT) writings frequently cite the Jewish Scriptures, identifying their words as divine speech. Long before the Old Testament (OT) canon was closed or its writings completed, however, a concept of Scripture had come into being that would have an enduring effect on Jewish and Christian understandings of sacred writings.[16]

Deuteronomic Torah: The Authority of Sacred Law

The earliest datable reference to a written document whose words are identified, at least indirectly, as the words of God is found in the account of Josiah's reforms (ca. 621 BCE). The "book" (or "document") discovered during the course of repairs to the temple is identified more specifically as the "book of the law" (2 Kgs 22:11) and "book of the covenant" (2 Kgs 23:2). Although the narrative does not use the expression "law of God," it makes clear that the words read before the king were understood as none other than Yahweh's words and that in failing to obey the "words of this book," Israel had disobeyed Yahweh's commands (23:13; cf. vv. 16, 19).

Both the language used to describe the book and the covenant-making that accompanies its reception link it with the book of Deuteronomy,

---

15. Exceptions in the OT are the book of Deuteronomy (1:1–3) and a number of the Minor Prophets whose superscriptions identify the contents of the book as "the word of the LORD" spoken or revealed to the prophet (Hos 1:1; Joel 1:1; Mic 1:1; Zeph 1:1; Mal 1:1). In the NT, only the book of Revelation 1:1–2) makes a comparable claim, placing itself in the OT prophetic tradition. In contrast, the Letters of Paul are clearly pastoral writings that make no attempt to present themselves as divinely inspired.

16. Since the time of Origen, the two parts of the Christian Bible have been referred to as the OT and the NT. Several candidates to replace the confessional nomenclature with more neutral descriptive terminology have been suggested, e.g., *Hebrew Bible*, *Hebrew Scriptures*, or, less frequently, *First Testament*. These necessary and useful attempts to find nondiscriminatory language do not, however, represent the customary or current use of either of the two faith communities involved. Since this article is concerned with the meaning of these writings precisely in their function as authoritative for faith, the traditional nomenclature has been retained. Postscript (2015): Today "Hebrew Bible" has become standard in many Christian churches, but usually mismatched with "NT." The effort to correct this disparity by pairing "Hebrew Scriptures" with "Christian Scriptures" is even more problematic, however, suggesting that only the NT constitutes Christian Scripture and so embracing Marcion's heresy.

whose central section (Deut 4:44—28:68) is introduced as "the law that Moses set before the Israelites" (4:44, NRSV), and more specifically as "the commandments of Yahweh" (4:2). According to Deut 4:13-14, the book contained the covenant stipulations declared to Israel by Yahweh at Horeb (Sinai) and expounded by Moses at Yahweh's charge.

Torah as Constitution

Deuteronomy is unique within the HB in its claims to embody a written deposition of authoritative law and as a book whose text is referred to elsewhere in the OT.[17] References to it abound in the "Deuteronomistic" exhortations and accusations of the books of Joshua and Kings, as well as in various prophetic writings (e.g., Josh 1:7, 8; 1 Kgs 2:3; 2 Kgs 10:31; 17:34, 37; Jer 9:13; Amos 2:4). The collective term used to designate this body of writings is *tôrâ* (*torah*), traditionally rendered as "law," but etymologically identified with "teaching" or "instruction." In Deuteronomy's usage it refers to a body of stipulations having normative and prescriptive force, but it is not an umbrella term for every rule, decision, or enactment of Israelite legal authority.[18] It is more specifically covenantal law, the implementing legislation of the covenant made by God with Israel at Horeb.

This special sense of Deuteronomic *torah* as Israel's "constitution" was recognized by Josephus, who rendered it with the Greek term *politeia* ("polity") rather than *nomos* ("law"/"lawcode"). Interpreting the Pentateuch for a Gentile audience in the first century CE, Josephus described the book of Deuteronomy as preserving the "divinely authorized and comprehensive 'polity' or national 'constitution'" that Moses had delivered to Israel, in both written and oral forms, in the final days of his life.[19] The *torah* of Deuteronomy sets forth the principles and policies of a "divinely authorized social order that Israel must implement to secure its collective political existence as the people of God."[20]

The notion of divinely issued decrees and commands contained in a written document and intended as a normative guide for a people bound to God by a covenant relationship is specific to Deuteronomy and the

---

17. McBride, "Polity," 231.
18. Ibid., 232-33.
19. Ibid., 229.
20. Ibid., 233.

Deuteronomic "school," but it has played a foundational role in Jewish and Christian understandings of Scripture. It contains the essential notions of a communal document, which is to be appropriated individually and internally by each member of the community. It is a gift of God, the consequence of divine initiative in creating a new people. In its demands it reveals the character of its giver. It is both written and oral in nature and, therefore, not limited to the word once spoken. It is a word that always addresses a new generation, with demands for new covenant commitment.

The term *torah* was ultimately extended to the Pentateuch as a whole and with it the claims of divine origin and authority, as well as Mosaic "authorship." In that context *law* would come to have a broader meaning, and the Deuteronomic ordinances would find their place as the climactic word of a story of God's purposes and action from the creation of the world to the creation of Israel, a story to be continued on the other side of the Jordan. In that narrative context, the words of Moses spoken on the plains of Moab are for the new generation that will claim the promise and enter the land. The book of Deuteronomy is fully aware that the Israel it addresses no longer stands at Horeb. It recalls, and refashions, the words spoken at the mountain, so that they remain true to the character of the divine speaker and the changing historical circumstances of the audience.

The Two-Part Structure of Covenantal Law

Deuteronomy represents a critical stage in the transformation of tradition, but it was neither the beginning nor the end of the process. Behind Deuteronomy stands the covenant tradition of the older narrative sources of the Pentateuch; after it stand the later prescriptive collections of the Pentateuch and the body of oral and written decisions of the rabbis, which continued to give instruction to Israel in ever-new circumstances of life. Within this continuing tradition one feature deserves special note, since it points to the essential combination of stability and flexibility in Israel's notion of "law" and Scripture. Deuteronomy, like the older tradition on which it rests, is presented as a two-part composition, consisting of the Decalogue (Deut 5:6-21; cf. Exod 20:2-17) followed by a diverse body of ordinances or "rulings." While the Decalogue remains essentially unchanged, the collection of rulings is greatly expanded in Deuteronomy, not only by new and different cases, but also by interpretive and hortatory elaboration.

Two classes of divine commands are recognized in this arrangement. The "Ten Words" may be understood as statements of policy or basic norms that Deuteronomy insists were heard by Israel directly from the voice of God at Horeb and received on tablets written by the finger of God (Deut 4:12–13; 5:4, 22; 9:10). The "statutes and ordinances" may be understood as implementing legislation that Yahweh had charged Moses to teach to the Israelites for their observance in the land they are about to occupy (Deut 4:14; cf. 5:31). The distinction between the two classes involves differences of form, function, terminology, and historical setting, but not of authority. Both are covenantal law and expressive of divine will, but the latter body is mediated and historically conditioned in a way that the former is not.

Deuteronomy's interpretation of the two-part structure of covenantal law employs both historical and theological arguments. The covenant made at Horeb must be reappropriated by every generation (Deut 5:3; 11:2–7). Its basic demands of loyalty and justice are unchanging; they are heard and stamped upon the mind as the direct address of God (4:10–13; 5:22–24), and their constancy is assured by memoranda on stone tablets. But changed and changing circumstances are reflected throughout the book and signaled by the constant refrain of "today" (Deut 5:1; 11:2, 8, 13, etc.). Deuteronomy's "today" is a dynamic concept and must be understood as such. The social and political circumstances reflected in the book clearly point to the seventh century BCE as the time of its composition[21] rather than to the eleventh century of its narrative setting. To Hebrew readers of Josiah's day, the references to the "nations" and their practices would have been transparent allusions to religious and political relations of their own day.

Mediated Word

Deuteronomy contributes one further element of Israel's understanding of Scripture: the fundamental role of human mediation in divine communication. The divine law is spoken and expounded by Moses. But

---

21. Current scholarly debate on the date of Deuteronomy, in which some date it to postexilic times, does not affect the basic argument that the book was created at a much later time than its Mosaic setting and was a response to the conditions of that later time.

mediation implies contingency. At the heart of Israel's traditions concerning God's revelation to Israel lies a tension between the absolute and unchanging nature of God and God's will for the covenant community and the changing (historical) circumstances of life in which Israel must live out its covenant faithfulness. Both are acknowledged, and bound together, in the traditions of God's revelation in the wilderness—and Moses is the figure who unites them. All divinely authorized law or instruction in Israel was "Mosaic," identified with the formative period of Israel's life, located in the wilderness narrative. Yet the several collections of laws in the Pentateuch and the obvious accretions to the earlier laws clearly point to later times. The later laws do not replace the earlier ones but stand side by side as witness to a continuing "Mosaic" function.

Torah in Post-Exilic Judaism

A century after Josiah's reforms, Mosaic *torah* figures prominently in another account of national renewal. Nehemiah 8 relates how Ezra, the priest and scribe, read from the "book of the law of Moses" (8:1) to an assembly of returned exiles at their request. The assembly comprised "both men and women and all who could hear with understanding" (8:2, NRSV), and the reading was accompanied by interpretation (8:7–8). Whether this is to be understood as translation (into the Aramaic vernacular) or exegesis (spelling out meanings and implications) is uncertain, but the narrative makes clear that the law was understood as both authoritative for the community and requiring interpretation by skilled experts. It also introduces us to a new religious title, "scribe" (8:1, 4, 9, 13), apparently designating a new class of scholars who study and expound the law (cf. Ezra 7:6, 21). The context of the reading (from a raised platform, with accompanying acts of homage and blessing) and the subsequent action by the heads of the ancestral houses (who gather on the following day to "study the words of the law") appear to reflect late practice associated with the synagogue, where public reading and private study were the central activities of religious life. But whatever the date, *torah* in this account has assumed a new place in communal life.

    The book designated alternately as the "law of Moses" (8:1) and "law of God" (8:8, 18) appears to have been substantially identical with that read by Josiah to "all the people, both small and great" (2 Kgs 23:2, NRSV), although it may have been contained in a larger pentateuchal corpus. In both instances, it is understood to represent the authoritative word of God, binding on the community as a whole; but the meaning of the book has changed with the changing circumstances of the community.

Mosaic *torah* as defined by Deuteronomy contained directives for life, more specifically the life of the nation. It was communal in its orientation and political in its implications: The king was to meditate upon it and govern in accordance with its commands (Deut 17:18-20; cf. 2 Kgs 22:10-13; 23:1-3, 24); foreign alliances were to be rejected (Deut 7:1-2); and the fate and welfare of the nation depended on obedience to its commands (Deut 30:16-18; 2 Kgs 17:19; 22:23). But it also laid demands on every Israelite able to understand its commands (Deut 31:12; 2 Kgs 23:2; Neh 8:3, 12). It was to be read publicly before the entire assembly (Deut 31:10-12; cf. 2 Kgs 23:2; Neh 8:2) and to be an object of study and meditation (Deut 6:6-7; Neh 8:13). It was not simply policy for rulers or guidance for judges and cultic officials. Its primary audience was the covenant community, individually and collectively.

In the postexilic setting, the political dimensions of the law are absent, and the problem of foreign alliances is now a problem of marriage with foreigners (Neh 9:1-2; 10:28-30; Ezra 9-10; cf. Deut 7:3). A scribe of the law holds the book, and the people take the initiative, not the king. The community has been redefined as a body constituted by the reading and hearing of the word of God. Authority for governing the community is now invested in a book and its interpreters.

Implications for Christian Understanding of Scripture

All these features of the understanding and use of Israel's earliest Scriptures have relevance for Christian understanding of the nature of Scripture and scriptural authority, and all have received confirmation in Christian doctrine and use. The fundamental affirmations of this tradition are that Scripture is both communal and individual in its address, and its authority must be realized at both levels. Understanding is necessary to assent, and understanding requires interpretation. Interpretation involves special knowledge and skill, but study and meditation are the obligation of all who are capable. The authoritative word is from the past, but is directed anew to each generation. Its message is heard differently in different contexts, requiring different responses. The word lays demands on its hearers—for the ordering of community, family, and individual life—but it also provides the means to fulfill those demands. It is a means of grace, God's gift, in which the nature and will of the giver are revealed. Its purposes are life and well-being. If later interpretations of the "law" narrowed and perverted this understanding in frozen literalism and false contrasts with the "gospel," the Deuteronomic understanding of *torah* continued nevertheless to dominate the evolving corpus and conception of Scripture.

Expanding Torah: The Authority of Sacred Story

Although the law occupied a position of primacy in Israel's Scriptures, it was not the only form of sacred writing recognized as authoritative in Israel, or the earliest composition. Before the "book of the law" had received its final form, other writings had come into existence that would ultimately form part of Israel's sacred canon.[22] Some were joined to the "book of the law" to form the Pentateuch. Others found their way into later collections of Hebrew Scriptures, and some were lost, forgotten, or circulated outside the finally authorized canon. During the whole period of canon formation, new writings continued to be produced. The question of when these writings became "Scripture," and for whom, is difficult to answer. Originally composed and cherished by particular groups within Israel, as the law itself was, they served limited purposes related to particular institutions or occasions, and only gradually became part of a "national" literature. Outside the Pentateuch, they never formed a single unified corpus but retained the character of a library, even in their final canonical form.[23]

The history of the growth of the canon, and of individual books within the canon, shows that the authority of the Scriptures depends on the recognition of a community but also that recognition may be accorded in a variety of ways for a variety of reasons. Before the individual

---

22. The history of the Pentateuch is currently debated, both in respect to its component parts and in respect to the circumstances of its final composition. That it is a composite work, however, is recognized by the majority of scholars, who also acknowledge the separate character of Deuteronomy within the "Five Books." This article assumes the existence of early narrative traditions employed in the construction of the larger work, along with smaller complexes of traditions of various sorts.

23. The view of canon formation presented here is essentially that of McDonald, *Formation*, 48–66. For a view that minimizes the differences among Jewish canons as well as between the Jewish and Christian (OT) canons, see Beckwith, *Old Testament Canon*.

writings were assembled into a body of "Scripture," each had established its authority in respect to its own peculiar character and use: laws, to guide and govern the community; ancestral tales and historical narratives, to create and confirm a sense of identity and trace the activity of God in past experience and event; prophetic oracles, to illuminate God's action in the present and to warn; proverbs, to counsel; psalms, to direct prayer and praise; didactic tales, to instruct and encourage steadfastness. Similar distinctions of purpose and use, and consequently distinctions in types of authority, characterize the NT writings.

The distinctive character and authority of the individual writings is maintained by continuing distinction of form and boundaries within the canonical collection. But the unity of the collection, however loose or variable, imposes a new demand on interpreters to relate the component parts to each other and to the new whole—and a corresponding new demand to reconceive the authority of the whole and its parts. The unified collection has a new locus, or loci, of interpretation—the synagogue and the church—and it is in relation to the new needs of these two new institutions that the authority of Scripture came to be defined. The shift to a new communal context of interpretation and use began with the liturgical reading of Scripture in the postexilic period, as evidenced by Nehemiah 8, but the move from Scripture to canon extended over centuries. Not until the end of the first century CE was there a definitive Jewish canon; the OT canon, together with the NT of the Christian Bible, was not fixed until the fourth century CE—without final unanimity. Thus even as collections of writings began to be formed for use by new religious bodies, the boundaries of the collections varied, reflecting differing theological emphases and interests and differing views of the authority of individual writings as well as criteria of authority.

The Narrative Setting of Israelite Law

Mosaic *torah* played a determinative role in Israelite understanding of Scripture, but in its present literary context, it is embedded in a narrative that is decisive for its interpretation. The Pentateuch presents an account of Israel's origins, set in the context of world history and looking to the occupation of a homeland in the mountains of Canaan. In various recensions, the underlying narrative attempted to comprehend, and defend, Israel's identity and vocation as the people of Yahweh and spell out the terms and consequences of that relationship. Thus history complemented law in revealing God's nature and purposes for Israel by supplying the story of divine initiative and action that had given birth to the nation and preserved it through various threats.[24]

Covenantal law had a narrative setting, which was finally fleshed out, from many sources, to compose the present pentateuchal account. In this literary context, *torah* as divine instruction was extended from sacred law to sacred story. Within this context the words of the law are given a specific historical setting and purpose, appearing as the historically conditioned terms of a relationship set within God's overarching purposes and actions in the world. Fixed in time, Mosaic law opens the way to new teachings and new commands in relation to God's new actions in history. But it is also located outside of time and history. The place of revelation is the mountain of God, located in the wilderness, in a place apart. Mosaic law is isolated and magnified as the model of all subsequent teaching. Thus *torah* is both absolutized and historicized in its pentateuchal setting.

Prophetic Word and Prophetic Authority

The Pentateuch, as the first corpus of writings to acquire the shape and authority of canonical Scripture, was composed of testimony to God's revelation in deed and word. So too was the second major section of the Jewish canon: the historical books from Joshua through Kings together with the prophetic writings. Here, however, the divine word is mediated not by Moses but by prophets. The Deuteronomists represented the prophets as continuing the Mosaic office (Deut 18:15, 17-20; cf. 34:10). In their construction, the word once spoken at Horeb is spoken anew to successive generations through the prophets, giving divine direction to a new age. In contrast to the word from the mountain, however, the prophetic word is timely, specific, and bound to the circumstances of its delivery—or so it would appear. As a divine word, however, it also had the potential of disclosing God's nature and will in a way that might instruct future generations as well. Ultimately, prophetic words, like Mosaic commands, were preserved in collections that were studied, expounded, and amplified.

---

24. See Sanders, *Sacred Story*, 18-19, for a view that emphasizes the priority of story in the canonical process.

The attempt to link the two forms of divine communication represented by prophecy and law is clearly a secondary effort. It is nevertheless instructive as an attempt to claim the authority of written *torah* for prophetic speech and at the same time to subordinate prophecy to Mosaic law. While the activity of prophets is attested from premonarchic to postexilic times, and prophetic speech may have been viewed by some as the primary and preferred form of divine communication, prophetic oracles do not appear to have been gathered into books until the eighth or seventh century BCE, the same period in which the Deuteronomic book of the law was being formed and promulgated; and they did not achieve the status of Scripture until the exile, at the earliest.

Prophetic speech in its primary setting was marked by directness and immediacy; it provided divine guidance for specific occasions and needs, solicited and unsolicited. And it carried the authority of divine speech; the prophet spoke in the divine first person, as God's messenger or as one possessed by God's Spirit. These very attributes, however, made the prophetic word a problematic source of divine guidance. It was sporadic, occasional, tied to passing events, and sometimes unavailable (Mic 3:7). It could not be obtained at will, and when it could, it was suspect (1 Kgs 22:5–7; Jer 23:16, 21–22, 25–32).

The question of authority in claims of divine communication is raised in its earliest and most acute form in relation to prophetic words. Conflicting messages (1 Kgs 22:5–28; Jer 28:1–17), predictions that failed (Jer 28:11; 29:18–19; cf. 2 Kgs 24:6), and lying or deluded prophets (Jer 23:16–32; cf. 1 Kgs 13:18; 22:19–23; Mic 3:5–8) are among the issues that attended prophecy, especially in the final years of the Judean state, a time in which the question of truth in prophetic pronouncements had come to have life-and-death significance. Who had the true word from God? By what signs could one recognize it? On these questions hung the fate of the nation—and the future of prophecy itself.[25]

In this period, tests were formulated that have significance for contemporary debates. First, the truth of a word, and hence the assurance that it was a message from God and not simply an invention of the prophet's own mind or desire, could not be assured by any formula of speech or professional title. False messages, described as "lying" or "deceptive" words, were spoken by persons bearing the title prophet and introduced by the standard formula of introduction: "Thus says the LORD"

---

25. See Sanders, "Hermeneutic"; Crenshaw, *Prophetic Conflict*; Childs, *Old Testament Theology*, 133–44; and Sheppard, "True and False Prophecy."

(Jer 28:1–5, 10–11; cf. 12–16). Attempts to distinguish true from false messages by the manner of reception or delivery are accorded limited credibility. "False prophets" (a term coined by the Greek translators but unknown in Hebrew) are said to receive their messages through dreams or visions of their own heads rather than by direct audition or access to the divine assembly (1 Kgs 22:19–23; Jer 23:16–32); false prophets are also said to "steal" one another's words (Jer 23:30). They may also be characterized by frenzied behavior (1 Kgs 18:26–27). But most of these criteria are not easily discernible, or may be applied to canonical prophets as well (Jer 29:26–27). Another effort to establish criteria of credibility was associated with signs, but this too was judged inadequate (Deut 13:1–5). In the final analysis, the truth of a word could be judged only by its content and by the vindication of time (Deut 18:21–22; Jer 28:9)—a criterion of little use to the hearer, who must decide immediately which word to follow.

If the message itself held the clues to its origins and truth, then the hearer's, or reader's, chief resource for assessing its claims was the faith tradition. For the Deuteronomists, this core of belief was embodied in the law given through Moses, and more particularly in the Decalogue and the first commandment. This was no strange word or new command, not difficult to obtain or comprehend, and not dependent on dreams or esoteric interpretations, but available to all (Deut 30:11–14). It was to be recited, bound to head and hand, written on the door post, and taught to the next generation (Deut 6:4–9). Nine centuries later, early Christian theologians would make a similar appeal to the "rule of faith" as the criterion for judging the claims of various writings to authoritative status in the church's Scriptures. Such appeals to tradition have their own pitfalls, however, tending to make past formulations and experience a norm rather than a guide for discerning the divine presence and will in new situations and new forms. The tension between prophecy and law characterizes the whole history of the canon and of the church.

The Writings: New Models and Meanings of Scripture and Authority

The Law and the Prophets formed the heart of the Jewish Scriptures, which the church inherited from Israel, but those Scriptures embraced a far more diverse collection of writings, whose boundaries were still in flux when the first Christian writings were being formed. The third section of the Hebrew canon, designated simply the Writings, was a loose assemblage of works that had for the most part arisen subsequent to the earlier collections or did not fit the recognized categories of form or content. It included a collection of sacred songs and prayers drawn from public worship and private devotion (Psalms) and a number of compositions from the world of wisdom, including a collection of maxims and instructions (Proverbs), a skeptic's monologue on the apparent meaninglessness of life (Qoheleth), and a dramatic poem on the justice of God explored through the dialogue of a sufferer with his would-be comforters (Job). Love songs (Song of Solomon), elegies (Lamentations), didactic novels and heroic tales (Ruth, Esther, Daniel [1–6, together with apocalyptic visions, 7–12]), and new historiographic writings (Ezra-Nehemiah, Chronicles) completed the collection that ultimately won the approval of Pharisaic Judaism. Other works contended for inclusion, however, and are cited as authoritative by Jewish writers in the first two centuries BCE and even as late as the fourth century CE, although the shorter canon was generally accepted after 90 CE.

The final segment of the Jewish canon involves a debate concerning the nature and scope of Scripture and the manner of divine revelation in which the emergence of Christianity as a distinct movement within sectarian Judaism played a critical role. The closing of the OT canon was precipitated by a crisis of identity in which two religious communities defined themselves, in part at least, by their differing uses of common Scriptures and their eventual construction of distinct canons. The process was complex, especially in the first century CE, when both Judaism and Christianity were marked by great internal diversity, including diversity of views about the authority of Scripture and the canon of sacred books.[26] The final outcome of this internal and external debate was a contracted Jewish canon and an expanded Christian OT.

The third section of the Jewish canon is a miscellany, lacking any clear center or overarching conceptual framework. In Greek canon lists, these writings do not constitute a distinct unit, but are combined in varying order and arrangement with the prophetic and historical books, thus extending the category as well as the corpus of "the Prophets." This segment of Scripture has played an important role in a series of critical questions concerning definitions and boundaries of canon, Scripture, church, and synagogue. It also contributes more specifically to the question of scriptural authority.

---

26. Greer, *Christian Bible*, 120–21.

First, the diversity of the writings that completed the Jewish canon, even in its short version, extends the notion of Scripture to include works that cannot readily be interpreted as the record of divine speech or action, even when broadly defined as "sacred story." The authority of these books must rest on broader grounds, which cannot be identified by a single concept of origin or agency but must be related to their function in shaping and sustaining community identity—a function that is also central to the earlier collections.[27] The concept of Scripture must be recast in relation to this broader corpus, as the collection of writings that informs and instructs Israel in its identity and vocation as the people of God. In myriad ways it tells Israel who it is, why it has been created and preserved ("chosen"), and what is expected of it.

It performs this function by means of multiple voices and genres. The internal diversity of the Scriptures is magnified in the third division of the Hebrew canon, which preserves voices of conflict and dissent, defenders and critics of tradition, even religious skeptics. Thus it is the witness of a community in debate—a feature also discernible within the older canonical writings. Theological diversity and debate are a fundamental feature of both testaments, and any doctrine of biblical authority must be consonant with this aspect of the Bible's character.

The Scriptures are not simply multivocal but historical in their essential nature. They grew—through accretion and selection. They were not handed down from heaven or created in a single moment, but are the product of a particular community and changing circumstances of life. They testify to the eternal out of their own historical and cultural particularity. Their authority is one of historical and historically conditioned writings. That is equally true of the Christian canon, which added a final chapter to the collected writings—but not to the history of dialogue and witness, which continued beyond the boundaries of the canon.

Canon and Authority

The formation of the Jewish canon as a bound collection of sacred writings was the final stage in the community's recognition of the authority of these works, a process that would be repeated in the church's formation of

---

27. See Kugel, *Early Interpretation*, 40–51, for a helpful attempt to discern the primary themes and motives in this diverse literature. Kugel suggests that many of the writings from the Restoration and its aftermath exhibit attempts to link current history and experience with a "canonical" past or "canonical" models (ibid., 46).

its own canon. The canon did not establish the authority of the writings but acknowledged existing authority. And it did not contain all of the writings judged to be inspired, true, and profitable for knowledge of God and conduct of life, but only those deemed essential and having broad appeal within the community. The criteria for inclusion remain one of the most debated issues; what is essential to affirm here is that the canon represents a selection, based primarily on use.

Canon implies boundaries, which have significant consequences for interpretation and use. Different degrees or types of authority are accorded to works inside and outside canonical boundaries, as may be seen in differing Protestant and Catholic uses of the deuterocanonical/apocryphal writings. Canon does not, however, imply fixed or unchangeable boundaries. The Hebrew canon grew—and contracted—and differed according to the community of reference. The Pentateuch appears to have acquired the status and function of a canon for Second Temple Judaism, and a small prophetic "canon" may have been recognized by some Jewish circles as early as the exile.[28] In the century before the closing of the Jewish canon, however, Sadducees, Essenes, and Pharisees all had different canons, with the Sadducees recognizing only the Law of Moses as authoritative and the Essenes employing the widest selection of writings.

Canon is a function of political power as well as theological persuasion. The canons of both Judaism and Christianity reflect the views of the dominant parties—and the survivors. To the extent that canonical status was determined by use, it was weighted in favor of use by the largest or most prestigious cities, churches, and religious leaders. Modern historical scholarship has allowed us to see the losers and dissenters in earlier battles over the Bible and to recognize that early Judaism and Christianity were far more diverse than the later orthodoxy of each tradition has suggested.

The church inherited a canon of Scriptures that was still in flux, in respect to both the number of books and the written text. From the evidence of first-century-BCE and -CE manuscripts, and from what can be reconstructed of the history of the OT text, it is clear that the notion of inspired and authoritative writings did not mean for the ancient guardians of those texts that the words themselves must remain unchanged—even where those words are represented explicitly, as in the prophetic writings, as the direct communication of God. Until the end

---

28. McDonald, *Formation*, 50.

of the first century CE, a dynamic understanding of divine communication in Scripture seems to have prevailed. This is exhibited in its early stages in redactional activity, evident in virtually all the OT books: New understandings of the divine purpose and will were incorporated directly into the received Scriptures. With the closing of the canon, however, that continuing interpretive effort had to take its place outside the canon and alongside the received text in various types of commentaries.[29] Thus at the time the church was coming into existence, the concept of Scripture as the "Word of God" had not yet acquired the literal interpretation it received in the second century CE.

Scripture in the time of Christian origins also did not imply that all "canonical" writings had the same type or degree of authority. Within the Hebrew Scriptures a hierarchy of authority was recognized, which is discernible in NT citations. The Pentateuch had preeminence, as the earliest body of writings to achieve its final form and as a corpus identified with Mosaic teaching and authority. Prophecy had succeeded *torah* as the means of continuing revelation in the post-Mosaic age and had given rise to a second corpus of authoritative writings, which appears generally to have been accorded secondary status within early Judaism. By 200 BCE a relatively closed prophetic canon was recognized by the dominant group, which held that the period of prophecy had ceased.[30]

For those holding this view, inspired and authoritative writing had also ceased. Those writings that were ultimately recognized as the third division of the Jewish canon had either to claim continuing inspiration or to establish their authority on other grounds. One attempt to formulate a criterion of authority that did not depend on the concept of prophetic inspiration is exhibited in the argument of "defiling the hands" that was used to assert the canonicity of certain contested works (Ecclesiastes and Song of Songs). The expression appears to refer to a quality of holiness recognized in the liturgical reading of Scripture, particularly the Law.[31]

---

29. Sanders, *From Sacred Story*, 140; and Sanders, *Torah*, xiv-xv.

30. Associated with the time of Ezra in 1 Macc 9:27; 4:45-46; Josephus, *Against Apion* 1.8.14; McDonald, *Formation*, 50-51.

31. The precise origin and meaning of the expression are debated. See Anderson, "Canonical," 114. What is clear, however, is that this manner of designating authoritative Scripture rests on liturgical use rather than on concepts of divine origin (inspiration). Liturgical orientation is also exhibited in the term that rabbinic Judaism came to use for the Scriptures as a whole: *miqra'*, "that which is read [aloud]." Judaism never employed the term *canon* (Greek *kanōn*, "standard"), which Christians adopted in the fourth century CE to designate their authorized corpus of Scriptures. (See ibid., 114,

This was ultimately extended to the whole corpus of authorized Scriptures, distinguishing them from other popular, but "noncanonical," writings, especially the so-called hidden or apocryphal works.[32] In seeking a term to describe writings that could not be included within the prophetic corpus, the creators of the three-part canon simply named them "the Writings" (in Greek, *hagiographa*, "Holy Writings"). In some circles of first-century Judaism, however, the concept of "inspired" or prophetic writing appears to have been extended to include all the writings outside the Pentateuch (evidenced by Septuagint canon lists). Some believed that prophecy had not ceased, among them Christians, who attempted to portray their movement as a revival of prophecy in the latter days.[33]

THE BIRTH OF THE CHRISTIAN BIBLE

Jewish and Christian Scriptures in the First Century CE

Christianity was born as a sectarian movement in first-century Judaism, and for a century at least some Christians continued to think of themselves as Jews. For all Christians in the formative period, "Scripture" was the Jewish Scriptures, whose authority and importance for the church's self-understanding are evidenced in the multitude of citations and allusions in early Christian writings. The center of the earliest Christian canon was the Law, and references to Scripture as a whole employ the two-part designation "the law and the prophets" (Matt 5:17; Luke 24:27; Acts 28:23). Only one NT reference suggests a three-part canon (Luke 24:44 [NRSV], referring to "the law of Moses, the prophets, and the psalms"). The notion of divine authorship and agency in the Scriptures can be seen in citations of OT passages that attribute the words directly to God or the Holy Spirit, without reference to the intermediary author, even where the OT lacks the rubric "says the Lord."[34] Little or no distinction of author or literary type is made; all words are understood as God's words and, therefore, as having equal authority.[35]

134, 156).

32. Ibid., 134, 156.

33. McDonald, *Formation*, 53; cf. Barr, *Holy Scripture*, 55–56.

34. Shires, *Finding*, 21; cf. 62.

35. Thus, e.g., Psalms (the most frequently cited book) is used in the same way as Deuteronomy and Isaiah (the most frequently cited books of the Pentateuch and Prophets), although as literature it has an entirely different character. And while its

The church inherited a canon and a concept of Scripture, together with means of interpreting it. In developing its own distinctive hermeneutics, it adapted current Jewish theory and practice. Where the church differed from its parent faith in respect to a common Bible was primarily in the relative weight it attached to scriptural authority. For Christians, the primary focus of divine revelation was not Scripture, but Christ, to whom Scripture was understood to bear witness. Christian preaching ("the gospel") was the primary authority for faith in the first centuries, and Scripture was interpreted in its light.[36] Christians believed that God's purposes for Israel as revealed in the Scriptures had reached an end in Jesus. As a consequence, they sought to show how Scripture pointed to Christ. Scripture, as the authoritative word from the past, had a decisive role to play in confirming and interpreting the new revelatory event, but it had no meaning, or could not properly be understood, apart from that event (2 Cor 3:12-18). It was still the authoritative Word of God, but it no longer communicated salvation.[37] This orientation toward Christ as the center and source of faith distinguished Christianity from the beginning and determined Christian understanding of Scripture, including the new Christian writings that would eventually stand alongside the OT canon. Christians, in contrast to Jews, were not primarily a people of the book.[38]

Christian use of Scripture shifted emphasis from God's activity in the past to God's activity in the present, a shift that affected the shape of the Christian OT and also the Jewish canon. Christians shared the belief of certain Jewish groups that the time of revelation was not past. In their conviction that the new age of the Spirit, predicted for the final days, had dawned, Christians were attracted to Jewish apocalyptic and messianic literature, which likewise expected a dramatic reappearance of divine activity in history. Christian use of these writings, as well as their "misuse" of the older canonical literature, seems to have been one factor behind the move by the dominant Jewish party to fix both the corpus and the text of the Jewish Scriptures at the end of the first century CE. The resulting canon admitted only one apocalyptic writing (Daniel) and no writings

---

words are typically identified with David, the Holy Spirit is understood to speak through them. See Shires, *Finding*, 126-27; see esp. 35-64 for analysis of varying uses of Scripture by different NT authors, as well as the extent of the corpus of sacred writings. See also Greer, *Christian Bible*, 126-54.

36. Greer, *Christian Bible*, 114.
37. Barr, *Holy Scripture*, 14.
38. Greer, *Christian Bible*, 112, 114, 202; McDonald, *Formation*, 66.

composed originally in Greek, apparently in reaction to the Christian adoption of the Septuagint (the Greek version of the Jewish Scriptures, produced in Alexandria).[39] Thus hermeneutics had a decisive influence on *which* books were considered authoritative as well as on *how* their authority was understood.

The Christian OT canon remained open for two more centuries, with continued, and ultimately unresolved, debate concerning some of the later writings, but a general preference for an expanded corpus based on the Septuagint.[40] Nevertheless, the main corpus of the OT had already attained such a degree of authority by the time Christians appropriated it as their own that no significant challenge was made against any individual book of the shorter Jewish canon. The real challenge to the authority of the Jewish Scriptures was directed to the corpus as a whole, and from that challenge the Christian Bible was born.

The Shape and Authority of the Christian Bible

The first century and a half of the church›s life was marked by wide diversity of understanding and practice as different communities attempted in different ways to relate the new faith to its parent religion and to other religious and philosophical movements. The consensus that finally emerged charted a course between two extremes, represented on the one hand by Jewish Christians, who insisted on maintaining their Jewish heritage and denied the divinity of Christ, and on the other by gnostic Christians, who depreciated the created order and the Jewish Scriptures and denied the full humanity of Christ.[41] By the mid-second century the primary challenge came from the gnostics and gnostic-influenced thinkers.

Marcion, a lay member of the Roman congregation who was heavily influenced by gnostics and Paul, had come to believe that the Jewish Bible was incompatible with the gospel. Moreover, he argued, the God of the Jewish Scriptures was not the God of Jesus Christ, but a vengeful and changeable god, whose eye-for-eye morality was superseded by Jesus's ethic of love. Christ had not only rendered the law obsolete but also revealed a new God. Marcion insisted that the church sever its Jewish roots completely, including the Jewish Scriptures; and he rejected attempts to

---

39. McDonald, *Formation*, 61–62; cf. Froehlich, *Biblical Interpretation*, 2–3.
40. See Sundberg, "Bible Canon," 58–59; McDonald, *Formation*, 178.
41. Greer, *Christian Bible*, 116.

hold on to these (in his view) outmoded and antithetical texts by such arbitrary methods of interpretation as allegory and typology. Establishing a counterchurch in 144 CE, he also proposed a counter Scripture. In place of the Jewish Scriptures, he proposed a canon of Christian writings consisting of an expurgated version of the Gospel of Luke (with all OT influences eliminated) and a freely edited collection of ten letters of Paul.[42]

The church ultimately rejected Marcion's theology and his canon, but in so doing it had to rethink its understanding of Scripture. In the end it reappropriated and reappraised the Jewish Scriptures in relation to a new collection of Christian Scriptures.

Christian Writings

Christian writings had begun to appear soon after the birth of the church, but they were intended to assist, not replace, oral proclamation, which was the authoritative form of the apostolic witness in the first century.[43] The circulation of written gospels, referred to as "memoirs of the apostles," did not mean, however, that they were immediately treated as Scripture.[44] The creation and adoption of a canon of Christian Scriptures had multiple sources and motives. The death of the first witnesses and the delay of the parousia gave impetus to the recording of the oral tradition, as did the difficulty of certifying oral tradition. Apologetic motives played a role in the composition and use of some of the NT writings, as did the needs of community worship and instruction, and the need to communicate with a rapidly expanding church for which personal communication was no longer possible. Practical reasons dictated the composition of most of the writings.

The growth of the NT and final establishment of a closed, authoritative canon paralleled in many ways the process by which the OT canon came into being. The sayings of Jesus were considered authoritative from the beginning and had the status of Scripture before they were recorded in any collection or gospel. Citations of Jesus's words became frequent in the second century, typically coupled with OT citations, and often

---

42. McDonald, *Formation*, 86–88; Froehlich, *Biblical Interpretation*, 10–11.

43. McDonald, *Formation*, 76–77.

44. Although the words of Christ were accorded Scripture-like authority from the beginning, scholars disagree about when in the second century that authority was extended to the books as a whole. See ibid., 74; von Campenhausen, *Formation*, 118–21.

derived from written Gospels (mostly Matthew). Citations from NT epistles also appear in this period, though less frequently, and there is evidence that Paul's letters were being circulated among a number of churches in Asia Minor and beyond. There is also evidence of liturgical use of the Gospels for public reading in worship—alternating with the Prophets. Whatever the original purpose and occasion of these writings, when they were placed alongside the OT Scriptures in worship and in appeals to authoritative teaching, they functioned as Scripture, whether they were formally accorded this status or not.

The Twofold Canon

The NT canon was not finally fixed until the fourth century, but the principal and the core literature had been established by the time of Irenaeus (writing ca. 170–180), who provided the nomenclature and the theory for uniting the two canons in a single Christian Bible. Irenaeus, who appears to have been the first to designate the two-part Scriptures as OT and NT, conceived of the history revealed in the two testaments as that of salvation in which the Hebrew Scriptures had a positive role in preparing the Jewish people for Christ. The incarnate Word of God was the head of this history, uniting and summing up all in God, but present in it from the beginning, revealing God the Father in creation and in the whole history of Israel. The revelation of the Word as attested by the Scriptures occurred in stages, marked by four covenants (Adam, Noah, Moses, Christ), in which the form and content of the message were appropriate for the particular dispensation in which it was given. Consequently, each testament was necessary to this progressive revelation of the one God, with the OT providing an indispensable pedagogy for Christ.[45]

Irenaeus's main contribution to the developing Christian Bible was his recognition of the need for an authoritative collection of NT writings to represent the apostolic witness. He did not define the limits of the canon but focused on the Gospels, which he saw as the primary source for the tradition held by the church. His insistence on a fourfold Gospel, rather than on the selection of one (as Marcion's Luke or the Ebionites' Matthew) or on a harmony (Tatian's *Diatessaron*), was based on use in the churches of his day. But his arguments (four were dictated by the

---

45. Greer, *Christian Bible*, 155–57, 163–74.

four quarters of the world and the four winds)[46] are a reminder that the whole process of Scripture formation, including canonization, is stamped by finite and culturally determined human reasoning.

Irenaeus's effort to establish a Christian Bible was motivated by his concern to defend the Christian message from heresy. For him, the primary form of that message was the apostolic witness, entrusted to the church and guaranteed by the succession of bishops. Its key, and the true canon of the church, was the "canon [or "rule"] of faith" (*regula fidei*), a summary of the essential content of the apostolic preaching resident in the church. While not verbally fixed, Irenaeus's formulation of it corresponds closely to the content of the later creeds.[47] It represented the essential content of "the one faith" that "the church, though dispersed throughout the whole world . . . [had] received from the apostles and their disciples." It was with this canon that heresy was opposed, but it needed the fuller witness of the Scriptures.

For Irenaeus, the rule of faith was the key that unlocked the Scriptures and the standard of truth by which all writings and teachings were to be judged, but it also depended on the Scriptures, deriving its categories of interpretation from them. Irenaeus likened the Scriptures to a mosaic, made up of many distinct passages, and the rule of faith to the "hypothesis" that enabled one to arrange the passages in the right order. Elsewhere he described the two as twin brothers whose message was in principle identical. For Irenaeus, Scripture and tradition could not be opposed or ranked; they needed each other and were mutually dependent.[48]

Irenaeus's understanding of Scripture and scriptural authority became the common property of Christian orthodoxy. It included a two-part canon, a hermeneutical principle derived from it and applied to it, and an authority structure capable of determining valid interpretations of Scripture. He also found a way of holding on to the Jewish Scriptures without resorting to allegory or other methods of interpretation that ignored their plain meaning and ancient context.

In his defense of the Jewish Scriptures as essential to Christian theology and authoritative for Christian faith, Irenaeus addressed a fundamental problem of all Scripture: its dual character as a word from the past, which is always to some degree alien and unrepeatable, and as a

---

46. Irenaeus, *Against Heresies* 3.11.8, 9.
47. Ibid., 1.10.1.
48. Greer, *Christian Bible*, 124, 157.

word for the present, informing and forming faith. With his view of progressive revelation and his concept of the educational purposes of past failings and punishment, Irenaeus was able to claim the continuing truth and revelatory power of the past while expressing a clear realization that elements in the ancient writings no longer represented the understanding of the community—and might even stand in opposition to it. That recognition is not new with Irenaeus but is a constitutive feature of the whole process of Scripture formation and transmission. What is new is the explicit recognition of a historical dimension: revelation as suited to the times and conditions under which it occurs. With this view of accommodation, both past and present are freed from the constraints of forced harmonization or unanimity of thought.

Criteria of Canonicity

The primary test for authority made by the early church was faithfulness in conveying the apostolic witness, which came to be formulated in terms of authorship. The underlying concern was to ground the church's faith in Jesus in reliable tradition. Yet the notion of reliable transmission of the Jesus tradition did not rest on historical connection alone. Neither Mark nor Luke could claim apostolic authorship, and the *Gospel of Thomas*, which did, was rejected because its message did not conform to what the general church understood as apostolic teaching, even though some of its sayings may actually have originated with Christ. Thus the claim of apostolicity, which was eventually extended to the whole NT canon, was a claim about the content of the message rather than the history of its origins.[49]

The notion of orthodoxy as a criterion of authority is even more strained. The church opted for a canon characterized by a plurality of theologies, because the church itself, from its earliest days, did not have a single unified theology. The unique contribution of Scripture, over against the rule of faith, was and is its irreducible pluralism, its articulation of the one faith in multiple voices—which requires prioritizing in the act of appropriation. The truth in the notion of orthodoxy as a criterion is that the recognized writings needed to lie within a general range of accepted belief.

---

49. For a discussion of several criteria for a NT canon, see McDonald, *Formation*, 146–63.

Inspiration is the criterion most commonly cited by modern interpreters to explain the authority of the canonical writings, but without elaboration it is inadequate and misleading. All of the competing canons consisted of writings understood to be inspired, but writings that claimed no canonical status were also recognized as inspired. Thus inspiration was a necessary, but insufficient, criterion. Moreover, many noncanonical writings claimed inspiration, while few canonical writings did so. The Montanists, with their new Scriptures, made the church wary of inspiration as a criterion, especially in the East, resulting in a neglect of prophetic literature—and suspicion of the book of Revelation as late as the fourth century.[50] The Montanist excesses illustrate an important feature, however, of general early Christian understanding of inspiration—namely, the belief that inspiration had not ceased with the canonical writings—and that it was a gift to the whole church, not simply a possession of certain writers.

In the final analysis, the formation of the NT canon and the Christian Bible closely paralleled the process for the OT Scriptures. Both rested ultimately on the recognition of a community through its use, but in neither case does this supply an adequate criterion of judgment. At the base of the recognition was the community's belief that these writings conveyed a true representation of God and of the saving acts that constituted the community, that they offered trustworthy guidance for the present, and more particularly that they served the needs of the community at the time of the closing of the canon. Thus truth in representing the tradition and suitability for meeting current needs were the twin tests of authority in the creation of the Christian Bible.

AUTHORITY IN THE WESTERN CHURCH

Wherever the question of biblical authority has been raised in the history of the canon, it has been linked to the question of meaning and the underlying question of purpose. For most of that history, belief in the Bible as a source of divine revelation and a guide to salvation was unchallenged, but

---

50. Montanism was an enthusiastic revival movement that spread rapidly through the church in the late second century, emphasizing the imminent return of Christ and the new gift of the Spirit. The Montanists stressed the new revelation given by their prophets and set forth their visions in new apocalypses, claiming superior authority for the "New Prophecy of the Paraclete" over the former revelation. See von Campenhausen, *Formation*, 221–23.

it could be maintained only by hermeneutical means that enabled readers to discern the spiritual message in the human words. Modern critics of the Bible's primitive cosmology and ethics are not alone in finding much within the Scriptures incredible or offensive, and Marcion was not the first to expose the defects in the OT's portrait of God.

The Jewish philosopher and exegete Philo of Alexandria (ca. 20 BCE–50 CE), recognized that the biblical stories were filled with "impossibilities," "impieties," and "absurdities" when read literally. But his Hellenistic understanding of inspiration, as affecting the production of the text itself, led him to seek a deeper, spiritual meaning through the use of allegory—a method of interpretation developed by Greek exegetes as a means of discovering higher cosmological or ethical truths behind the ancient Greek mythical texts. He also found a rationale for the OT"s anthropomorphic representations of God in the concept of accommodation. The anthropomorphisms, he argued, were an accommodation of God to human thought, enabling finite human minds to apprehend the infinitely great and unknowable God.[51]

The great Christian theologian and exegete of the early church, Origen of Alexandria (ca. 185–254 CE) built his own hermeneutical theory on these foundations. Origen found the model for God's condescending or accommodating to human weakness in the incarnation, which he saw as revealing God's manner of communication from the beginning. In Scripture, God had stooped to speak human language, which was like children's speech. Like a schoolteacher or a father, God adopted "baby talk" to lead his children according to their ability to comprehend. The means of communication, Origen argued, was suited to its purpose. The Bible was a book of salvation, not of human science; it suited God's salvific purposes, not the human search for knowledge. For Origen, Scripture was a guide for the soul in its ascent to its true home in the Platonic realm of spiritual reality. The "stumbling blocks" placed before the reader by the divine author were a sign of the Bible's higher purpose and an invitation to search it out. Origen's hermeneutical theory enabled readers to move from the limited, literal sense of the text to the higher,

---

51. Froehlich, *Biblical Interpretation*, 6–7; Rogers and McKim, *Authority of the Bible*, 11–12, view the notion of accommodation as a key and constant feature of premodern exegetical theory, which was lost by Protestant orthodoxy and its heirs in their defense of the Bible against modern criticism. Their reconstruction of the historical understanding of biblical authority has been challenged on several grounds, especially in regard to the concept of inerrancy. See, e.g., Woodbridge, *Biblical Authority*. Nevertheless, it remains a useful historical survey.

spiritual meaning, but it also lent itself to uncontrolled speculation, arbitrary equivalences, and even denial that the ancient writers had spoken for their own time at all.

In the fourth and fifth centuries a rival school arose in Antioch, challenging the excesses of Alexandrian spirituality. Antiochene exegesis drew upon a different pagan and Jewish philosophical heritage in its grammatical-historical approach to the text. Rabbinic exegesis, aimed at applying the text to practical questions, and a concern for history, textual criticism, and classical rhetoric provided the foundations for the Antiochene emphasis on the natural meaning of the text in its historical context. For John Chrysostom (ca. 347–407), the principle of accommodation exemplified in the incarnation led to a focus on the humble text, rather than on the lofty meanings spun out by philosophers. But he too recognized that some statements could not be understood literally and that mere literalism, with no concern for the divine purpose and character of the words, could easily result in "utter absurdity." Antiochene exegesis was also governed by a stronger emphasis on the apostolic tradition as a guide to interpretation.

Despite the differences between the two ancient exegetical schools, they shared a common belief that the primary purpose and content of Scripture was salvation, and that whatever did not accord with that message was not authoritative. They also recognized a distinction of content and form, in which the form of the message represented a divine accommodation to human thought and speech. That meant that the literal meaning of the text, however incomprehensible or offensive, had a purpose in God's communication in the Scriptures and could not be dismissed entirely. Thus readers were able to acknowledge difficulties in the text without jeopardizing the fundamental authority of the Scriptures.

Elements of both Alexandrian and Antiochene exegesis combined in the hermeneutical theory of Augustine (354–430). He, like Origen, sought the higher meaning of the text by means of allegorical interpretation, but he also affirmed the root historical meaning, preferring to give both a literal and a spiritual meaning of the same text. This did not, however, affirm their equal value but rather showed that the one prefigured the other. His preference for the spiritual meaning led at times to strained interpretations, but his exegesis was generally more restrained than Origen's because of his appeal to the rule of faith and the authority of the church in interpreting Scripture.

Augustine believed that the goal of Scripture was to induce love for God and neighbor and thus to order Christian life toward its heavenly home, but this love was to be found in its true form only in the church. Against various heretical sects who based their beliefs on private interpretations of Scripture, Augustine appealed to the authority of the church, declaring that he would "not believe the gospel except as moved by the authority of the Catholic Church."[52] For Augustine, as for Irenaeus and Chrysostom, the rule of faith supplied the basic principles for interpreting Scripture and for resolving ambiguities.

Augustine developed a hermeneutical theory that became the foundation for exegesis throughout the Middle Ages. Recognizing four "senses" to be sought in every biblical book (if not every text), he brought together all the major exegetical streams of the earlier period. Attention to the *literal* sense preserved the Antiochene tradition of grammatical-historical exegesis; the *allegorical* sense continued the tradition of typological interpretation; the *tropological* meaning made room for the moral message emphasized by Chrysostom and the rabbis; while the *anagogical* sense maintained the Alexandrian emphasis on the spiritual sense. Appeal to the fourfold sense of the text permitted the Bible to serve a variety of practical and speculative needs, as the foundation for doctrine and ethics and as a guide to the spiritual life. Recognition of multiple senses was an ideal solution to a problem inherent in the concept of Scripture as it had developed in Jewish and Christian tradition and in the character of the text. A clearly composite text of different types of material and levels of insight, divergent views, and conflicting statements was to be read as the authoritative record of God's self-disclosure and saving action in the past and as a present source of divine guidance. But the notion of multiple meanings also led to uncontrolled speculation and ecclesiastical control, which undermined the authority of Scripture while maintaining the principle of Scripture as norm.

The authority of the Bible, understood as the inspired and inerrant word of God, was maintained throughout the Middle Ages without formal challenge. Although Scholasticism[53] revived the question of the place of philosophy in apprehending divine truth, suggesting a role for reason alongside revelation, the greatest of the Scholastics, Thomas Aquinas (ca. 1225–1274), gave precedence to Scripture in his magisterial synthe-

---

52. Augustine, *Against the Letter of the Manichaeans*, chap. 5 (6), *NPNF* 4:131.

53. *Scholasticism* refers to the teaching that flourished in the schools of the eleventh through the fifteenth centuries. See Rogers and McKim, *Authority of the Bible*, 36–48.

sis of reason and faith. While he sought to secure a place for reason in leading to faith, he recognized the divinely revealed truths of Scripture as surpassing reason. The means of apprehending those truths, however, was through the literal sense of the text. In his concern to be scientific, Aquinas turned away from allegorical speculation to the grammatical-historical sense of the text, insisting that it must be the basis of all other meanings.

The Protestant Reformation

Luther

Where Luther differed from his medieval colleagues was not in asserting the authority of the Bible but in denying the authority of the church and pope. Forced to acknowledge a conflict between the two authorities to which he had appealed, he chose Scripture. Luther's choice, and his view of opposing claims, widened a rift between the church and Scripture that had begun developing in the fourteenth century. Prior to that time Scripture and the tradition maintained in the church were understood to "co-inhere"; there could be no ultimate discrepancy between the two sources, because each derived authority from Christ, the living Word who spoke through both. In his earliest arguments, Luther still tried to hold on to the belief that church and Scripture spoke with a common voice. When he could no longer reconcile the two, however, he chose Scripture as the firmer foundation and surer guide. Although his view of alternative, and opposing, authorities had antecedents,[54] the political and theological crisis in the church of Luther's day made his appeal to *sola scriptura* ("Scripture alone") a revolutionary cry, whose echoes still resound in a fractured church.

Luther's attempt to reform the church of his day appealed to the Bible as the norm of faith and doctrine, setting it over against the church's teaching. As the primary and unchanging source of the gospel, it stood as witness against ecclesiastical perversions and served as a source of both judgment and renewal for the church. Moreover, it was accessible to every believer, or at least potentially so. Luther's opposition to the ecclesiastical establishment of his day was directed at its control, not only of souls, but also of Scripture. The fanciful interpretations characteristic of medieval

---

54. E.g., Henry of Ghent (d. 1293); see Tavard, *Holy Writ*, 22–79.

biblical exegesis served mainly, he believed, to obscure the meaning of the text, setting human invention in the place of the divine word. For Luther and his Reformed colleagues, the "plain" or literal (grammatical-historical) meaning, rather than the allegorical sense, conveyed the intention of the divine author—hence the true "spiritual" sense.

The Reformers' appeal to the Bible as the primary source and norm of faith, and their understanding of Scripture as the self-interpreting word of God, set Scripture over against, or at least alongside, the church and its teaching office as an independent, and privileged, source of authority. Thus the Reformation reversed the two interpretive principles of the preceding age, setting literal reading over spiritual or allegorical and the word of Scripture over the word of the church.

Luther never gave systematic formulation to his understanding of the authority and inspiration of the Bible. While he regarded both the book and the authors as inspired and referred to the Scriptures as the "Word of God," he never simply identified that word with the words of Scripture. Rather, the word of God was Christ; but like Christ, whose humanity Luther emphasized, God's Word in Scripture was incarnate, communicating the divine message in weak and imperfect human speech. The authority of the Bible for Luther came from the One to whom it bears witness, and must be confirmed in the heart of the believer. Thus it was both objective and subjective.[55]

Luther recognized the Bible as both a divine instrument and a human document of decidedly uneven quality. The aim of exegesis, in his view, was to discern the gospel, contained in both testaments, and distinguish it from the law. Those portions of Scripture that did not "urge" Christ were not worthy of belief. With this criterion of authority for faith, Luther boldly dismissed some Scripture as unworthy, including the books of Esther, James, and Revelation; yet he retained them in his canon, honoring tradition over his own discernment. He also reopened the question of the OT canon, which had never been formally settled, opting for the shorter canon of Jerome and Jewish orthodoxy.

---

55. See Gerrish, "Biblical Authority," 342–43; Rogers and McKim, *Authority of the Bible*, 75–88.

Calvin

Calvin's understanding of Scripture was close to Luther's but was given more systematic and theoretical expression in his theological writings and commentaries.[56] For Calvin, the key to the understanding and authority of Scripture was the activity of the Holy Spirit speaking in Scripture but also prompting the heart and mind of the believer to recognition and assent. This "internal testimony of the Holy Spirit" is essential to the acknowledgment of Scripture as "the word of the Lord." The words themselves are merely the record of God's speaking and are not themselves either inspired or authoritative. The content of Scripture, apprehended through the internal action of the Spirit, is the word of salvation, but the words of Scripture in their human and historical meaning constitute the essential and sole access to that divine word.

Both Luther and Calvin gave new emphasis to the authority of Scripture, drawing on traditional views of the Bible as the inspired "word of God," but both emphasized the continuing activity of the divine speaker and the necessity of encounter with that speaker in the heart and mind of the believer. Consequently, the authority of Scripture could not be located exclusively either in the words themselves or in the historical authors. The two great Reformers had opened the door to a new understanding of the inspiration and authority of Scripture that had ancient roots and combined emphases on faith and reason, which had tended to diverge in medieval exegesis. Their successors, however, fell back on the medieval underpinnings of the Reformers' thought, attempting to defend the Bible against the counterattack of the Roman Catholic Church and new critical forms of interpretation by means of a rigid theory of verbal inspiration. Protestant orthodoxy also extended and absolutized the claims of scriptural authority, vesting in the biblical text the authority previously given to tradition, philosophy, and ecclesiastical structures. By the seventeenth century, the Bible had become a compendium of fixed theological statements. Gradually a new apparatus of interpretation was imposed upon the text in which doctrine again held the key.

---

56. See Rogers and McKim, *Authority of the Bible*, 89–176; Reid, *Authority of Scripture*, 29–55.

Roman Catholic and Protestant Proclamations and Praxis

Roman Catholic response to Protestant elevation of scriptural authority took a variety of forms, exhibited in the debate on Scripture that took place at the Council of Trent (1545–1563).[57] While all of the participants were intent on upholding the authority of the church against Protestant assaults, they differed on the mutual relations of the church and Scripture and the connection of each with revelation. The Council had to reconcile differences that ranged from "Scripture alone" to "the church alone," as well as the priority of "continuing revelation." The statement that was finally adopted affirmed two modes of revelation, declaring that the pure gospel was contained and handed on in *libris scriptis et sine scripto traditionibus*, "in written books and unwritten traditions," and that both were to be received and venerated *pari pietatis affectu ac reverentia*, "with equal feeling of piety and reverence."[58] The compromise displeased those who objected to placing tradition on the same level with Scripture, but by refusing to specify how each authority related to the other, it permitted a view of the priority of Scripture.

The mainstream of Roman Catholic thought interpreted the Tridentine declaration as affirming Scripture and tradition as "two sources" of revelation, in which the content of revelation was divided materially between the two. This interpretation has recently been called into question, but it stood for almost five centuries as the dominant view and "one of the most important points of controversial theology" directed against the Protestant doctrine of *sola scriptura*. The Council itself apparently rejected this interpretation when it removed the *partim ... partim* from an earlier draft that had declared that the "truth [of the gospel] is contained partly (*partim*) in written books, partly (*partim*) in unwritten traditions."[59] Moreover it defined Scripture as *norma normans et non normata*, "the norm that governs, but is not governed," suggesting an understanding of Scripture as the norm for the traditions of the church, which appears close to the views of Protestant orthodoxy.[60]

---

57. See Tavard, *Holy Writ*, 196–209 for a detailed account of the debate, and 113–91 for the various positions taken in the preceding three decades.

58. Schroeder, *Canons and Decrees*, 17, 296.

59. See Tavard, *Holy Writ*, 202, 205, 208, 244–45.

60. See the Lutheran description of Scripture as *norma normans*, "the norm that governs," and the tradition or the confessions as the *norma normata*, "the norm that is governed [by Scripture]" (*Book of Concord*; see Gnuse, *Authority of the Bible*, 8).

Despite similarities in formal pronouncements and doctrines affirming the authority of Scripture, the Bible played a quite different role in Protestantism than in Roman Catholicism or the Eastern churches. The two branches of the Western church had different canons and different authoritative texts, and they differed markedly in their views of interpretive authority. Against Luther's preference for the Jewish OT canon favored by Jerome, the Council of Trent endorsed the longer canon drawn up at the council of Hippo (393 CE), declaring that all of the books of the OT and the NT, including the deuterocanonical/apocryphal books, were of equal authority. It also authorized the Latin Vulgate as the "authentic" edition for public reading, exposition, and disputation, in contrast to the Reformers' appeal to the original Hebrew and Greek. But the Council went beyond the establishment of an authoritative text and canon, attempting to secure authoritative interpretation as well. No interpretation should be considered valid, it decreed, which was "contrary to that sense which holy mother Church has held and now holds," for "it is her office to judge about the true sense and interpretation of Scripture."[61] This reassertion of the principle that Luther had opposed resulted in continuing ecclesiastical control of Roman Catholic biblical interpretation.

Protestants, following Luther, shifted authority for interpretation from the teaching office of the church to the individual conscience informed by the Holy Spirit.[62] Despite latent conflicts and unresolved tensions concerning the actual locus of authority for interpretation, Protestantism took a generally "democratic" approach, marked in some traditions by a strong populist emphasis.

The Bible also functioned in a quite different way in the congregational life and personal piety of Protestants. The symbolism of the word, read and expounded, at the center of the traditional Protestant service of worship points to a fundamentally different way of understanding scriptural authority than that of the traditional Roman Catholic mass. Similarly, the subordination of Scripture to the liturgy, or incorporation of Scripture into liturgy, in Orthodox practice signals a different

---

61. Schroeder, *Canons*, 19, 298; Collins and Brown, "Church Pronouncements," 627; cf. Gerrish, "Biblical Authority," 339.

62. Formally, the Protestant claim locates the authority in Scripture itself, speaking of the "self-interpreting word." In practice, however, authority rests with the individual interpreter and with the faith community of the believer, or with both. Recent Protestant critique and ecumenical discussion have led to the recognition that the authority exercised by Protestant confessional groups closely resembles that formally claimed by the Roman Catholic magisterium.

disposition toward Scripture, even where common affirmations may be made concerning its authority for faith. Moreover, the Bible functions for many Protestants as the primary medium of communion with God, hence it plays a critical role in Protestants' experience of God—a major factor distinguishing Protestant and Catholic approaches to feminist theology.[63] The dominant image of evangelical Protestantism today is of a Bible-centered faith, and Protestants in predominantly Roman Catholic or Orthodox countries typically identify themselves as "Bible believers." Whatever the accuracy of this claim and implied contrast, it is an important witness to the authority accorded to the Bible by a major stream of the Reformation.[64]

In its practice, as well as its confessions, Protestantism centered its life on the Bible and looked to the Bible for guidance in all matters of belief and practice. As a consequence, the challenge to traditional understanding of the Bible and biblical authority occasioned by the Enlightenment had an especially traumatic and far-reaching effect on Protestantism. Although it eventually made an impact on Roman Catholicism, in the modernist controversies of the late nineteenth and twentieth centuries, the ancient church remained intact, while the younger churches were shaken to their foundations, many sustaining irreparable breaches.

AUTHORITY IN AMERICA

Scenes of Battle: Setting the Stage

American Protestantism, together with its descendants around the globe, is characterized by a unique interest in the question of biblical authority, which arises from its peculiar history and distinguishes it from its European ancestors and confessional kin.[65] Both the shape of the church, with its multiple denominations and independent churches, and its theological discourse have been deeply marked by battles over the Bible—

---

63. Tolbert, "Protestant Feminists." See Rogers and McKim, *Authority of the Bible*, 147–261.

64. The distinction between Bible-centered and liturgy-centered worship is breaking down today as a result of liturgical changes occasioned by Vatican II and the growing phenomenon of communal exegesis in base communities.

65. An exception to the dominant Protestant pattern has been the African American church, which developed its own distinctive (counter) hermeneutics and in which biblical authority was not tied to textual or scientific claims. Trust in the message was combined with suspicion of its interpreters, ancient as well as modern.

battles that are being replayed in many denominations today. The major battles were fought in the period between the 1880s and the 1920s and have their roots in the particular confluence of two streams of influence, Renaissance learning and Reformation piety, as they met on the American frontier. The history of their antecedents and earlier interactions in Europe is important for understanding the modern debate, but the constraints of this chapter limit consideration to a few key developments.

The Doctrine of Inerrancy

Post-Reformation Protestantism, especially on the Continent, responded to the Roman Catholic Counter-Reformation by adopting its weapons, reverting to an older scholastic mode in attempting to systematize the work of the Reformers.[66] Fighting battles on several fronts, including battles with humanists and intra-Protestant disputes, both Lutheran and Reformed traditions developed confessions aimed at securing the faith, in which the doctrine of Scripture was the key article.[67] Theology, conceived as a science of systematically ordered truths, was grounded in Scripture, whose sufficiency and trustworthiness had to be defended. Viewed as a book of revealed truths, which together presented a comprehensive system of knowledge, the Bible's technical accuracy took on heightened importance, especially in the new intellectual climate created by the revolution in science and philosophy. The meaning and efficacy of Scripture came to depend on a conception of the Bible as verbally inspired and inerrant; and the work of the Holy Spirit was now conceived primarily as ensuring the Bible's accuracy, rather than as awakening faith in the believer.

In seventeenth-century Reformed scholasticism, inerrancy became the key claim on which the Bible's authority rested, a claim that directed interpretive efforts to resolving apparent conflicts in the text and focused attention on the form of the text—even including the Hebrew vowel points. Thus the Reformed theologian Francis Turretin (1632–87) argued:

66. See Rogers and McKim, *Authority of the Bible*, 147–261.

67. See ibid., 462–72 ("Appendix: Reformed Confessions on Scripture") for a useful collection of texts. The articles on Scripture commonly stand at the head of the confessions and tend to become progressively longer and more detailed, as illustrated by the Second Helvetic Confession of 1566 and the 1646 Confession of Faith of the Westminster Assembly of Divines (known as the Westminster Confession).

> We have always thought the truer and safer way to keep the authenticity of the original text safe and sound against the cavils of all profane persons and heretics whatever, and to put the principle of faith upon a sure and immovable basis, is that which holds the points to be of divine origin ... and therefore, that the adversaries err who wish to impugn the authority of the Hebrew manuscript from the newness of the points.[68]

These efforts at securing the authority of the Bible would later serve to undermine it as new historical and scientific data challenged the premises of the claims. The battle over inerrancy had its roots in the seventeenth century, but it did not break in full force until two centuries later.

Renaissance Scholarship

The Renaissance revival of classical learning brought with it a new interest in the study of the Bible and new linguistic and historical tools for the task. In contrast to the ecclesiastical exegesis of the Middle Ages, whose aims were theological and devotional, the new scholarship was primarily historical in its interest, broadly humanistic in character, and marked by a spirit of critical and open inquiry. Its focus on the literal and historical meaning of the text corresponded to the new Reformation emphasis; and many Protestant scholars welcomed the new learning with enthusiasm, viewing it as a means of recovering the original meaning of the ancient authors and freeing the Bible from dogmatic interpretation and ecclesiastical control. But the alliance was an uneasy one, and many within the church saw the new scholarship as a direct threat, not only to traditional interpretation of the Bible, but also to the Bible's authority as a source and norm of faith. Their apprehension was fueled by freethinkers, as well as others, openly hostile to the church, who saw in the new criticism a means to unmask religion and reject its supernatural claims by exposing the Bible's human character, crude expression, and fallibility.

The new biblical scholarship analyzed the Bible in the same manner and with the same tools that had been used to study classical literature,

---

68. Cited by ibid., 180. Turretin was a key figure linking seventeenth-century Reformed theology in Europe to nineteenth-century theology in America. His textbook, *Institutio Theologiae Elencticae* (1674), dominated the theology of Princeton Seminary during its first century (1812-1912). In it, 355 pages were devoted to the doctrine of Scripture, which he believed to be the most important subject in theology (Rogers and McKim, *Authority of the Bible*, xvii, 175-76).

making comparisons of content, concepts, vocabulary, and style between different writings, both inside and outside the Bible. The results challenged traditional views of authorship and chronology, which had been the linchpins of a biblical history of salvation. Historical-critical scholarship transformed salvation history into "mere history" and judged it historically false, or so it appeared to many. In its reconstruction of the history behind the texts, it resembled the old allegorical readings in finding the key to the "true" meaning of the text in a reality behind the text; only, it reflected the new spirit of the times by seeking a historical explanation rather than a spiritual one.

For pious advocates, the new method liberated the Bible from traditional dogmas of interpretation that had been imposed on the Scriptures and did not arise from the text itself. It allowed the Bible to speak in its own voice, or better, voices. Recognition of multiple authors and circumstances of composition made it possible to explain discrepancies and contradictions that had troubled exegetes from earliest times. It was no longer necessary to deny or disguise the discord by harmonizing readings. Many welcomed the new clarity and believed they could now hear the ancient authors' words as they had intended them, unobscured by intervening interpreters. One could now know, or hope to know, the historical Jesus behind the dogmatic portrait. After encountering initial resistance, the new learning made rapid progress in the universities, especially in Germany.

Among most believers and ecclesiastical authorities, however, the new interpretation caused deep consternation. In its focus on the human words of Scripture and natural causality, it appeared to deny or exclude the notion of divine authorship and to leave no room for the action of the Holy Spirit. Whether directly or indirectly, it challenged traditional understandings of the authorship, inspiration, and authority of the Bible. It replaced a divine oracle with a collection of human words, robbing believers of the one sure foundation of faith and casting doubt on the wisdom of the past. At a time when Protestants had elevated the Bible to the position of supreme authority and infallible guide, critical scholarship appeared to many to have turned it into a babble of voices from an alien past without a clear and authoritative word for the present. A new scholarly elite had taken away the Bible so recently restored to the people.

Resistance took many forms and varied according to regional and confessional context, personal disposition, and education. For the broad base of believers, historical-critical scholarship was, and remains in much of the Christian world today, an esoteric science that has obscured the plain meaning of the text. The seeming alliance of Christian scholars with humanists of anti-ecclesiastical and even atheistic bent served to reinforce a latent suspicion of all critical scholarship, leaving a legacy of anti-intellectualism deeply embedded in some streams of Protestantism, in particular in American evangelicalism. The embrace of the new criticism by the Deists in England and its contribution to a radically atheistic rationalism in France led to ecclesiastical responses by both Protestants and Catholics, which attempted to maintain the authority and traditional interpretation of the Bible by means of prescriptive confessions and declarations. Scripture was once again subordinated to the ruling authority of the church.

Protestant rhetoric invested supreme authority in the Bible but left unclear where authority for interpretation lay. One stream of the Reformation emphasized the individual conscience, illumined by the Holy Spirit, as the final interpreter, with the Bible as the ultimate source of truth. This emphasis on individual interpretation apart from, or in opposition to, church tradition encouraged fragmentation into new denominations and sects based on differing understandings of particular biblical teachings (e.g., baptism and sabbath observance). The mainstream of Lutheran and Reformed tradition, however, retained a strong sense of the church's teaching and disciplining authority, exercising that authority in attempts to demonstrate and defend the Bible's truth and primacy.

New Locus and Form of Authority

Protestant orthodoxy's attempt to control biblical interpretation was a response, not merely to new interpretations that were deemed false and dangerous, but also to a new locus of interpretive activity, hence authority, that was largely outside ecclesiastical control. The early and strong opposition of Roman Catholic and orthodox Protestant ecclesiastical authorities to the new biblical scholarship had the effect of branding it secular and forcing it into opposition to the church, or at least independence from it. Thus the church contributed to the autonomy of biblical criticism, freeing it from clerical supervision, but also severing its ties to the dogmatic tradition that continued to dominate private devotion and preaching. "Precritical" interpretation continued to be the norm long after critical study had become established in the university, and attempts to open the church's door to the ostracized criticism were hampered by its history of secular development.

It was not simply the secular character of the new biblical scholarship that created a problem of authority in the church, but the independence of the new discipline from dogmatic theology—and from the new "scientific" theology that had emerged from the old biblically oriented dogmatics. The new discipline of biblical studies raises a number of critical new questions concerning authority in biblical interpretation: What is the authority of biblical scholarship in its historical and literary judgments for theological construction and for the faith of believers? Are some methods of interpretation more valid, or more appropriate, than others for use of the Bible as a resource for faith? Are some excluded, and if so, on what grounds? What are the criteria for judging the adequacy or truth of the methods and results of modern critical study of the Bible, and who is qualified to make such judgments?

The questions raised for the church and for traditional belief by all forms of new knowledge and investigation, including biblical studies, are not easily answered. Appeal to old standards in response to new questions may actually serve to undermine the Bible's authority, since these are commonly formulated in propositional forms involving extrinsic norms (such as plenary verbal inspiration, Mosaic authorship, or concepts of historicity and facticity foreign to the biblical writers). Attempts to defend traditional understandings also tend to deny the essential character of Scripture as a bridge between the past and present action of God, by means of which God addresses new generations through words from the past. The expectation of hearing a word for today—hence a new word—is fundamental to the church's understanding of Scripture. This means, however, that the message for the present generation cannot simply be equated with the message spoken to the ancestors. The problem with both historical and dogmatic interpretations of Scripture is that they tend to fix as normative a single meaning at a single time, thereby missing the essential dynamic character of Scripture as the meeting place of past word with an ever-changing present. The word of God becomes imprisoned in the text rather than freed for fresh hearing and response.

Behind the Scenes: Roots of the Great Debate

The roots of the American debate lay in the German universities and the English and Scottish churches. General ecclesiastical resistance to the new criticism was first broken in Germany during the eighteenth and nineteenth centuries, where the relative freedom of the universities from church restraint provided an environment in which the new exploration could take place. But the universities were also the primary centers for theological debate and the training of pastors, so that the new study had a significant impact on the church. The result was that Germany pioneered historical-critical study of the Scriptures—as an expression of faith rather than doubt.

The Battle in Britain

England lagged behind the Continent in accepting a critical approach to the Bible. Ecclesiastical control of the universities and the early Deist controversy gave a different cast to the discussion, as did the Evangelical Revival, which largely ignored the questions raised by the rationalist critique. In Germany, discussion had focused on the problem of relating historical fact to religious truth, or dogma. German theologians responded by developing a science of interpretation (hermeneutics) that would enable movement from historical exegesis to contemporary faith within the framework of the church's traditional confession. By contrast, the English debate focused on the problem of science and faith, and more specifically on the conflict of reason and revelation as defined by early eighteenth-century Deism.[69] This debate decisively affected the American understanding of the problem.

Deist denial of special divine action or communication in history and its insistence on a universe ruled by divinely instituted laws of nature as revealed by modern science left no room for revelation (identified with miracles) or prophecy and cast doubt on the credibility of the biblical "reports," and hence on the authority of the Bible. An overconfident young science, embraced by critical religious thinkers, forced the argument onto its ground. Defenders of Scripture were pressed into an uncritical stance and responded by asserting the infallibility and the scientific credibility of the Bible in all its statements. Biblical apologists attempted to give scientific proof for the Genesis account of creation, to find evidence of the deluge and Noah's ark, and to defend the Bible's chronology as well as its miracles. In this defense, however, the problems of literalism became ever more evident and the arguments more strained.

69. Neil, "Criticism."

The publication in 1859 of Darwin's *On the Origin of Species* directly challenged the literalists' attempt to defend biblical cosmology with a six-day creation in 4004 BCE. Scientists and religious skeptics acclaimed the new theory, as did numerous theologians who saw it as generally supporting current studies on the Pentateuch (which had recognized a development of ideas exhibited in a succession of "documents" discernible within the Pentateuch). But for those who linked the authority of the Bible to literal infallibility, it was a call to arms. In 1864 some eleven thousand clergy signed the Oxford Declaration, aimed at countering the new "heresy" by denouncing all who denied that the whole Bible was the word of God. In the view of the signatories, Genesis said all there was to be known about origins; any other view was blasphemy.[70]

The victory, however, was short-lived; within three decades, biblical faith had made peace with natural science through the mediation of devout but critical biblical scholars. Contributing factors were the broad support for Darwin's theory of evolution by the scientific and philosophical communities and the arguments of a new generation of biblical scholars influenced by German criticism, who insisted that the Bible should be treated on its own terms, not forced to fit the categories of modern science. The Bible was a book of religious testimony, they insisted, not a manual of science.[71]

New Awakening, New Science

In America, critical biblical study was a foreign import, which did not finally take root until the end of the nineteenth century—although it had been introduced almost a century earlier.[72] The early decades of the nineteenth century saw a new wave of revivalism sweep the country and establish itself on the frontier, giving rise to new denominations and sects, and reshaping older ones. This movement, which determined the character and shape of American religion for the rest of the nineteenth century and much of the twentieth, elevated emotion as the sign of authentic religion and emphasized individual decision and simple propositional faith. The Bible figured prominently in the new religious wars over

70. Ibid., 257-63.
71. See ibid., 268-72, 279-82, 287-89.
72. Brown, *Rise of Biblical Criticism*; summary treatment in Bird, *Bible as the Church's Book*, 59-61.

the "essential" content of faith, but the major battle over the Bible did not break until the end of the century.

Renewed contact with the intellectual world beyond America's shores after the disruption of the Civil War brought in rapid succession two new waves of assault on the thought world of most Americans, challenging a broad stratum of the population to come to terms with the scientific worldview. Darwin's evolutionary theory had an impact in America similar to that in England, with public debate by national leaders and immediate general rejection. But its rapid acceptance in the scientific community and among the more broadly educated segments of the population led ultimately to wide acceptance of a critical scientific-historical worldview. The crisis this caused for traditional religious views was profound and prolonged, however, because the religious regeneration that America had experienced in the New Awakening had been linked to a theological retreat into a rigidly anticritical defense of "traditional doctrines." The key to the reintegration of the intellectual and religious worlds of devout, but thinking, Christians was critical biblical interpretation. Although its advance was marked by bitter resistance, heresy trials and church divisions, this time it had come to stay.

Inerrancy on Trial: Scholastic and Populist Defense

The Briggs Trial

Biblical criticism came to America in the latter part of the nineteenth century as a mature and established discipline, part of a broad influx of German learning. Many American biblical scholars embraced it eagerly, and conservatives rallied to meet them in battles that affected virtually every American denomination. None was more deeply torn than the Presbyterian Church, whose conflict was symbolized in the heresy trial of Charles Briggs.[73] At his inauguration in 1881 to the chair of Biblical The-

---

73. Debate over the authority of the Bible centered in the Reformed tradition as carried in this country primarily by the Presbyterian Church; hence my attention to this debate, which made front-page news at the time. The resulting polarization in that church, however, has affected most American denominations, especially those that define themselves as theologically conservative or have significant segments that do. Churches with strong liturgical traditions (Roman Catholic, Orthodox, Episcopalian), liberal orientation (Congregationalist/United Church of Christ), or charismatic emphasis (Pentecostals, until recently) have been less affected, or differently affected, by these debates. See below for the continuing debate.

ology at Union Theological Seminary in New York, Briggs had defended historical criticism, characterizing the dogma of inerrancy as an attempt to "prop up divine authority by human authority." Such errors as historians find cannot destroy the authority of Scripture, he argued, which is from God. Moreover, he insisted, the claim of inerrancy is nowhere made by the Bible itself nor sanctioned by the creeds of the church.

The immediate target of Briggs's attack was an article in the *Presbyterian Review* (April 1881) by Princeton theologian A. A. Hodge and NT scholar Benjamin Warfield. In it they produced a classic statement of the doctrine of scriptural inerrancy. According to them, the Scriptures not only contain the word of God but are the word of God; hence all their elements and all their affirmations are absolutely errorless. Apparent inconsistencies and conflicts with other sources of information are due to imperfect copies of the now-lost originals ("autographs") or failure to realize the point of view of the author. In their view, "the historical faith of the Church has always been, that all the affirmations of Scripture of all kinds, whether of spiritual doctrine or duty, or of physical or historical fact, or of psychological or philosophical principle, are without any error, when the *ipsissima verba* of the original autographs are ascertained and interpreted in their natural and intended sense."[74]

This statement was adopted as the official position of the Presbyterian Church, and Briggs was suspended from the Presbyterian ministry on grounds of heresy—retaining his chair, however, as the seminary severed its denominational ties. The "Princeton theology" had won the battle of the Bible, at least for the time—but its time was measured. A half century later, biblical study at Princeton was taught with the same critical assumptions and the same methodologies as at Union. By the third decade of this century, a critical approach to the Bible was the norm in the seminaries of all of the older denominations, if not in the pew. And in the middle of the century the Roman Catholic Church, the only Western church that had officially condemned historical-critical study of the Bible, opened its doors to it and commended it as a pastoral tool. Today many evangelicals are also cautiously appropriating its methods and perspective. The shift in stance, which is still contested in significant segments of the church, came about as the church came to see the new scholarship as an ally rather than an enemy of faith.

---

74. Cited by Rogers and McKim, *Authority of the Bible*, 169.

The backbone of Presbyterian resistance in the twentieth century was the Princeton Theology, an expression of post-Reformation scholasticism deriving from Turretin and the Westminster Confession.[75] Hodge contributed to this theology by shifting attention from the Confession to the Bible as the final authority for the system of theology presented therein. He also gave the first systematic treatment to the doctrine of inspiration. "Inspiration," he wrote, "was an influence of the Holy Spirit on the minds of certain select men, which rendered them the organs of God for infallible communication of his mind and will. They were in such a sense the organs of God, that what they said, God said."[76] Maintaining that this view was "the common doctrine of the Church" since the beginning, Hodge appeared unaware of the concept of accommodation common to the early church theologians and the Reformers.

The Princeton Theology linked the authority of Scripture to its inerrant words, treating the Bible as a repository of information on all manner of things, whose accuracy had to be defended by current standards.[77] Scripture was understood as divine speech in universally valid and universally intelligible form, in which historical and cultural contexts played an insignificant role. This frozen view of Scripture had widespread appeal, and continues to appeal to those who seek a changeless word in changing times. In America the last decades of the nineteenth century and the first decades of the twentieth century were times when the world was changing too fast for many. Current revival of the debates of that period is likewise a response to rapidly changing times and uncertain, or conflicting, values.

The Scopes Trial

A distinctive feature of the inerrantist debate in America has been the coupling of rationalistic scholasticism, as represented by the old Princeton school, with fundamentalist, and populist, anti-intellectualism.[78]

75. To which all Princeton faculty were required to subscribe (ibid., 200–203, 279–80, 357–58).

76. Hodge, *Systematic Theology*, 1:154.

77. E.g., Hodge declared that "the Bible is to the theologian what nature is to the man of science. It is his store-house of facts; and his method of ascertaining what the Bible teaches, is the same as that which the natural philosopher adopts to ascertain what nature teaches" (ibid., 1:10).

78. Anti-intellectualism does not define fundamentalism but represents a

These two strains within the inerrantist camp are symbolized by the two debates that galvanized opinion: the Briggs trial of 1891, featuring two eastern seminary professors, and the Scopes trial of 1925, featuring a frontier school teacher, represented by an atheist "big-city" lawyer, and an evangelical populist politician. The latter trial was a key battle for fundamentalism, which had made inerrancy its touchstone. It provided a national forum for its cause but also subjected it to a devastating media attack.[79]

Fundamentalism arose in the early decades of this century[80] out of the old revivalist evangelicalism that had been the Protestant establishment in nineteenth-century America but found itself increasingly challenged or eclipsed by the rise of new philosophies of life and new religious perspectives. Its primary target was the new liberal theology (later called modernism) that attempted to integrate the findings of science, biblical criticism, and historical studies and to reformulate Christian doctrine in their light. Distrusting the new syntheses, traditional Protestants emphasized a simple Bible-centered theology, whose appeal was strengthened by the perplexing array of new alternatives. Between 1920 and 1925 the movement gave particular attention to the teaching of evolution in the public schools, culminating in the Scopes "monkey trial," which served as a public debate between fundamentalism and modernism.

John Scopes, a Tennessee biology teacher, was charged with violating a state law against the teaching of Darwinism in the public schools. He was defended by ACLU lawyer Clarence Darrow, whose primary aim was to ridicule and humiliate those who would bring such a charge. While Darrow's immediate target was the lawyer for the prosecution, the famous politician and orator William Jennings Bryan, he meant to

---

deep-seated and broad impulse in American religious consciousness. It does provide fertile ground, however, for fundamentalist arguments, as illustrated by Harold Lindsell in his widely read book *The Battle for the Bible* (1970). In it, he attempted to win over the Southern Baptist Church to the inerrantist position by sounding the alarm against the critical biblical interpretation invading the seminaries. "Godly men through the ages," he argued "have come to the Scriptures without advanced theological training and have been better interpreters and more spiritual leaders than many who have undergone the most rigorous theological training" (7). Lindsell's is not the first, nor the last, attempt to rally devout laity against the seminaries, or to control intellectual inquiry.

79. See Wills, *Under God*, 97–124 for a discerning analysis of the religiopolitical aspects of the trial.

80. —Ed.: this twentieth century.

discredit fundamentalists generally as well as the "stage of civilization" of the state of Tennessee.

Bryan, a lay preacher and ardent champion of social reform, had become obsessed with the question of evolution because of the social Darwinism he identified with it. Opposing the notion that the strongest must prevail in society, he entered the fray but allowed himself to be discredited when he attempted to defend the Bible's science. With the national media covering the debate, Darrow forced Bryan into an untenable literalist position, and although Darrow lost the case (later reversed on a technicality), he succeeded in portraying the fundamentalist position as intellectually untenable. Americans in the 1920s were generally enthusiastic believers in science, and that included many moderate Protestant conservatives, who quietly withdrew their support from the fundamentalist movement after 1925.

That did not mean the end of the movement, however; nor did it signal a general willingness to accord religious scholarship the same trust and awe as scientific expertise. Fundamentalism continued to thrive in local congregations, Bible schools, mission organizations, and through various media, and it remains a significant force today, although splintered into a number of factions. Distrust of biblical scholarship continues among a wide spectrum of believers who share Bryan's conviction that "the one beauty about the word of God is that it does not take an expert to understand it."[81]

CURRENT ISSUES AND OPTIONS

New Evangelicalism

Contemporary evangelicalism represents a complex phenomenon, whose diversity has been analyzed in a variety of ways.[82] Despite wide differences of theology and ecclesiology, evangelicals share a common emphasis on the final, or sole, authority of the Bible. In their emphasis on the primacy of Scripture, they understand themselves as maintaining the ancient faith of the church in the tradition of the Reformers, defending it against modern forms of perversion and erosion.

---

81. Quoted in ibid., 112.
82. See Marsden, *Understanding Fundamentalism*; cf. Sheppard, "Biblical Hermeneutics," 82–83.

Within evangelicalism, differing theological positions are associated with differing ways of describing or appealing to the authority of the Bible.[83] Thus fundamentalists and other conservative evangelicals generally prefer the term *inerrancy* to describe their understanding, insisting that it is "the badge of evangelicalism."[84] The language of "inerrancy" emphasizes the necessary relationship between the accuracy of the words and the authority of the message, often extending the claims to historical and scientific statements as well as spiritual and moral teachings. An example of this position is provided by the Chicago Statement on Biblical Inerrancy (1979), which bears a close resemblance to the Hodge and Warfield statement.[85]

The Chicago Statement represents an attempt to reassert an older view of scriptural authority in the face of a new evangelicalism, which began to emerge in the 1940s and departed in various ways from its fundamentalist roots. Neoevangelicalism represented a resurgence of evangelicalism in a postmodern milieu in which neither the old liberal positions nor fundamentalist positions seemed adequate. Arising from a stagnant and defensive fundamentalism, the new evangelicals rejected the separatism, sectarianism, and social conservatism of their once-vital parent. In their attempts to move evangelicalism into the mainstream of American society and religion, they have been drawn increasingly into the world of contemporary biblical scholarship. Thus new evangelicals commonly exhibit some degree of openness to modern, historically informed understandings of Scripture and doctrine and consequently reject efforts to bind Scripture to eighteenth- and nineteenth-century understandings of inspiration and truth.

---

83. See McKim, *Bible in Theology*, 52–62, 76–86; Noll, "Evangelicals"; and Sheppard, "Biblical Hermeneutics" for evangelical views and uses of Scripture.

84. Lindsell, cited by McKim, *Bible in Theology*, 89; see Noll, "Brief History of Inerrancy," for a survey of evangelical debate over the term.

85. The Chicago Statement on Biblical Inerrancy is a nineteen-article statement defining the "biblical and historic position on the inerrancy of Scripture," formulated by the International Conference on Biblical Inerrancy, an ecumenical assembly that met in Chicago in 1978. Norman Geisler, who edited the papers from the conference, introduces the "Statement" by highlighting the connection with authority: "The authority of Scripture is a key issue for the Christian Church in this and every age ... Recognition of the total truth and trustworthiness of Holy Scripture is essential to a full grasp and adequate confession of its authority" (Geisler, *Inerrancy*, ix). In the statement, both "inerrancy" and "infallibility" are used to describe "the total truth and trustworthiness of Holy Scripture" (ibid., 493). See articles 11, 12, and 19.

While new evangelicals represent a considerable spectrum within evangelicalism and define their positions in different terms, most tend to prefer the language of "infallibility" to describe their confidence in Scripture as the authoritative word of God. They are no less committed than fundamentalists to upholding the authority of the Bible, but they understand its message and purpose differently—and thus operate with different hermeneutics. For new evangelicals, the purpose of Scripture is to "bring people to faith and salvation in Jesus Christ." It accomplishes this purpose as "a book that presents a gospel message of salvation received, interpreted, and handed over by men," not a timeless truth or idea. The authority of its message is established by the witness of the Holy Spirit, not by rational argument. Thus inerrancy is viewed as an inappropriate and misleading term for describing the basis of the Bible's claim to authority. Given that the Bible is a book whose purposes are theological, rather than scientific or historical, its "complete trustworthiness and its ability to accomplish its purpose" is better affirmed, they believe, by the term *infallible*.[86]

Ecumenical Perspectives

The prominence of evangelicalism in the history of American religious life has meant that its preoccupation with the question of biblical authority has generally set the terms for addressing the subject. Ecumenical discussion fostered by the World Council of Churches and the contributions of a vigorous and theologically grounded Catholic biblical scholarship in the last half of this century have brought new perspectives and a broader horizon to the question, which is still largely neglected in most general treatments of the subject.[87] Ecumenical consideration of the place of the Bible in the churches' attempts to articulate their unity has led Protestants to acknowledge a much greater role of tradition in shaping doctrine and uses of Scripture than confessions generally admit. And although evangelicals have generally remained outside these discussions,

---

86. McKim, *Bible in Theology*, 87–99.

87. Exceptions seem to depend on Roman Catholic contributors, exemplified by the final chapter in Gnuse, *Authority of the Bible*, 113–21; and Dulles, "Scripture." Space is lacking in this article for an adequate review of the important series of consultations and documents sponsored by the World Council of Churches, in which both Roman Catholic and Orthodox views were represented, as well as a broad spectrum of Protestantism. See Flesseman-van Leer, *Bible*.

a similar recognition has begun to emerge concerning the role of church and tradition in evangelical interpretation. What has been learned from ecumenical discussion is what the history of the Bible itself has taught us: The Bible is the creation of the church and reflects, as well as directs, the church's understanding in its continuing interpretation and use. Behind slogans of "Scripture alone" are the realities of community faith and doctrine, which have an inescapably particular, and therefore plural, character when viewed from the perspective of the church as a whole.[88]

While Protestants have gained new appreciation for the church and tradition in their understanding of Scripture and scriptural authority, Roman Catholics have elevated the place of Scripture within the church and redefined tradition. It is now widely believed that the traditional two-source theory misrepresented the Council of Trent, which held a more unified view of Scripture and tradition, and that its equation of the two sources is unacceptable. In reinterpreting the Tridentine statement, Vatican II substituted "tradition" for "traditions," understanding it as a fluid and dynamic process, rather than a collection of beliefs, directives, and the like. Tradition is described as "the presence of Christ in the faith of the Church manifesting itself anew for each generation . . . [It] makes Scripture available and understandable to a changing and imperfect world where the biblical text must be reinterpreted."[89] This understanding has much in common with Protestant notions of the living Word and the Holy Spirit as the author and interpreter of Scripture. The main difference between converging Protestant and Roman Catholic views of Scripture remains authority for interpretation, with Protestants unwilling to hand this over to the church, and Catholics unwilling to entrust it to unqualified or unscrupulous exegetes.

At the same time that greater variety has been recognized in understanding and using the Bible, and hence variety in the ways its authority is conceived and actualized, a new and broad consensus has been achieved concerning the meaning of the Scriptures in their ancient contexts of origin.[90] This consensus spans confessional, and even religious, divisions, creating a new meeting place for biblical scholars—and a new set of questions for the churches. But it also contributes positively to

---

88. Ibid., 1–12.

89. Gnuse, *Authority of the Bible*, 116.

90. Scholarly disputes generally remain within a common realm of discourse, however disparate the views; and they are not primarily governed by confessional differences.

reformulating the question of authority. Through its recognition of the irreducible plurality of perspectives and theologies within the Bible itself, modern biblical scholarship has occasioned a more dynamic conception of the Bible's message, a search for continuities rather than a center and acknowledgment of contextual factors in the communication of divine truth. It has thereby provided a bridge to the pluralistic and conflicted world of the present, in which the word of Scripture can carry the authority of the word of God only as it addresses individuals and communities in their specific needs while simultaneously witnessing to the oneness of God, whose purposes are the redemption and *shalom* of the whole creation. Modern historical understanding of the Bible also suggests that the Bible's authority does not rest in its word alone, as declarative utterance or command, but in its nature as the witness of a community to the source of its life and the record of its continual struggle to comprehend the new thing God is doing in creation. Thus the Bible presents itself as a book of questions as well as answers, and it has authority insofar as it compels us to engage those questions with our own experience.

Feminist Critique

As early Christians found much within the Jewish Scriptures morally and intellectually incompatible with their faith in Christ, so feminists today find much within the two-part canon morally offensive and incompatible with the message of the gospel as they have come to understand it. And as early Christians took different paths in responding to the perceived defect of the Scriptures, so too do feminists today.[91]

Those in the early church whose position would ultimately receive the stamp of orthodoxy insisted that the witness to God's activity in the ages prior to Christ was essential to Christian understanding. In order to retain that witness, they developed various means of interpretation that subordinated, reinterpreted (by figurative and allegorical means), or dismissed as no longer relevant passages that appeared incompatible with later belief. A similar approach is taken by some feminists today. But the enterprise of recovering a liberating message from a sexist text involves a more radical assessment of the problem of Scripture, for it is apparent that the patriarchal and/or androcentric bias that feminists identify as a

---

91. See Sakenfeld, "Feminist Perspectives"; Osiek, "Feminist"; cf. McKim, *Bible in Theology*, 172–91.

sinful betrayal or denial of the gospel is deeply embedded in the texts of both testaments—and also in the communities behind the texts.

Feminist theology shares in large measure the basic hermeneutical stance of other liberationist theologies, but it exhibits a stronger sense of disparity between the gospel as transmitted historically through Scripture, creeds, and church teaching and God's intention for humanity as discerned through the contemporary working of the Holy Spirit, in communities outside the church as well as within.[92]

For most feminists, in contrast to other liberationists, the record of the past contains no model for the future, no core of tradition untainted by patriarchy—although some find a message of equality in an original Jesus tradition and in selected texts and traditions of both testaments when read with a feminist hermeneutic. Whether they acknowledge such a "subversive memory" in the text, feminists in general regard the memory of the past as recorded and brought into the present by Scripture as failure to grasp and actualize the will of God, rather than faithfulness. The Bible, they insist, presents a deficient and distorted witness to God's nature and purposes by virtue of its androcentrism.

Reaffirmations

Feminist critique represents the most radical form of the contemporary questioning of biblical authority, often extending to the notion of authority itself.[93] Any affirmation of the authority of Scripture today must take

---

92. Feminism is a complex movement uniting women inside and outside the church and in other religious bodies. Despite wide differences, most are united in condemning biblical patriarchy, and for many, including some feminist theologians and biblical scholars, this means rejecting the Bible's authority. Feminism is also characterized by an emphasis on the authority of experience, in particular, women's shared experience of oppression. Thus a key issue in feminist theology is the question of how this source of authority relates to the authority of the Bible and tradition. On the special problem of the Bible for Protestant feminists, see Tolbert, "Protestant Feminists." There is no single feminist theology, and affinities with liberation theologies are not claimed by all feminists.

93. Feminists are not alone in questioning or rejecting the concept of authority. Rejection of authority has commonly been associated with liberal theology and a modern critical spirit. The association of authority with hierarchical systems of social organization and value is, however, closely tied to feminist analysis of patriarchy. Much of feminist, as well as general, critique of authority falsely identifies it with authoritarianism. Authority can be expressed in forms of mutual respect and obligation and does not depend on hierarchical structures or arbitrary exercise of power. For a

account of that critique, which requires clarification of what is essential to the claim. Different assessments and different formulations will be made according to the believer's experience, theology, and social or ecclesial context. The following is one attempt to reaffirm the authority of the Bible in light of feminist critique and modern biblical scholarship. It is not intended as a comprehensive statement but as a concluding summary of the preceding arguments.

Feminist critique contributes two fundamental assertions that correlate closely with two essential affirmations of traditional understanding of the Bible and biblical authority. The first is the recognition of the pervasive androcentrism in the text and the culture, which serves as a needed reminder that Scripture is a human product and instrument and, therefore, culturally conditioned and limited—a feature of Scripture that has been affirmed in every age, even as every age has attempted to deny or minimize it. The Bible conveys the word of God, or becomes the word of God, only as fully human words, the record of human thought and experience. The temptation in claiming divine authority for Scripture has always been to deny its fundamental human character. The offense of the Bible's androcentrism provides a needed reminder that its words and ideas, as our own, are culturally conditioned. It is also a reminder that the Bible is the record of a sinful people—fearful, shortsighted, rebellious, like ourselves—a record of betrayal as well as faithfulness to the revelation they had received. The authority of Scripture does not depend on infallible words or model behavior but on the ability of its words to confront readers with the story and the presence of a God who redeems sinners by assuming their weakness, and empowers the weak and the silent (or silenced) with visions and with speech.

The second assertion is the ground of the first: Feminist critique of androcentrism is rooted in the conviction that it is a perversion of the gospel, or of God's intention for creation. The condemnation points to continuing recognition of a norm within the tradition, and the Scriptures with which the tradition is bound. Feminist critique is rooted in the gospel, or in an ideal of full humanity that is consonant with the gospel. Whatever the ultimate origin of the shared sense of injustice over patriarchal structures of social organization and meaning, Christian feminists find resources of judgment and alternative vision in the gospel transmitted by the church and informed by the Scriptures. That affirmation, which

---

feminist attempt at reformulating the concept of authority, and debate over the usefulness or necessity of the concept, see Russell, *Household of Freedom*.

is made in different ways by different feminist theologians, is evidence of the Bible's continuing authority, even where it is sharply limited or formally denied. And it is consonant with the traditional understanding of a norm within Scripture, interpreting and judging Scripture. The Bible's authority rests in its ability to confront readers or hearers with the gospel so that it is heard not merely as a historical word but as a present assurance and demand.

The authority of the Bible is communal, requiring individual confirmation. It is, therefore, marked by inevitable tension and is always in the process of being reconstituted. Affirmation of biblical authority is indispensable to Christian identity and belief, but it does not compel assent to any particular interpretation of content—only hearing, with a disposition to hear a word from God. That predisposition to hearing is a sign of the Bible's authority. The Bible comes to each reader or hearer with the church's commendation and testimony that God has spoken through its words and will continue to speak through them. For Christians, the Bible is not a neutral or unknown entity, however unknown its actual content; it bears credentials and a burden of expectations. But the authority that gives it a hearing can be retained only as it is reconfirmed through fresh encounter with the text and appropriation of its message. This reappropriation is both an individual and a communal task.

The Bible means different things to different people, but Christians are not free to construct their own meanings apart from the community that created and transmitted the Scriptures—however painful that relationship. The Bible is the church's book and never stands alone, despite Protestant declarations of *sola scriptura*; nor does it simply stand alongside tradition, as the traditional Catholic theory of two sources suggested. Rather, Scripture is both a product of tradition and a part of the church's ongoing tradition, and it cannot be interpreted as a document of faith apart from that context of communal interpretation and use. Communal authority does not demand consensus, but it does demand engagement. The Bible exercises no authority for those who cease to listen or to struggle with it. While the degree of dissent tolerated by communities and individuals varies widely, unanimity of belief is not a demand of biblical authority.

The Bible's authority is grounded in past experience, which is never sufficient for an ever-changing present.[94] The insufficiency of past for-

---

94. This is not a denial of the sufficiency of Scripture to awaken faith or to serve as a ground and norm of belief; it is, rather, recognition of the inadequacy of all past knowledge.

mulations of belief as contained in Scripture, and tradition, is seen with particular clarity by feminists in their identification of the patriarchal stamp of all our inherited institutions and ideas. Feminist insistence that past understanding, however profound and essential to Christian identity, is not sufficient for the future exposes false bases of biblical authority. The reason why the Bible continues to exercise authority for successive generations in ever-new situations is that it points beyond itself to God, whose purposes and nature are never fully or finally expressed in historical communications. Even in its function as memory, the Bible witnesses to a dynamic relationship at the heart of its testimony.

The Bible's authority derives from God, but it must be understood in terms appropriate to the medium in which it operates. The Bible comes to us as literature, a human, historical product combining memory, art, and reason in the attempts of a community to comprehend and confess its encounter with the divine. Its multivocal and multivalent witness comprises the testimony of more than a millennium, framed in different languages and idioms, in different political and cultural contexts. As the record of many voices, speaking in harmony and discord, its authority is exercised through the conversation, not by suppressing or harmonizing the multiple voices. The church is obliged by the form of its Scriptures to listen for the voice of God in the dialogue of a community. It acknowledges the authority of Book and Author by continuing that dialogue.

The Bible's authority does not rest in the infallibility of its statements but in the truth of its witness to a creating and redeeming power, which can and must be known as a present reality. The Bible as the word of God in human words exhibits the cultural limits and sinful distortions of humanity in every age, witnessing thereby to the central affirmation of Christian faith that God is most fully and truly revealed in assuming this same human nature. The Bible shares the incarnational character of the One to whom it bears witness. It proclaims by its composition as well as its declarations that the Creator has chosen to be revealed in creation, even coming among us as one of us. But that manifestation does not exhaust or circumscribe the divine presence or power, and the word by which that action is recalled and re-presented is only the servant of the living Word. The words of God spoken to prophets and poets are essential to Christian faith and carry the authority of their Speaker, but the word of God cannot be contained in any document; nor can it be comprehended apart from the Word made flesh, which is both the center and the norm of Scripture.

4

The Bible in Christian Ethical Deliberation Concerning Homosexuality

Old Testament Contributions

INTRODUCTION

The current debate in the church concerning the status of homosexual[1] persons, acts, and relationships requires us, as in every theological and ethical debate, to seek the counsel of Scripture, but it also requires us to clarify our understanding of the nature of Scripture and the way it informs and norms Christian ethical judgments. The debate is occasioned because changed practice and perceptions have created tensions between

---

1. For convenience I have used the terms *homosexual* and *homosexuality* to refer to the whole complex of biological and social factors relating to homoerotic attraction and relationships, recognizing that a single term does not do full justice to the range of phenomena encompassed thereby or to the lack of consensus concerning etiology and expression. The term is a modern one, without correspondence in the biblical writings or in the cultures from which they stem. The hermeneutical significance of this observation is treated below. See Nissinen, *Homoeroticism*, v–vi, 5–17, 123–40, 142–44. This important Finnish study of homoeroticism in the biblical world became available to me in a preliminary English translation after I had completed this article. I have expanded my treatment to include discussion of Mesopotamian sources, drawn largely from Nissinen, and have included some references to his general discussion of gender roles, but I have not attempted to "update" my treatment of the OT texts by systematic inclusion of references to his interpretation, which is very close to my own.

traditional norms and current understandings and raised questions for which existing rules and guidelines do not provide clear answers. In a situation of uncertainty and conflict the church seeks to discern the will of God by searching the Scriptures, probing the tradition, and seeking the counsel of science, reason, and experience. But the Bible, to which the church turns for guidance, is already present in this debate, appearing to many as the source of the conflict. On the question of homosexual practice, the Bible's word is both known and clear, or so it seems—and it is a word of unambiguous and unconditioned condemnation. Upheld through the ages by both secular and ecclesiastical authority and justified by traditional theological and scientific reason, this condemnation seems to pit the full weight of Scripture, tradition, and reason against the weak authority of divided and ambivalent experience. It has not succeeded, however, in silencing the voice of experience. Homosexuality is a subject of debate in the church today because faithful Christians who understand themselves as homosexual and seek fulfilment of their sexual needs in same-sex relationships have insisted that their identity and practice as gay men and lesbians is consonant with, and even expressive of, their identity as Christians. It is also a subject of Christian debate because other homosexual Christians, faced with a perceived conflict between biblical norms and their own sexual needs, have been driven to the tragic options of divided lives, divided consciences, denial of sexual expression, contorted rationalizations, rejection of biblical authority and the Bible itself, self-hate, and even self-destruction.

For most Christians struggling with the conflicting testimony of Scripture and homosexual experience, the conflict is understood as a conflict of revelation with experience. This perception rests, I believe, on a faulty understanding of Scripture and its relationship to experience. It treats the Bible as divine oracle or law, abstracting its words from their literary and social contexts and absolutizing them as statements of timeless rules or principles that stand over against changing social practices and values. The Bible does indeed contain attempts to formulate governing principles for a variety of ethical situations, exemplified in the Decalogue and the "love command." But these are set within contexts of deliberation concerning specific and changing demands for personal and communal righteousness and an overarching narrative of God's continuing action in creation. When the dynamics of interchange with specific historical situations are lost, or when particular judgments are cast as absolutes, the Bible's ethical witness is distorted.

The Bible does not present us with a distinct mode of revelation, but a privileged locus—in which the divine self-disclosure is mediated by the same processes of tradition interacting with experience and reason that we recognize as sources of continuing revelation today. As a foundational document and as a medium of continuing communication with God, the Bible has an essential and primary place in Christian theological and ethical deliberation. But it is the starting point of the church's conversation, not the end; a conversation partner, not an oracle.

My approach to the Bible as a source of ethical guidance in the current debate is in fundamental agreement with Christopher Seitz's insistence on the two-part canon of Old and New Testament Scriptures viewed together as the relevant corpus for Christian theology and ethics.[2] My focus on the Old Testament is dictated only by the space allotted to me and my conviction that this portion of the Christian Scriptures has been both neglected and misused. Where I differ from Seitz is in my insistence on the historical character of the biblical witness and hence in my employment of historical-critical tools (including social analysis) to inquire into the ancient literary and sociohistorical contexts of the writings. I reject the view that traditional interpretation must determine Christian understanding of these texts and insist that they be allowed to speak on their own terms—however discordant this may appear either to traditional interpretations or to contemporary demands.[3]

Limits of space require me to eliminate the fuller exegetical arguments that underlie my interpretations and abbreviate treatment of texts I have dealt with in previous publications. The fundamental issues in the current debate are hermeneutical, however, rather than exegetical, so I begin with a brief statement of my understanding of the nature and authority of Scripture.

The Christian Scriptures are a collection of diverse documents bound together in a two-part canon, whose center is the witness to Christ as the new revelation of the God made known to Israel. As a collection of writings, the Bible is pluriform and multivocal—as are many of its

---

2. My references to Seitz are to a prepublication version of his article, "Sexuality and Scripture's Plain Sense."

3. In articulating my own position, I do not wish to argue for a single normative approach or construction—either as dictated by tradition or as demanded by present needs. The option I have chosen takes its clues primarily from the Bible itself and locates the authoritative word of God in the dialogue between ancient and modern witnesses, rather than in the sacred page.

constituent parts. Thus the Bible is characterized by an irreducible pluralism that requires constructive effort to grasp the unity within the diversity and to discern patterns that give coherence to the whole. While the church has an interpretive tradition that shapes every Christian reading, such preunderstanding holds the constant danger of inhibiting, rather than enabling, fresh encounter with the text and with the totality of its witness. Attempts to formulate the Bible's essential message tend to silence dissident voices within the canon and suppress the dialogical character of its witness. Debate is a constituent feature of the biblical canon, reflecting its origins in the conversation of a community over time.[4]

What holds the Scriptures together is the community that created, preserved, and transmitted the writings, Israel and its daughter the church.[5] United in canonical form, the Scriptures present an overarching story that moves from the beginning of creation to a vision of new creation and, within that framework, the conversation of the community about the implications of that story for its life. That conversation spans a millennium in its recorded memory, but it does not end with the last canonical writing; it continues today, as the story itself continues. I will not rehearse that story here or attempt to characterize the distinct voices that contribute to the dialogue, except to emphasize that they are many.

One voice requires special note, however, for its absence. As many of us have become painfully aware in recent times, the voices we hear in Scripture and through whom we claim to hear the word of God, do not represent the full testimony or experience of the people of God, but rather that of its male members, and an elite among them. Thus the conversation of Scripture is both incomplete and biased. This means, I believe, that the testimony of Scripture may not be absolutized, or viewed as final revelation. It does not mean that the Scriptures lack authority; rather it makes unavoidably clear that the authority of Scripture is the authority of historical witness. Standing in time, the Scriptures point beyond time, but always and only as a product of the cultures out of which they speak. The word of God in Scripture is always an incarnate word, and therefore limited.[6]

---

4. For a fuller statement of my understanding, see Bird, "Authority" (chap. 3 in this volume).

5. I stress the continuity here while recognizing two distinct communities, each internally diverse. The problem of unity is posed within each Testament as well as in their union.

6. The relative absence of women in the text serves as a pointer to the more

Although I find the Bible's limits most serious in its inadequate and distorted representation of women's experience, I believe its testimony is true in its essential message, and sufficient both to direct us in the way we must travel and to provide sustenance for the journey. The Bible's message of God's creating power, redeeming grace, and demand for righteousness, together with its proclamation of God's suffering and reconciling love in Jesus Christ that breaks the bonds of sin, has made it possible—and necessary—within the biblical period and beyond, to redefine the boundaries of the community that lives by that message, and to reformulate the rules for participation. In my lifetime it has meant a fundamental change in the roles of women in the church, and a revolution in theology—changes that are still in process and are leading us into new perceptions and questions we could not have known or anticipated in an earlier age.

Today the question of homosexuality presents the church with another case that calls it to reexamine its understanding of the boundaries of the community, the terms of membership, and the forms of leadership and service to which it calls members. I do not intend to suggest a parallel to the case of women except in a very general way. There are distinctive factors in the biblical tradition and in the current phenomenon that demand individual and differentiated treatment. One of these, which makes deliberation so difficult, is that homosexuality is not a single question, and there is no consensus concerning the nature of the phenomenon, or phenomena, identified by this term. Thus the first problem that confronts us in seeking biblical guidance is the question of where to look and what to look for.

OLD TESTAMENT TEXTS WITH EXPLICIT REFERENCES TO HOMOSEXUAL BEHAVIOR

I begin with the texts that have traditionally been understood to relate to homosexuality, although these are not the texts to which I would appeal in constructing ethical guidelines for church policy today. This starting point is dictated by the course of debate in the church and the need for biblical scholars in the service of the church to engage that debate with

---

fundamental character of the texts and the culture as governed by patriarchal and androcentric norms—features of direct consequence for all questions of sexual identity, activity, and roles.

corrections as well as alternatives. I limit my treatment to Old Testament texts, recognizing that they cannot stand alone. Biblical references to homosexual behavior are rare in both Testaments, exclusively negative, and commonly associated with other types of immoral or excluded behavior. They treat only acts, not relationships,[7] and with the exception of Rom 1:26 speak only of acts between males. Richard Hays rightly observes that "in terms of emphasis, it [homosexuality] is a minor concern, in contrast, for example, to economic injustice."[8] Why that is the case is less obvious, however, and paucity of reference may not simply be equated with either ignorance or tolerance.[9]

Narrative Texts: Genesis 19:1-29 and Judges 19:22-24

Hays comments that the notorious account of the men of Sodom (Gen 19:1-29) is "actually irrelevant to the topic [of consensual homosexual intercourse]," since the men's intent was apparently gang rape of Lot's two visitors.[10] I believe he is right in insisting that this text does not address the cases under consideration today, but I do not think it can be dismissed as testimony to the OT's attitude toward homosexual activity. In both the Sodom account and the story of the Judean Levite and his concubine among the Benjaminites of Gibeah (Judges 19, a story modeled on Genesis 19), "foreigners" or outsiders are depicted as exhibiting moral depravity in their inhospitality toward visitors.[11] The honor due a guest

---

7. Jonathan's love for David (1 Sam 18:1) does not belong to the OT's understanding of homosexual relations, which is interested only in acts, not affections. Similar disinterest in affections also characterizes rules governing heterosexual relations. Sex, love, and marriage are not correlated in the same manner in ancient Israel as in contemporary western society. It is precisely the OT's disinterest in affective bonds and the quality of relationships that makes the Bible's pronouncements on prohibited sexual unions problematic as guides to contemporary sexual ethics. Nissinen (*Homoeroticism*, 17) uses the term "homosociability" to describe interaction between people of the same sex where the erotic-sexual aspect is not emphasized or essential. See ibid., 53-56.

8. Hays, "Awaiting," 5.

9. See Dozeman, "Creation," 172.

10. Hays, "Awaiting," 5. See also Seow, "Heterotextual Perspective," 15-16; Nissinen, *Homoeroticism*, 46.

11. The issue of foreign mores is clear in Gen 19:9 when the men of Sodom dismiss Lot's protest as that of an "alien." Although the Judges account deals with an intertribal conflict, the Benjaminites are presented there as acting like the wicked Sodomites (i.e., like "foreigners").

is violated (at least by threat) in the most objectionable way conceivable, by sexual humiliation.

In both texts, the request for sexual favors by the men of the city uses language employed elsewhere for normal (hetero)sexual relations: "to know."[12] The verb itself contains no sense of coercion, which is supplied by the context—the demand that the host "bring out" his male guest(s) (Gen 19:5; Judg 19:22) and the depiction of the threatening crowd. The response of the host, who pleads with his "brothers" not to act wickedly (*ʾal-naʾ ʾaḥay tārēʿû* [Gen 19:7; similarly Judg 19:23]) and offers female substitutes, confirms the view that it is the male object that makes the action offensive—so that it is branded a *nĕbālâ* (an "outrage")[13] in Judg 19:23. The analogy is clearly with rape, as exhibited by the language used in reference to the female substitute. In Judg 19:23-24 the old man offers his virgin daughter and his guest's concubine in place of his male guest, inviting the men to "ravish them" (*wĕʿannû ʾôtām*).[14] Thus desire for a male sexual partner, represented as a "simple" request, is countered by an invitation to violate a woman, and her sexual honor, in its most prized and protected state—an offer made by the male charged with protecting that honor, whose own honor must suffer from the invited action.[15]

The account carries the clear message that male honor is threatened by homosexual intercourse, and that it is valued even above a daughter's virginity. The parallel and contrasting language of "ordinary" sexual intercourse (with a male) and abusive sex (with a female) equates homoerotic relations with rape; and the portrayal of the request as a threat suggests that the Israelite authors could conceive of participation in male homoerotic acts only as forced. It is not clear whether they viewed homoerotic activity among the inhabitants of these wicked cities as consensual

---

12. See, e.g., Gen 4:1, 17, 25 and 1 Sam 1:19, of sexual relations as a prelude to conception. Cf. Gen 38:26 (NRSV "lie with") and 1 Kgs 1:4.

13. NRSV: "vile thing." The term is translated variously as "senselessness" (in disregard of moral or religious claims [BDB]), "wanton crime," "disgrace," "vile outrage," and "folly." It is not specifically related to sexual outrages, although it is used to characterize the rape of Dinah in Gen 34:7 and the outrage against the Levite's concubine (together with the threat to the Levite himself?) as reported in Judg 20:6, 10. It describes a violation of a community norm or taboo and is used in the older narrative sources with much the same sense as *tôʿēbâ* ("abomination") in later sources.

14. Cf. Gen 19:8: "do to them as you please." The reported action in Judg 19:25 combines the term *ydʿ* with the verb *yitʿallĕlû* ("act wantonly"), to give the sense of "wanton intercourse."

15. Cf. Gen 34:7, 31.

and habitual or only as perverse sport with visitors. They do appear to suggest, however, that no Israelite male would consent to engage in homoerotic relations — at least not as the passive partner. In these accounts we catch glimpses of an undergirding code of sexual behavior governed by views of gender roles and sexual honor that are rarely, if ever, spelled out, only exemplified. Inferring the unarticulated norms from the biblical narratives and laws is an essential, if uncertain, task of biblical ethics.

These two texts strongly suggest that the ancient Israelites had no experience or conception of male homoerotic relations as consensual or expressive of a committed relationship. They appear to view the "use" of a male in sexual relations (initiated by a male) as a violation of male honor, more serious than the worst violation of female honor. This interpretation is corroborated by Martti Nissinen's cross-cultural study of homoerotic activity in the ancient Near Eastern and Mediterranean world, in which a distinction of active and passive partners is seen to be fundamental and universal, and in which the passive role is always defined as feminine. Hence engaging in homosexual acts in the passive role involves a threat to male identity. Sexual acts, whether heterosexual or homosexual, were not conceived as a relationship between equals.[16]

Legal Texts: Leviticus 18:22 and 20:13

The OT contains two explicit prohibitions of homosexual activity, both in the larger collection of laws known as the Holiness Code (Lev 17:1—26:46) for the governing idea that informs its demands: "You shall be holy, for I YHWH your God am holy" (Lev 19:2). The two texts occur in parallel series of prohibitions and are essentially duplicate statements, employing the same terms and differing only in style, as dictated by the individual series. They are positioned differently, however, in the two series, creating different contexts of interpretation. Both have entered the growing corpus of priestly law at a relatively late stage and are closely related to the theological perspectives of the final document.[17]

---

16. Nissinen, *Homoeroticism*, 26; see below.

17. I assume an exilic date for the final work, although both chapters show stages of growth. Individual laws and collections of laws may go back to much earlier times, while additions continued to accrue to the already-completed work. Cf. Elliger, *Leviticus*, 14-20, 229-35, 263-72; Noth, *Leviticus*, 127-28, 134, 146-47. Nissinen (*Homoeroticism*, 37) assumes a postexilic setting, while Joosten (*People*, 202-7) argues for a preexilic dating of the Holiness Code as a whole.

Leviticus 18:22

Leviticus 18 has been shaped into a literary and rhetorical whole by a theological framework in verses 2b–5 and 24–30, which begins and ends with the declaration "I am YHWH your God." In both opening and closing exhortations, Israel is enjoined not to follow the practices of the Canaanites who preceded them in the land, but to observe YHWH's statutes and ordinances, which assure life to those who do them. With this hortatory framework legal custom is proclaimed as divine law. The concluding exhortation spells out the consequences of disobedience with a lesson from history, cast in cultic terms: the previous inhabitants, through their "defiling" actions, caused the land to become defiled, so that God punished the land, making it vomit out its inhabitants. I note this theological framework to highlight two fundamental differences in reasoning from our own: (1) issues of prohibited sexual relations are presented here in essentially cultic rather than ethical terms: they defile, and therefore endanger the community; and (2) historical process and divine agency are understood in terms that are foreign, and unacceptable, to most modern American readers. Any contemporary appeal to these texts must consider these differences.

Within the hortatory framework of Leviticus 18 is a collection of laws whose core (vv. 7–16) is a unified series of ten prohibited classes of sexual relations with relatives, (re)interpreted as marriage prohibitions (v. 6). Both the apodictic form of the series (direct and absolute prohibition, as in the Decalogue, without specification of punishment) and the nature of the protected relationships, which describe a circle of persons living together in a three-generational extended family, point to an early period of Israel's history, marked by kinship-based organization. The laws forbid promiscuity within this family circle constituted by marriage as well as "blood" relationships, and all are addressed to adult males.[18] This older series of prohibited sexual relations with female family members, which lacks any religious language, has been extended in verses 17–23 by further sexual (and in one case, cultic) prohibitions of quite disparate nature, couched in cultic terminology. This has the effect of creating a more comprehensive list of proscribed sexual practices, but it also shifts the emphasis of the whole from family ethos to concern for ritual purity.

---

18. On the significance of the male address, see Melcher, "Holiness Code," esp. 91–93.

Verses 17–18 are closely linked to the preceding series but concern marriage rather than sexual relations. Verses 19–23 form a block distinguished by language of (ritual) uncleanness or *tomʾâ* (vv. 19, 20, 23). This language links it to the concluding paraenesis, which begins with the summary statement "You shall not defile yourselves (*ʾal-tiṭṭammĕʾû*) in any of these ways" (v. 24), and concludes with the admonition not to commit any of "these abominations (*ḥuqqôt hattôʿēbôt*) which were done before you," and not to "defile yourselves (*wĕlōʾ-tiṭṭammĕʾû*) by them" (v. 30). The appendix is a miscellany of defiling practices, including having intercourse with a menstruating woman (v. 19), engaging in sexual relations with a kinsman's (or neighbor's) wife (*ʾēšet ʿămîtĕkâ*, v. 20), sacrificing offspring to Molech (v. 21), having sexual relations with a male "as with a woman" (v. 22), and having sexual relations with an animal (v. 23). The Molech prohibition appears as an exception to the common subject matter of sexual violations, but it has the effect of identifying the supplementary prohibitions with alien cultic practice, and perhaps more specifically with alien gods.[19] Standing at the center of the appendix, it characterizes the act as "profan[ing] (*ḥll*) the name of your God," following this with the declaration "I am YHWH," which connects it to the opening and closing words of the chapter. Thus it serves to link the appendix as a whole to the governing ideas of the chapter in its final edition.

The prohibition of homosexual relations is formulated as follows: "With a male you shall not lie (as) lyings with a woman; it is an abomination" (*wĕʾet-zākār lōʾ tiškab miškĕbê ʾiššâ tôʿēbâ hī[w]ʾ*, v. 22). The formulation emphasizes the inappropriateness of a male as the object of the (male-initiated) sexual act, which is defined by reference to a woman. The use of the term "male" (*zākār*) is not coupled here with the corresponding biological term "female" (*nĕqēbâ*), as in Gen 1:27–28, but simply "woman" (*ʾiššâ*). Thus it does not appear to echo the creation account or emphasize procreative function but simply describes the normative pattern of sexual relations.[20] The prohibition is accompanied by the declaration, "it is an abomination (*tôʿēbâ*)."

The term *tôʿēbâ* is concentrated in exilic texts (forty-three times in Ezekiel) and cultic contexts, where it serves to characterize practices

19. See Noth, *Leviticus*, 136; cf. Elliger, *Leviticus*, 24; Albertz, *History*, 1:190–94; Heider, *Cult*, 248–49; Day, *Molech*, 22–24.

20. Cf. Judg 21:11, 12. The use of *zākār* ("male") is not confined to texts concerned with physical attributes or sexual function but also appears in texts stressing male gender roles, rights, and obligations (e.g., Exod 23:17).

as incompatible with Yahwistic practice, or "taboo."[21] It is lacking in the old legal collections, as well as in the older narrative traditions (where *nĕbālâ* functions as an equivalent, as in Gen 34:7 and Judg 19:23), but is common in late Deuteronomic texts (seventeen times in Deuteronomy), where it carries connotations of foreign/pagan cultic practice.[22] In Leviticus it occurs only in the duplicate prohibitions of homosexual acts and the epilogue of chapter 18 (four times). It is not an ethical term but a term of boundary marking. In its basic sense of taboo it describes a feeling of abhorrence or revulsion that requires or admits no rational explanation. It may be given a theological grounding by reference to the deity: "X is an abomination/abhorrent to YHWH."[23] The attachment of the *tôʿēbâ* declaration to the homosexual prohibition serves in Leviticus 18 not only to characterize this act but to link the prohibition to the concluding paraenesis with its fourfold repetition of *tôʿēbâ* (vv. 26, 27, 29, 30), closely associated with the idea of defilement. It belongs to the language of separation and of distinctness from the nations, which came to expression during the exile and was applied retroactively to earlier stages of Israelite history.

The prohibition of homoerotic relations, like all of the prohibitions in the chapter, addresses males and thus only considers relations with another male. In view of the fundamental orientation of the OT laws toward the rights and responsibilities of males, primarily in relation to other males, I do not think we can conclude anything from this formulation about the incidence or acceptance of lesbian relations, except that sexual relations confined to the realm of female activity were apparently not considered threatening to the male-dominated community. If the primary issue in the condemnation of homosexual acts is male honor, then female homoeroticism is of no interest or concern.[24]

---

21. See Gerstenberger, "*tʿb*"; Humbert, "Le Substantif"; L'Hour, "Les Interdits." In its basic use and meaning it describes something that is "not done (here)," or is "unthinkable (to us)," i.e., practices unacceptable in Israelite culture. See Seow, "Heterotextual, Perspective" 14, for examples.

22. E.g., Deut 13:14 (Heb. 15) and 27:15. The term has no specific associations with "fertility rites," and is only associated with cult-related sex in Deut 23: 17–18 (Heb. 18–19; see appendix A).

23. *tôʿăbat yhwh*, esp. in Deuteronomy and Proverbs. Cf. *KAI* 13.6 (a sixth-century-BCE Phoenician grave inscription forbidding damaging of the grave as an "abomination to Astarte").

24. See Nissinen, *Homoeroticism*, 35–36, 43.

Leviticus 20:13

Leviticus 20 appears in its present form to be a later composition than chapter 18 and to draw upon both chapters 18 and 19. Although it covers many of the same cases as chapter 18, the arrangement is different and the core series of sexual prohibitions appears to have arisen separately.[25] The chapter opens with an extended treatment of the Molech sacrifice (vv. 1–5), followed by mentions of "turn[ing] to mediums and 'wizards'" (v. 6).[26] These religious practices are described in terms of idolatry; the descriptions employ the language of harlotry (*znh*), rather than the language of defilement, as the key interpretive term.[27] The opening section concludes with an exhortation to be holy, and a new series of capital crimes begins in verse 9.

Verses 10–21 detail sexual offenses, but these are introduced in v. 9 by a case of "curs[ing] father or mother." The curious inclusion of this case suggests that the chapter has been constructed on the pattern of the Decalogue: cases involving the violation of YHWH's honor (by worship of other gods) are placed first, while the dishonoring of parents serves as a transition to the second division of laws, concerning the violation of a neighbor's or kinsman's honor. The primary concern in this series is with relations within the larger community and the immediate family—not the extended family, as in Lev 18:1–16.[28] Thus homoerotic acts (v. 13)[29] and bestiality (vv. 15–16) are included in the primary series of sexual of-

---

25. Elliger, *Leviticus*, 25–72; Noth, *Leviticus*, 146.

26. Heb. '*ōbōt* and *yiddĕ'ōnîm*, which Heider (*Cult*, 249–50) convincingly identifies with the practice of necromancy, establishing a connection with the Molech cult in a common association with the cult of the dead (ibid., 250–51).

27. The metaphorical character of the "whoring" language is especially clear here, since neither of the two cases suggests any association with "sacred prostitution" or a fertility cult.

28. The cases treated are as follows: sexual relations with a neighbor's wife (v. 10, using the specific language of adultery, *n'p*), a father's wife (v. 11), a daughter-in-law (v. 12), a male (v. 13), [marriage to] a woman and her mother (v. 14), an animal (by a man or a woman, vv. 15–16), a sister (v. 17), a menstruating woman (v. 18), a mother's or father's sister (v. 19, in apodictic form), an uncle's wife (v. 20), and [marriage to] a brother's wife (v. 21).

29. The prohibition here is formulated in the same terms as in chap. 18 but in the casuistic style of the series and with an additional declaration of guilt: "A man who lies with a male (as) lyings with a woman: the two of them have committed an abomination; they shall surely be put to death; their blood is upon them" (*wĕ'îš 'ăšer yiškab 'et-zākār miškĕbê 'iššâ tô'ēbâ 'āśû šĕnêhem môt yûmātû dĕmêhem bām*, v. 13). The guilt of both parties is also emphasized, in keeping with the series.

fenses, with adultery (v. 10) heading the list. Verses 17–21 (together with v. 14) have the character of an appendix, exhibiting a mixture of styles and sentences and evidence of internal accretions. The *môt yûmat* ("he shall certainly be put to death") formula is applied to all of the cases in vv. 1–16 but is lacking in the appendix, suggesting less serious infractions. The main series of capital offenses appears to be graded, with the most serious placed first.

The chapter concludes with an extended paraenesis (vv. 22–26), introducing themes picked up from chapter 18 including the theme of separation from the nations (vv. 23–24, 26b), the theme of the land's vomiting out its inhabitants (v. 22b), and the theme of possession of the land (v. 24), here expanded. It closes with an exhortation to be holy, as YHWH is holy (v. 26; cf. 19:2). Thus, as in chapter 18, so here in chapter 20 an interpretive framework has been supplied to the laws, which stresses holiness as the governing theological principle and links the demand for holiness with separation from the peoples. Here, however, these themes lack linguistic connections with the individual laws. In chapter 20 the homosexual prohibition is simply another sexual taboo, without clear cultic associations, and its characterization as an "abomination" finds no echo in the paraenesis.

The Inclusion of the homosexual prohibition in the main series of sexual offenses raises the question whether this represents an understanding of (male) homosexual acts in primarily ethical terms, in contrast to chapter 18, where ritual/cultic associations predominate.[30] There does appear to be an attempt in both Leviticus 18 and 20 to create comprehensive lists of sexual acts that undermine community and family relations, with the list in chapter 20 presenting a more integrated conception. But neither is complete, and neither has any place for circumstantial considerations, such as questions of age, initiative, or consent. This lack of interest in essential ethical criteria is strikingly clear in the assessment of penalties. In all of the cases in chapter 20 both the sexual partners are subjected to the same punishment, including the animal, who is to be put to death together with the man or woman who has used it sexually. In verse 16 both the woman and the animal are explicitly declared "guilty," in the same terms applied to those who engage in homoerotic activity ("their blood is upon them"). Thus the fundamental character

---

30. Cf. Rom 1:26-27, which places homosexual conduct in the context of pagan practice and impurity, rather than with other sexual offenses such as adultery, rape, or incest.

of the prohibitions in both chapters as boundary-defining, as well as their judgment of sexual acts in purely objective terms, their interpretive framework based in cultic notions of purity and defilement, and their exclusively male orientation limit their usefulness for contemporary sexual ethics.

Neither the OT nor the NT offers a comprehensive approach to sexual ethics, but these two chapters of Leviticus mark an important step on the way toward bringing the "private" and "secular" realm of sexual relations into the sphere of religious concerns and lay groundwork for the development of a theological ethics of sexual relations. What is lacking here, in addition to the deficits and biases already noted, is an articulation of the underlying principles and examples of how the judgments were applied.

Conclusions and Implications for Contemporary Use

1. The OT prohibitions of homosexual relations may not be understood as timeless decrees that can be applied to contemporary situations on the assumption of one-to-one correspondences. The language and contexts of these formulations betray a worldview and a theology that is both inconceivable and unacceptable to most Western Christians. The theological issues that govern the introduction of the homosexual prohibition into the biblical canon are purity and defilement, of people and land—notions that place sexual relations with a menstruating woman (including a man's own wife) and child sacrifice in the same category of offenses as homosexual relations (Lev 18:19, 21–22).

2. Although the prohibitions are presented as absolute and unconditioned decrees in first-person divine speech, the two series of laws in their settings within the Holiness Code and in the larger canonical context witness to a more dynamic and historically conditioned understanding of divine law than the individual compositions suggest or the historical literalism of modern readers commonly recognizes.[31] The difference between the two occurrences of the prohibition is not simply a matter of spelling out the penalties in chapter 20. It involves a fundamental reor-

---

31. When the ancient writer spoke of the need for Israel to separate itself from the nations that YHWH was driving out before them, his seventh- or sixth-century-BCE audience understood this as a transparent reference to their own need to maintain, or redefine, their identity as a people distinct from the peoples among whom they were living.

dering of the categories, eliminating some cases and rearranging others to indicate different orders of seriousness and different types of infractions. The second series (chapter 20) moves in the direction of more distinctly ethical reasoning—though it still leaves that reasoning unarticulated.

The two lists of sexual prohibitions within the Holiness code point to *changing* views of sexual relations in response to changing social, political, and religious conditions. Urban society and a more cosmopolitan milieu, including perhaps the experience of foreign domination under Assyrian or Babylonian rule, or both, and concomitant exposure to other peoples and practices, have required a rethinking of categories and a reordering of priorities relating to sexual practices, even within the relatively homogeneous theological tradition represented by the Holiness Code.[32] Even more striking differences and changes in perspectives, issues, and emphases are evident, however, when the Holiness Code is compared with other collections of laws within the larger OT legal tradition.

3. The absence of the prohibition in any of the older law codes and its first appearance in a context characterized by themes of purity and separation from the nations/peoples point to the emergence of the issue of homosexual practice as a theological concern in the context of an attempt to redefine the boundaries of the community in terms of praxis rather than in geographical or ethnic terms, a praxis governed by a cultically derived notion of holiness, extended from ritual practice to personal relations. The "Israel" of these laws is no longer a geographical entity, and the geographically based and kinship-ordered agricultural village is no longer the controlling social organization. Homosexual practice belongs to the behavior that is understood to break community solidarity at a time when the community is under stress and the old kinship-based mechanisms of social control are threatened or no longer operative. The first move of Leviticus 18 is to appeal to old family law controlling sexual relations, redefining it as incest prohibitions; the second is to prohibit "pagan" sexual practices as defiling.

4. From the position of the prohibition in Leviticus 18, where it stands apart from the family-oriented law, it appears that male homoerotic

---

32. It is not essential to my argument to determine precisely the date of the Holiness Code or the individual collections of laws within it, which have been dated from late preexilic to postexilic times. While greater precision would help to clarify the particular dynamics at work in the formulation and reformulation of these two series, it is sufficient for my purposes to argue that the essential features of the context in which they have emerged are a breakdown of an older, unwritten consensus and increased exposure to and/or involvement with alternative practices.

activity was not viewed as threatening to male interests within the family. Prior to Leviticus it also does not appear to have been recognized as a threat to community norms, in contrast to beastiality, which is treated in both of the older law codes (Exod 22:19; Deut 27:21). If we consider the narratives of Genesis 19 and Judges 19, homoerotic activity seems to have been considered a threat only in "foreign" cities—where the threat is to male honor and clearly not to marriage, since a spouse and marriageable daughters are offered as a substitute! I believe we must conclude from this evidence that male homosexual relations were rare, and abhorrent, in the tightly knit patriarchal village life of ancient Israel.

5. The language of "abomination" that attaches to the prohibition in both chapters of Leviticus reinforces the view of a history of abhorrence, rather than tolerance. The term appears nowhere else in Leviticus apart from the parallel law in 20:13 and the epilogue of chapter 18, where it serves to associate the prohibited practices (as a whole) with foreign/pagan practice. The fact that the same declaration is found in 20:13, without the editorial connection, strongly suggests that it antedates both collections, or that its appearance in chapter 20 is dependent on chapter 18. Thus the testimony of the laws corresponds to that of the narratives.

The designation "abomination" is instructive, I believe, for our attempts to discover the underlying reasons for the prohibition. It points to a nonrational and pre-ethical judgment, a sense of revulsion toward a practice that is "not done here." The abhorrence may be rationalized or theologized in various ways, e.g., by association with "foreigners" or as divinely repudiated,[33] but such interpretations do not explain the socially grounded root response. It appears most likely in the patriarchal ethos of ancient Israel that homosexual activity carried a sense of male shame for the partner "forced" to assume the "female" role (or shamelessness for the male who assumed it voluntarily), a judgment corroborated by Mesopotamian evidence.[34] There is nothing to suggest that it was viewed as

---

33. It is noteworthy that the "unnatural" argument is not found in the OT, nor in any of the ancient Near Eastern texts that disparage or condemn homosexual relations (see appendix B). The language of "abomination" and the associations with defilement in Leviticus 18 contrast with the language condemning sexual relations with an animal (Lev 18:23), which characterizes the act as *tebel* "perversion" (from the root *bll* "to mix, confuse"). Attitudes toward homoerotic acts appear to relate primarily to issues of social order, not natural order.

34. That the fundamental issue is a transgression of gender roles is suggested by the prohibition of wearing apparel of the opposite sex (Deut 22:5), which is also branded an "abomination" (*tôʿăbat yhwh ʾĕlōhêkā*).

threatening the survival of the species—despite the fact that such an argument would have had far greater cogency in ancient Israel than it does today. There is no indication that homosexual relations in ancient Israel, or anywhere in the ancient Near East, were ever an exclusive option, and eunuchs played an important role in both Egyptian and Mesopotamian royal service as well as in Israel's own royal bureaucracy.[35] Behind the prohibition is, I think, a fear of deviation from the socially dominant pattern of male-female intercourse, a biologically favored pattern grounded in reproductive needs but by no means limited to them—as the toleration of prostitution evidences. In the final analysis it is a matter of gender identity and roles, not sexuality—which must conform to the socially approved gender patterns. Nor is it a matter of misuse of male "seed,"[36] a judgment relevant only to circumstances where a male has a duty to produce offspring (as in Gen 38:9-10)—and not applied to relations with prostitutes.

6. The suggestion that the prohibition of male homoerotic activity received explicit formulation in a context in which Israelite sexual norms were being defined over against those of other peoples requires a word of caution concerning attempts to locate and assess the practice against which it was aimed. It is possible that the breakdown of the old village culture, increased mobility (including forced migrations), and the anonymity and heterogeneity of city life were sufficient to permit or encourage the homoerotic encounters that are condemned in our texts, without positing significant foreign influence. The identification of abhorrent practices as "foreign" is a common polemical ploy and may be entirely baseless, or grounded in highly evolved "myths" whose origins can no longer be traced or confirmed.

a. Evidence for same-sex erotic interaction from the ancient Near East is meager and ambiguous but supports the view that sexual relations (of all types) were defined and judged according to gender-role prescriptions that identified the male as the active partner and the female as the passive.[37] No clear reference to homoeroticism is found in the Ugaritic or Hittite texts,[38] and only two Egyptian texts speak unambiguously of sexual acts between males. One suggests disapproval of pedophilia, while the

35. See Grayson, "Eunuchs"; and Nissinen, *Homoeroticism*, 31.
36. Cf. Dozeman, "Creation," 175-76; see below.
37. Nissinen, *Homoeroticism*, 19. Cf. Bottéro and Petschow, "Homosexualität." See appendix B for details.
38. Nissinen, *Homoeroticism*, 20.

other describes a case of anal intercourse as an act of sexual aggression intended to humiliate and demonstrate superior power.³⁹ Mesopotamian evidence, though fragmentary and scattered, offers instructive parallels to OT attitudes, but its contribution to the question of cultic sex as the source of the Levitical prohibitions is disputed.⁴⁰

(1) Assyrian law decrees harsh sanctions (including rape and castration) for a male who "lays" a "comrade" (i.e. an equal), and it also punishes a man who slanders a comrade with a false accusation of inviting, or consenting to, repeated sexual advances by other males.⁴¹ Omens, myths, and proverbs suggest that occasional homoerotic contacts were tolerated, on a consensual or contractual basis. Unlike the laws, these sources are not concerned with enforcing community norms; hence their references contain no moral judgments. They suggest nevertheless that the male who played the female role suffered social deprecation or belonged to a lower social class.⁴² No examples of female-female sexual relations are known from Mesopotamian texts.⁴³

(2) In addition to texts that speak directly of sexual relations between males, Mesopotamian sources attest a number of classes of male cult personnel (*assinnu, kurgarrû, kuluʾu,* and *sinnišānu*) that have

---

39. Ibid., 19. See appendix B.

40. Excluded from consideration here is the relationship between Gilgamesh and Enkidu, which Nissinen describes as a prime example of homosocial type bonding in an "equal relationship between men with no clear social or sexual role division." In Nissinen's words, "They experience unity and share each other's worlds — unlike a man and a woman who lived in separate worlds" (ibid., 24; see further 20-24; cf. Leick, *Sex*, 254-69). Although this represents the bonding of two superheroes, it has analogies in the male friendships that are formed in patriarchal societies, best illustrated in the OT by the friendship of David and Jonathan (n. 7 above).

41. Nissinen, *Homoeroticism*, 24-27; Bottéro and Petschow, "Homosexualität," 462.

42. Nissinen, *Homoeroticism*, 27-28; Bottéro and Petschow, "Homosexualität," 460-63. Nissinen's statement (*Homoeroticism*, 28) that "men could sometimes find amusement in taking the role of the opposite sex" would appear to apply primarily to partners of equal status.

43. Bottéro and Petschow, "Homosexualität," 468. The lack of documentary evidence appears, as in the OT, to reflect the male-oriented interest of the texts and society, which focused on the problem of a male assuming a "female" role. Thus the silence of the texts concerning lesbian relations is insufficient evidence to rule out the practice, though it could scarcely have been common. Nissinen (*Homoeroticism*, 35-36) underscores its rarity by observing that the one possible reference to lesbian relations (an omen apodosis) parallels it to the curiosity of two male dogs copulating.

frequently been described as male prostitutes,⁴⁴ although their role in homoerotic encounters is disputed, and evidence for their sexual activity is almost exclusively inferential. As devotees of the goddess Inanna/Ishtar, they reflect her androgynous nature as the Venus star and her control of sexuality, including her power to "change men into women." Their role in the cult was characteristically asexual rather than homosexual according to Nissinen, frequently (though not necessarily) involving castration, and marked by female dress and symbols, or a combination of male and female attributes (e.g., swords and spindles).⁴⁵ Since the *assinnu*'s prescribed cultic role required him to renounce the distincitive attributes of the male role, he would appear to provide an ideal passive partner for male homosexual encounters. There is no clear evidence, however, that such practice was a part of the cult, although one might say that wherever the *assinnu* practiced this trade he did so as a votary of the goddess. It is difficult to estimate the incidence of male prostitution (only one text speaks of "hire") since prostitution (both male and female) lies within the sphere of tolerated liminal activity and is not treated in laws or admonitions relating to infraction of sexual norms. There does not appear to be a "secular" term for a male prostitute corresponding to *ḫarimtu* (the "ordinary" female prostitute).⁴⁶ If the *assinnu*s or related classes supported themselves as male prostitutes, they had a cultic role to fall back on, unlike the *ḫarimtu*. This did not spare them, however, from the social denigration and ostracism that attached to their aberrant gender role.⁴⁷

---

44. Bottéro and Petschow ("Homosexualität," 463) refer to them as "professionals of passive homosexuality."

45. Nissinen, *Homoeroticism*, 30–31, 34. While Nissinen (ibid., 34) suggests that men of homosexual orientation (to use modern categories) may have sought out this role, as well as transsexuals or those born intersexed, he emphasizes that the role requirements determined the behavior and the sexual identity, not sexual impulse.

46. Unless it is the *sinnišānu* (lit. "man-woman"), mentioned in one text in connection with an inn or brothel (ibid., 33; cf. Lambert, *Babylonian Wisdom*, 218–19; Leick, *Sex*, 160). See appendix B. Nissinen (*Homoeroticism*, 28) includes this term with the other cult-related classes. None of the *assinnu* or *kurgarrû* texts that he cites contain references to a brothel or hire, and he does not use the term *prostitute* to describe the roles or activities of these classes. Nor does he treat the question of remuneration, either as a source of temple income or as a means of livelihood.

47. A passage in the Erra Epic describes *kurgarrûs* and *assinnus* as men "whose masculinity Ishtar changed into femininity to strike horror into the people," and as "bearers of daggers, razors, pruning-knives and flint blades who frequently do abominable acts [i.e., deeds under a taboo, forbidden to ordinary people] to please the heart of Ishtar" (Nissinen, *Homoeroticism*, 30, 148–49 nn. 63 and 64). The sense of fear

b. The frequently suggested association of the homosexual prohibition in the OT with Canaanite religion must be rejected for a number of reasons.

(1) Identification of homosexual activity with what is generally characterized as a "fertility cult" makes no sense—and finds no documentation in Canaanite sources. The "sacred marriage" model used to explain the phenomenon of female "sacred prostitution" cannot be extended to transgendered or asexual male cult personnel such as the *assinnu*, and the model itself is now seriously questioned as an explanation for cult ritual in ancient Syria-Palestine or Mesopotamia.[48] Generalizations about the sexual "depravity" of the Canaanites that indiscriminately combine all forms of nonmarital sexual activity do not help to explain the particular attention given to male homosexual acts in the Hebrew Bible—or Assyrian law.

(2) The *assinnu*s and other male devotees of Inanna/Ishtar who assumed female or androgynous roles in their identification with the goddess do not provide a model for the homosexual practice condemned in the Hebrew Bible. No clear evidence for this class of personnel or the cult to which they belonged has been demonstrated for the OT period.[49]

(3) The attempt to link male homosexual practice to Canaanite religion or culture through the language of "abomination" fails to distinguish homosexual relations from a host of other rejected practices, and fails to recognize the identification as a rhetorical weapon of an age

---

and abhorrence expressed in this text is close to the sentiment of Leviticus. The text pairs this reference with a reference to prostitutes and female devotees of the goddess (*kezertu*s, *šamḫatu*s, and *ḫarimtu*s) "whom Ishtar deprived of husbands and kept in her power." Both references reflect anxiety concerning transgression of gender roles and boundaries. As the *assinnu* transgresses the normative male gender role (dominance in sexual relations), so the (female) prostitute or devotee of Ishtar transgresses the normative female gender role (sex confined to marriage). Cf. Ereshkigal's curse of the *assinnu* (*kurgarrû* in the Sumerian version) in "Ishtar's Descent to the Underworld" (Nissinen, *Homoeroticism*, 32), which is virtually identical to Enkidu's curse of the prostitute Shamhat in the Gilgamesh Epic. Both curses are etiologies for a marginal and despised class living on the borders of the city and subjected to insults and abuse.

48. See Bird, "End"; Frymer-Kensky, *In the Wake*, 199–202; Renger, "Heilige Hochzeit"; cf. van der Toorn, "Cultic Prostitution," 510.

49. The cult of Cybele in Asia Minor and that of the Syrian Atargatis had a similar class of male devotees (the *galli*) who castrated themselves in honor of the goddess. Because Nissinen's main evidence comes from the Mesopotamian sources, I have focused on them. The Syrian evidence, though closer geographically, is later and derives largely from outside observers.

when Canaanites had long since disappeared. It belongs to the language of Israelite polemic that stigmatizes practices deemed unacceptable by identifying them with the "nations" that YHWH drove out before the Israelites, with much the same intention and effect as the terms *Communist* or *un-American* have had at times in American political and religious rhetoric.[50]

7. Despite the cultural differences (including theological understandings) that separate these texts from us and make it impossible for us to appropriate their words directly, they may still contribute to our current deliberation. The branding of male homosexual acts as an "abomination" suggests close correspondence to contemporary attitudes. What is shared, I think, is a deep sense of revulsion or ambivalence, or both, toward a practice that is perceived as "unnatural" or contrary to the fundamental order of society—conceived on a patriarchal model. The "reasons" given are secondary and culturally variable. Thus while Israel's attempt to associate homosexual practice with foreign/pagan peoples *may* reflect something of its encounter with surrounding cultures, it is no more adequate an explanation of the taboo than modern arguments that seek to ground it in the consequences of AIDS or the threat of genocide.

8. The context of the present debate is similar to that in which the subject of homosexual practice emerged as an issue of theological interest in ancient Israel and the biblical canon. The prohibition received "canonical" formation in a period of transition and breakdown of older community boundaries and norms, when the question of communal identity had become the central theological question. The answer provided by the Holiness Code applies a cultic concept to the community as a whole and creates legislation that redefines the boundaries of the community, interpreting them in cultic terms of purity and separation from defilement. Although the demand for holiness is spelled out elsewhere in this legislation in ethical commands that link reverence for God and respect for neighbor (with special provisions for protecting the weak neighbor in Leviticus 25), in the sexual realm its interest is solely in defining appropriate partners, not in the ethics of sexual relations and relationships.

---

50. If this language is understood to target practices introduced by Israel's conquerors or neighbors in the period of the nation's collapse or restoration, it is remarkably lacking both in specificity and in associations with identifiable foreign practices, such as divination, the Tammuz cult, and the cult of the Queen of Heaven (the Judean form of Assyrian Ishtar). Moreover, it also lacks associations with the Canaanite/Hebrew goddess Asherah, the clearest example of persisting Canaanite religion.

The Levitical response to the challenges of a changing political, social and religious order is not the only biblical model. Deuteronomy exhibits a different response, which may have been in part contemporaneous. The Deuteronomic move is toward restriction in cultic expression but greater inclusiveness in defining the cultic community. Women, slaves, and resident aliens are now explicitly brought within the provisions of the law and are the object of both cultic and ethical legislation.[51] The canon also witnesses attempts to define the identity and boundaries of the community in the writings of Ezra and Nehemiah (focused on the role of Torah and the problem of intermarriage with foreigners[52]), and various NT writings attest to the struggle of early Christian communities to define themselves over against their Jewish and pagan ancestors and neighbors.

9. Today the issue of Christian identity and the boundaries of Christian community is once more a critical issue, with its attendant concerns over rights and obligations of members. In the debate over these issues, the status of homosexual acts and persons has emerged as perhaps the most important case for testing our understanding of Christian identity and community. In this new situation none of the old answers will suffice, and those that are reaffirmed will be reinterpreted. But while the specific terms of the Holiness Code cannot serve our present needs, the legal tradition of the OT exemplified in the Covenant Code, the Deuteronomic Code, and the Holiness Code offers precedent and models in their attempts to create—and re-create—representative but encompassing statements of the principles and values that define community for a people that understands itself as the people of God.

a. The OT contributes to Christian ethics the conviction that the demands of love of God and neighbor must find expression in concrete acts and specific principles. Thus the OT legal tradition contains efforts to formulate general norms, as in the Decalogue, together with specific cases that are both expressions and tests of the general norms. Both are essential and both are subject to change as they are brought into new interpretive contexts. The successive, and in part competing, law codes

---

51. See, e.g., the recasting of the old law of the Hebrew slave (Exod 20:2-6) to include women in Deut 15:12-18, and the new legislation for the annual harvest pilgrim feasts in Deut 16:11, 14, which specifies inclusion of all of the landless classes: slaves, Levites, resident aliens, widows, and orphans. See Lohfink, "Poverty," 43-47.

52. Ezra 9-10 (which solves the problem by excluding foreign wives and their children) and Neh 13:23-30.

contained in the Hebrew Bible testify to an ongoing process of community deliberation concerning the rules that will govern its life, a process that continues today. Today cases relating to homosexual identity and practice are helping us clarify fundamental principles of Christian ethics.

b. The concept of holiness as embracing all of life and distinguishing life in Christ from life apart from Christ (to translate into Christian terms) is, in my view, a concept of continuing validity for Christian ethics, which requires reformulation. It is in many ways a revolutionary concept when applied to the realm of sexual relations.

c. The attempt of Leviticus 18 and 19 to bring sexual relations into the realm of theological interest, however limited, is an invitation to further theological reflection. It represents a step beyond the older collections of OT laws that show virtually no interest in relations, sexual or otherwise, within the private, male-dominated sphere of the family—or outside the family insofar as they do not affect the rights and/or honor of male citizens. From this point on, sex is not simply a "private" matter or a purely social concern.

d. The inclusion of the homosexual prohibitions within a larger collection of laws provides a model for contemporary deliberation. The question of homosexual ethics is properly situated in a broader consideration of the demands of Christian community that place sexual ethics alongside demands for social and economic justice. To isolate the question of homosexual practice from the other demands violates the biblical model.

10. While Leviticus 18 and 20 establish a claim of theological interest in sexual relations, the sphere of interest that they define and the factors they identify as relevant are far too limited in their exclusive concern with categories of sexual partners or defiling conditions (menstruation), both objectively defined. Because the laws are meant to establish boundaries, they do not address the more fundamental issue of sexuality and its appropriate uses and expression. That is true of the whole OT—and of the Bible as a whole. Just as gender is not a recognized concept or subject of debate in the biblical world, neither is sexuality, with all of its biological, psychological, and sociological aspects that must figure in any modern discussion. Sexuality and sexual ethics represent new concepts and arenas of discourse and discovery, to which we must attempt to relate the biblical testimony.

11. The OT laws, taken by themselves, are insufficient guides, even for the situations they address explicitly. They serve primarily to indicate

areas of interest, principles of justice, and underlying social and religious values. Thus the death penalty attached to the sexual prohibitions shows the intense level of interest in (male-defined) sexual rights and boundaries. But the prohibitions and judgments do not tell us how particular cases were handled or reveal the moral reasoning behind decisions. Here narrative texts may offer illumination, and qualification. The story of Judah and Tamar (Genesis 38) provides an instructive example of a violation of sexual norms in which the condemned woman receives not only a reprieve, but a judgment of "right(eous)" conduct—in view of the circumstances. It warns against absolutizing any of the sexual laws. Circumstances matter and so do motives—even when they are not explicitly articulated. This account reminds us that the laws do not stand alone. They function within a social and canonical context to which the OT narrative, prophetic, and wisdom texts give limited but essential witness.

EXTRALEGAL TEXTS AS SOURCES FOR OT ETHICAL DELIBERATION CONCERNING HOMOSEXUALITY

The OT legal texts may not be dismissed as sources for Christian theological and ethical reflection by appeal to Christ as the end of the law or because of their particular historical and cultic associations. The laws of the Christian OT do not bind but instruct, and their power to instruct is not diminished. But the law is only one mode of revelation in the OT canon, and one of the most commonly abused—by isolating individual sentences and absolutizing them as timeless decrees. The canonical context of OT law demands that it be read in the light of the Bible's full testimony to God's saving and revealing presence, and that it must be understood first of all as imbedded in a gospel story of God's gracious deliverance, leading, and instructing of a people invited into a covenant relationship and called to be witnesses to that divine action and self-disclosure.

In this larger canonical witness, where does one seek illumination and guidance for the new questions of sexual ethics facing us today, and in particular for the questions relating to homosexual persons and practice? The move from a small number of texts that make explicit, or implied, reference to homosexual activity to the larger canonical witness constitutes a major challenge, since these paths are neither as obvious nor as well explored. Recent discussion has turned increasingly to the creation texts as the primary source for a biblical understanding of sexuality and sexual relations against which to view the homosexual prohibition and contemporary issues of homosexuality. I believe that this move is both essential and problematic: essential because the Genesis creation accounts are foundational for all biblical reflection on the meaning of our common humanity and our sexuality, problematic because such appeals often fail to recognize the androcentric shaping and cultural presuppositions of these texts. The creation texts, no less than the laws, are products of an ancient patriarchal society and may not be absolutized. Moreover, their own interests are much more limited than we have traditionally recognized.

The Genesis Creation Accounts

Hays's appeal to the creation accounts may be taken as representative of current arguments in the homosexual debate. In his sketch of a wider biblical framework for the explicit references to homosexual practice, he begins with Genesis 1, under the heading "God's creative intention for human sexuality." "From Genesis 1 onwards," he writes, "Scripture affirms repeatedly that God has made man and woman for one another and that our sexual desires rightly find fulfillment within heterosexual marriage." He continues by citing Mark 10:2-9; 1 Thess 4:3-8; 1 Cor 7:1-9; Eph 5:21-33; and Heb 13:4, concluding that "this picture of marriage provides the positive backdrop against which the Bible's few emphatic negations of homosexuality must be read."[53] Hays's understanding does indeed reflect

53. Hays, "Awaiting," 10. Surprisingly, he does not treat either of the creation accounts but appears to interpret them through the NT texts. Cf. Mauser, "Creation," 47-49, for the NT interpretation of Genesis 1-2. A different approach to the creation texts is taken by Thomas Dozeman, who points to an intercanonical change in understanding of creation (from P to Paul) as consequential for biblical and contemporary theologies of sexuality (Dozeman, "Creation," 184). I am in fundamental agreement with his argument that the topic of sexuality belongs under the rubric of creation theology (ibid., 170-71), and I commend his attention to changing views within the canon as significant for current debate, but I differ with his interpretation of Genesis 1 in relation to Leviticus 18 and 20. My analysis of the OT texts has convinced me that the cosmological underpinnings of the Levitical prohibitions are to be found in the notion of gender identity and boundaries (cf. Frymer-Kensky, "Sex," 1145-46), not in the theme of procreation articulated in Genesis 1 and interpreted as a life/death option (Dozeman, "Creation," 175-76). Thus I cannot agree that the prohibition rests in the rejection of a "sexual act devoid of the possibility of reproduction" (ibid., 176). While the exact relationship of the H-Code to P remains disputed in terms of date and authorship, the characteristic concepts of H are recognizably distinct from those of P elsewhere in the Pentateuch, including Genesis 1 (Joosten, *People*, 193; cf. ibid., 13-14, 194-207). Drawing these texts together may serve the needs of contemporary

the history of interpretation in both NT and rabbinic exegesis, but it does not describe the intention of the Genesis creation texts. Moreover, the identification of marriage as the backdrop against which the homosexual prohibitions are to be understood reflects a contemporary understanding of the issues at stake, not an OT view. Homosexual relations in the OT are not viewed as an alternative or as a threat to marriage, and the creation texts are neither prescriptions nor models for heterosexual marriage as the context in which "sexual desires rightly find fulfillment." The creation texts are not concerned with right or wrong sexual behavior at all, and the notion of "fulfillment of sexual desire" is alien to these texts — and to OT understanding of marriage.

It is impossible to detail here arguments I have laid out elsewhere on the meaning of these texts in their ancient contexts and their implications for a contemporary theology of sexuality.[54] I can only offer a few summary comments related to common arguments in current debate, but they remain inadequate without a fuller discussion of the texts and their larger OT and ancient Near Eastern context. The main point that must be highlighted is that these texts *assume* the common pattern of sexual relations between male and female as the basis for the reproduction of the human species — as of the animal species (Gen 1:22, 27-28) — and interpret this gift of reproductive capability as God's good design; they further *assume* that the sexual drive that unites man and woman is the basis for marriage (Gen 2:24). They do not *prescribe* any behavior or institution. They are etiologies, explaining why things are the way they are — and in Genesis 3 explaining why the woman *is* subordinate to the man (in ancient Israelite society), not why she *should* be.[55] They are uninterested in variations or deviations from the dominant pattern. The theological problem posed by variations in nature, together with the related ethical

---

theology, but it misleads, I believe, when Genesis 1 is viewed as the historical matrix in which the homosexual prohibitions arose.

54. See esp. Bird, "Genesis 1-3"; for the exegetical foundations, see Bird, "'Male and Female'"; Bird, "Sexual Differentiation"; and Bird, "Authority of the Bible." Cf. Whitaker, "Creation" and Sheppard, "Use of Scripture."

55. The regulation of sexual relations and marriage belongs to the realm of law and custom. A noteworthy feature of the laws and traditions that did serve to regulate sexual relations and marriage in ancient Israel (at least those preserved in the OT canon) is that they never refer to the creation texts as models. See, e.g., the marriage blessing given to Ruth, which invokes the example of Rachel and Leah (Ruth 4:11), not Eve.

questions of appropriate social responses, is not adequately treated, or even recognized, in the canonical literature.[56]

The more important reason that we cannot expect help from the creation texts on the question of appropriate expressions and constraints of sexuality is that sexuality as we understand it today is not addressed in the Bible. It is a modern concept. The Bible treats sexuality only in limited forms of actualization. We can learn a great deal from the experience of Israel and the church in their attempts to comprehend and control sex as a divine endowment and as a human capacity subject to the distorting and alienating power of sin. But we cannot get a ready-made sexual ethic from the Bible, or even an adequate foundation. The terms of Israel's culturally shaped understanding will not satisfy our present need. In this field we must look to the ongoing revelation of science and of newly emerging voices of experience. That is to follow the pattern exhibited in the Bible itself. But the Bible also gives a more explicit mandate for the appeal to experience and science.

The Wisdom Tradition in the Old Testament

Appeal to experience is given theoretical undergirding by the wisdom literature, which affirms wisdom as a path to piety and observes creation (as mundane world and as cosmic wonder) for signs of the nature and designs of God.[57] In this literature and the intellectual tradition that it represents (including not only Proverbs, Psalms and Job, as well as the skeptic Qohelet, but also the creation account of Genesis 1) we find biblical authorization for the appeal to science to inform our understanding and judgment of homosexual orientation and practice. I will limit my comments on this underutilized tradition and its implications for our current debate to the following brief points.

---

56. Mesopotamian tradition preserves an attempt to account for abnormalities in creation and to provide a constructive social response. In the Sumerian myth of "Enki and Ninmah," the midwife goddess Ninmah, who has assisted Enki in creating humankind, continues to create in a drunken challenge to Enki, now forming misshapen creatures: a giant, a woman unable to bear, and a creature with neither male nor female organs. In each case, however, Enki is able to find a place in society for her creation and ensure it a living (Kramer, *Sumerian Mythology*, 68–72, esp. 71; and Jacobsen, *Treasures*, 113–14).

57. See Seow, "Heterotextual Perspective," 19–25 for a development of this argument.

1. Contemporary science, in all its ambiguity and fallibility, is a means of revelation of the nature of creation and the mind of the creator. It may not be contrasted to the science employed by the biblical writers (e.g., the cosmology of Genesis 1) in a manner that privileges biblical science as revealed knowledge.

2. Science is open-ended and characterized by multiple voices, achieving impressive consensus in some areas and characterized by unresolved tensions in others. The existence within the biblical canon of conflicting voices within the wisdom tradition is an authorization to keep open the debate today, and to give it a place within the witness of the community of believers.

3. Experience is irreducible. It is subject to distortion and error and is always culturally framed, but no other source, and no other's experience, may cancel or substitute for the experience of any individual or group. The book of Job offers a model for affirming the integrity of individual experience as it affirms Job's integrity in maintaining his innocence against his friends' pious interpretations of his predicament. The book of Job also provides a model in suggesting that particular attention must be given to those whose experience does not fit the reigning norms, including theological norms. Qohelet also demonstrates the Bible's openness to the skeptic. With respect to the current debate, I believe this means that the testimony of homosexual or bisexual persons to their experience of sexual need and fulfillment in same-sex relationships is testimony that may not be dismissed as deformed by social or ideological pressure or as incompatible with Christian identity and silenced within the Christian community. Experience must be allowed to speak, and it must be heard, which means that it must be aided in gaining a hearing when it is unpopular or unorthodox, or when it has been suppressed. Speaking and hearing are the first ethical requirements in the attempt to comprehend homosexual nature and practice and to devise guidelines for action.

4. Experience must be tested. Our problem today concerns the criteria for testing. My preference is for criteria that weigh personal and communal consequences in favor of options that conduce to health and wholeness, healing and the upbuilding of community, honor of God, and freeing for the work of the kingdom—tests that should apply equally to heterosexual as well as homosexual acts and relationships.

Implications for present action

Because we are currently in a situation where neither science nor experience has achieved a consensus concerning the nature of homosexuality and its individual and social consequences, the first ethical question that confronts us is how to make ethical decisions in a situation where experts do not agree. Although the analogy to the wilderness wanderings proposed by Kathryn Greene-McCreight is not as fitting as she first thought,[58] it is nevertheless suggestive to an OT exegete. We are not yet ready to settle the new land and build houses—not at least as united "tribes." But wilderness is a time of preparation, and an essential part of that preparation is trying out new options. The herding tribes in the biblical account requested and received permission to settle before their "brothers," in the pasturelands of the Transjordan that were suited to their lifestyle (Num 32), and even after the united settlement not all lived in the same manner. So one question that Israel's history and the complex testimony of the biblical canon places before us is, how much unity is necessary on this issue? And further, what type and degree of disagreement can be tolerated within the household of faith? In the wilderness, conversation and debate must continue, but it has to be informed by practice. Moving from the known land to the unknown, the preference in situations of uncertainty and conflict will always be to return to the security of the old ways—as evidenced by the Israelites who preferred bondage in Egypt to the uncertainties and hardships of the awful wilderness (Exod 14:12) and by the spies who preferred not to claim the promised land when confronted by its intimidating inhabitants (Num 13:30—14:4). Those individuals and church bodies today who are willing to challenge the intimidating defenders of tradition perform an essential service to the church by making available a new body of experience to be weighed in reformulating our codes of sexual ethics and our regulations concerning church membership and service. Thus while I agree with Greene-McCreight that we need a moratorium on legislative action designed to bind all members to a common position, I believe we need to encourage responsible experiments with alternative practices. We need spies in the new land who are

---

58. The references to Greene-McCreight are to arguments she presented at the Consultation on Homosexuality and Ethics (Brite Divinity School, 1996) for which this essay was originally prepared. For the published form of her paper, see Greene-McCreight, "Logic."

not afraid to set up colonies there, even if they must continue to live for a time in tents and booths.

APPENDIX A: DEUTERONOMY 23:17–18 (HEB. 18–19) AND "SACRED PROSTITUTION"

A key text linking sex and cult in the OT is Deut 23:17–18 (Heb. 18–19):

> (17[18]) *There shall be no qĕdēšâ ("consecrated woman") among the daughters of Israel,*
>
> *and there shall be no qādēš ("consecrated man") among the sons of Israel.*
>
> (18[19]) You shall not bring the fee of a prostitute (ʾetnan zônâ) or the price of a dog (mĕḥîr keleb) into the house of YHWH your God for [payment of] any vow, *for both of these are an abomination to YHWH your God.*[59]

These paired verses have commonly been understood as prohibitions directed against "cultic prostitution," in two forms and genders: "sacred prostitutes," male and female (v. 17[18]), and their secular counterparts (v. 18[19]), with "dog" (keleb) interpreted as designating a "male prostitute." Closer attention to the structure and context of the passage and the occurrence of the key terms elsewhere in the OT have made that view no longer tenable.[60]

The two verses parallel paired female and male subjects, but the verses are not parallel in structure or content. Verse 17(18) proscribes the *existence* of "consecrated women" and "consecrated men" among the Israelite population, employing a mimicking construction; v. 18(19)a prohibits *payment* of vows with funds described metaphorically as "whore's wages" or a "dog's price,"[61] employing a compound object. Verse 17(18), formulated in the third person, is an intrusion into an older series of

---

59. Italicized text represents later additions to an older law forming part of a series in Deut 23:18 (19)–23(24). See below.

60. In the original publication of this article, I accepted the identification of "dog" as a male homosexual prostitute, noting, however, that the law does not ban the practice or practitioner but only the proceeds as payment for vows. Reexamination of this text has led me to reject that view for the interpretation presented below, which is spelled out in fuller detail in my forthcoming article "Whores and Hounds."

61. mĕḥîr ("price") is commonly translated "hire" (RSV) or "wages" (NRSV) on the assumption that the "dog" represented a male prostitute, but it refers to the price in exchange for an article, as Goodfriend, "Prostitution," 508, has shown. See examples in Bird, "Whores and Hounds" (forthcoming).

2 m. sg. apodictic laws by a later editor, who also added the "abomination" clause in v. 18(19)b, encompassing the older law and reinterpreting it by binding the two laws together. This editor apparently understood the "dog" of v. 18(19) as a male counterpart of the (female) prostitute and created a "consecrated man" (*qādēš*)[62] to pair with the independently occurring "consecrated woman" (*qĕdēšâ*, elsewhere Gen 38:21-22 and [pl.] Hos 4:14).

Elsewhere in the OT the expression *ʾetnan zônâ* ("whore's wages") is used *only* metaphorically; it never refers to actual sexual encounters but is used figuratively to characterize other relationships.[63] "Dog's price" must likewise be understood figuratively. The dog in the OT is a scavenger, menacing, and unclean, a demeaning term when applied to a man[64]—and hardly something one would pay money for. Thus "price of a dog" can only mean "less than nothing," or, like the prostitute's fee, a payment that is "cheap," "dirty," or unworthy of temple use.[65] The clincher to this reading is found in 1 Kgs 22:38, where "whores" and "hounds" are similarly paired—as figures that add the final touches of dishonor to the portrait of King Ahab. There we read that when the king's bloody chariot was washed by the pool of Samaria, *dogs* licked up the blood and *prostitutes* washed themselves [in it]. Deuteronomy 23:18(19)a must be understood in a similar light, as targeting "cheap," demeaning, or "unclean" payments offered as fulfilment of vows.

But what of the *qādēš* (literally, "consecrated man") in v. 17(18), traditionally translated "sodomite" or "male (cult) prostitute"? This too yields no evidence of homosexual activity. A masculine form of the term for a woman dedicated to a diety (*qĕdēšâ*), *qādēš* /pl. *qĕdēšîm*) is found only in Deuteronomistic texts (1 Kgs 14:24; 15:12; 22:46 [Heb. 47][66]), all

---

62. For a detailed analysis of v. 17(18) and all texts containing the terms *qādēš*/ *qĕdēšîm*, see Bird, "End."

63. In much the same way that congressmen today, and President Obama, are described as "Wall Street whores."

64. See Goodfriend, "Prostitution"; and Goodfriend, "*keleb* in Deuteronomy 23:19."

65. As with all idioms, it is impossible to know with certainty what connotations attached to these expressions from a distant time and culture. What is critical is to recognize that we are dealing here with clichés, even if we cannot decode them. Deuteronomy 23:18(19) is about money matters, not (cultic) sex, and it stands in a sequence of laws that target postponing paying vows or failing to pay them (vv. 21[22], 23[24]).

66. On *qĕdēšîm* in 2 Kgs 23:7 as a misvocalization of *qŏdāšîm* ("dedicated gifts"), see Bird, "End," 73; and Naʾaman, "Dedicated Treasures." On the MT reading *qĕdēšîm*

interdependent and all later than the independently occurring feminine forms. The masculine noun appears to be a backformation from the feminine, originating in this verse as an attempt to create a parallel to the masculine *keleb* ("dog") of v. 18(19). The female-male order of presentation is unprecedented for nouns of dual genders[67] and points to the secondary and derivative nature of the masculine form. All other occurrences are plural or collective, suggesting uncertainty about the exact nature of the institution; and similar uncertainty attends their location, described simply as "in the land." All lack contextual associations with prostitution or sex. The references are confined to the editorial summaries of the reigns of three Judean kings, which record their presence "in the land" at the establishment of the independent southern kingdom under Rehoboam (1 Kgs 14:24), their "removal" "from the land" by the first reforming king, Asa (1 Kgs 15:12), and the "extermination" of the final "remnant" "from the land" by his son Jehoshaphat (1 Kgs 22:46 [Heb. 47]). Thus according to the Deuteronomistic History, the last vestige of the institution was eradicated by the ninth century BCE.

Appeal to Canaanite parallels yields no firmer evidence. Despite persistent references to "male cult prostitutes" in modern textbooks, which describe them as a characteristic feature of Canaanite religion and a symbol of its sexual depravity, no such institution or practice is known from any Canaanite texts. The masculine cognate *qdš* at Ugarit designates a class of married cult personnel subordinate to priests, with no associations with sexual activity, heterosexual or homosexual.[68] Attempts to interpret OT *qādēš/qĕdēšîm* by reference to the Mesopotamian *assinnu* or the *galli* of Asia Minor offer no better evidence for a "male cult prostitute," as noted above. And no comparable class is attested in Canaanite myths or cultic texts.

APPENDIX B: HOMOEROTICISM IN THE ANCIENT NEAR EAST

Evidence is limited to two references from Egypt and a scattering of Mesopotamian texts from different literary genres, with different purposes and perspectives, and covering a span of more than two millennia.

---

in Job 36:14, see Bird, "End," 75–77.

67. The masculine is always the "base form."
68. Von Soden, "Zur Stellung"; cf. Gruber, "Hebrew *qĕdēšāh*," 147.

Egypt

A confession in the Book of the Dead contains the twice-repeated statement, "I have not had sexual relations with a boy," suggesting that homoerotic relations between men (or more specifically pedophilia) was regarded as morally suspect.[69] More significant in revealing attitudes is an episode in the myth describing the power struggle between Horus and Seth, in which Seth abuses Horus sexually, by anal intercourse, while Horus is asleep. Seth's purpose, Nissinen comments, is to "show his superiority by forcing Horus to a position of a defeated and raped enemy." "This story," he concludes, "speaks about sexual aggression used in exercising power—not about homosexuality."[70]

Mesopotamia

The Middle Assyrian Laws contain two cases treating sexual acts between males.[71] Paragraph 19 concerns a man who spreads an unsubstantiated rumor about a "comrade" (*tappāšu* = "his equal"), saying "Everyone (m.) 'lays' him (*ittinikkūš*)."[72] The case is parallel in construction to §18, in which the accusation is, "Everyone 'lays' your wife." The punishments in the two cases are identical except for the number of blows the accuser is to receive: forty for the defamation of the woman, but fifty for the man.[73] This differential reflects values similar to those expressed in the OT narrative accounts where the violation of a woman is represented as a lesser offense than the parallel action with a man. The issue here is not forced,

---

69. Nissinen, *Homoeroticism*, 19.

70. Ibid. For additional Egyptian sources that may allude to some kind of same-sex interaction, see ibid., 144 n. 2; cf. Greenberg, *Construction*, 129-30.

71. *Middle Assyrian Laws* §§19-20 (KAV 1 ii 82-96), cited by Nissinen, *Homoeroticism*, 25. They follow a series of cases concerning adultery (§§12-18) and form part of a collection of laws known as the "Laws of the Woman" (Bottéro and Petschow, "Homosexualität," 462).

72. The verb *niāku*, which Nissinen translates "have sex with," always has the active and dominant party as its subject, but does not in itself imply force or violence (Nissinen, *Homoeroticism*, 25-26).

73. The punishment also included performing the king's service for a month, payment of one talent of lead, and some type of symbolic action (*igaddimu*) whose meaning is not clear (ibid., 25). It must indicate some form of shaming (cutting off the beard or hair?), though not castration (§20) (ibid., 146 n. 27; 26; cf. Greenberg, *Construction*, 125 n.4).

but willing, submission to the receptive role, with an emphasis (in both of the parallel accusations) on habitual promiscuity which amounts to a charge of prostitution.

Paragraph 20 concerns a substantiated charge that a man has 'laid' a comrade (*tappāšu inīk*). The punishment applies the rule of talion ("they shall have sex with him" [*inikkūš*]) and adds castration (*ana ša rēšēn utarrūš*: "they shall turn him into a eunuch")—a punishment that not only deprives the offender of his sexual "weapon" but creates a permanent change in his gender role.[74] This example makes clear that the offense was understood as dishonoring another man by forcing him into the role of a woman,[75] a view corroborated by Neo-Assyrian curses that threaten a disobedient (male) vassal with becoming a prostitute (*ḫarimtu*)[76] or that liken a man to a raped captive, a slave girl, or a woman.[77]

Male-to-male sexual acts are occasionally mentioned in dream omens, a genre concerned with exceptional phenomena and lacking any moral interest—in contrast to the laws, which seek to articulate and enforce community values.[78] The only clear examples come from the omen series *Šumma ālu*, which lists four cases of intercourse with a male in a series of thirty-eight dealing with various aspects of sex life. In the first (CT 39 44:13), the partner is identified as an equal, and anal penetration is specified: "If a man approaches [for copulation] (*iteḫḫe*) his equal (*meḫrīšu*) from the rear, he becomes the leader among his peers and brothers."[79] The following three cases (CT 39 45:32–34) involve social inferiors and appear to be associated with negative consequences.[80] They

---

74. Nissinen, *Homoeroticism*, 25.

75. Although the same verb is used here as in the two preceding laws, the case appears to be treated as an incidence of rape since only the man who is the active subject of the verb is punished. Cf. §12, where the woman who is raped incurs no punishment in contrast to the cases in which the woman is a consenting partner. In contrast, the accusation of §19 focuses on the shame of the receptive partner, who, analogous to a promiscuous wife, invites sexual advances.

76. Treaty of Ashur-nerari V of Assyria with Mati'-ilu of Arpad (SAA 3 30:1–4, 7), quoted in Nissinen, *Homoeroticism*, 26–27; cf. ibid., 146 n. 33.

77. Ibid., 26–27. Nissinen cites these as examples of "many other texts [that] know raping of a man as an ultimate act of disgrace."

78. Ibid., 27–28; Bottéro and Petschow, "Homosexualität," 460–61.

79. The omen apodoses often pronounce quite startling, and even conflicting, consequences and cannot be understood as logical results according to modern notions of causality.

80. The meaning of the apodosis in the case of the *assinnu* is not clear. See Nissinen, *Homoeroticism*, 27, 147 n. 39; cf. Bottéro and Petschow, "Homosexualität," 461.

identify, in descending order of status, an *assinnu*, a *gerseqqû* ("courtier," a member of the household, possibly a eunuch), and a house-born slave (*dušmu*) as the sexual partner. "Consensual," or contractual, relations seem to be assumed.

These cases suggest that male subordinates or members of special classes might provide a passive partner for homosexual encounters, in addition to occasional "exchange" of roles among equals. They do not fundamentally qualify the underlying assumptions concerning gender roles observed in the laws, which view sexual relations as inherently unequal and identify the active and superior role with the male and the passive with the female.[81] While a series of incantations refers to a man's love (*râmu*) for another man in the same terms as parallel references to a man's love for a woman, and a woman's love for a man,[82] this suggestion of common sentiment in different types of relationships remains in tension with the hierarchy of socially prescribed roles and actions. It is noteworthy that this triad of love relationships does not include love of a woman for another woman.

Although sexual allusions attend many of the references to the male devotees of Inanna/Ishtar, known variously by the names *assinnu*, *kurgarrû*, *kulu'u*, and *sinnišānu*,[83] there is no clear evidence for sexual activity as a part of their cultic role.[84] The single reference to an *assinnu* in a text treating male-to-male sexual relations[85] gives no information about the circumstances that would allow us to determine whether the contact was part of a cultic action or involved payment, or both. The one text that appears to speak of male prostitution is a proverb concerning a *sinnišānu*. On entering the "brothel" (*bīt aštammi*), he "raised his hands [gesture of prayer?] and said: 'My hire goes to the promoter[?] (*anzinnu*).

---

81. Nissinen, *Homoeroticism*, 27; cf. Bottéro and Petschow, "Homosexualität," 462; Locher, *Die Ehre*, 369-71. All the verbs used for sexual contacts are one-directional, with the active partner as subject; there is no Mesopotamian vocabulary for mutual and equal sexual relationships (Nissinen, *Homoeroticism*, 146 n. 31).

82. Bottéro-Petschow, "Homosexualität," 467-68, citing the "Almanac of Incantations" (BRM 4, 20); cf. Nissinen, *Homoeroticism*, 35.

83. Nissinen cites only one text referring to a *sinnišānu* (lit. "man-woman") (treated below). He notes (ibid., 28) that the group sometimes included the *kalû* lamentation priests.

84. On these classes, see ibid., 52-61; Bottéro and Petschow, "Homosexualität," 463-67; Leick, *Sex*, 157-69; cf. Greenberg, *Construction*, 96-97. Henshaw, *Female*, 284-311, offers an expanded list of titles.

85. The omen text CT 39 45:32, cited above.

You [Ishtar?] are wealth (*mešrû*), I am half (*mešlu*)."[86] The meaning of this statement is uncertain, as is the identity of the addressee. Sexual encounters (with men and women) seem to have taken place in the *bīt aštammi* (variously translated "tavern," "hostel," and "brothel"),[87] which was apparently attached to some temples, under the patronage of Ishtar.

---

86. Nissinen, *Homoeroticism*, 33, citing Lambert, *Babylonian Wisdom*, 218-19; cf. Leick, *Sex*, 160.

87. See Henshaw, *Female*, 312-23.

Bibliography

Achtemeier, Paul J. *The Inspiration of Scripture: Problems and Proposals*. Biblical Perspectives on Current Issues. Philadelphia: Westminster, 1980.

Ackerman, Susan. "'And the Women Knead Dough': The Worship of the Queen of Heaven in Sixth-Century Judah." In *Gender and Difference in Ancient Israel*, edited by Peggy L. Day, 109–24. Minneapolis: Fortress, 1989.

———. "The Personal Is Political: Covenantal and Affectionate Love (ʾaheb, ʾahaba) in the Hebrew Bible." *VT* 52 (2002) 437–58.

Albertz, Rainer. *A History of Israelite Religion in the Old Testament Period*. 2 vols. Translated by John Bowden. OTL. Louisville: Westminster John Knox, 1994.

———. "Religionsgeschichte Israels statt Theologie des Alten Testaments! Plädoyer für eine forschungsgeschichtliche Umorientierung." *Jahrbuch für biblische Theologie* 10 (1995) 3–24.

Alonso Schökel, Luis. *The Inspired Word: Scripture in the Light of Language and Literature*. Translated by Francis Martin. New York: Herder & Herder, 1972.

Anderson, G. W. "Canonical and Non-Canonical." In *The Cambridge History of the Bible*. Vol. 1, *From the Beginnings to Jerome*, edited by Peter R. Ackroyd and Christopher F. Evans, 113–59. 2 vols. Cambridge: Cambridge University Press, 1970.

Balch, David L., ed. *Homosexuality, Science, and the "Plain Sense" of Scripture*. 2000. Reprinted, Eugene, OR: Wipf & Stock, 2007.

Barr, James. *The Concept of Biblical Theology: An Old Testament Perspective*. Minneapolis: Fortress, 1999.

———. *Does Biblical Study Still Belong to Theology? An Inaugural Lecture delivered before the University of Oxford on 26 May 1977*. Oxford: Clarendon, 1978.

———. *The Garden of Eden and the Hope of Immortality*. 1993. Reprinted, Eugene, OR: Wipf & Stock, 2003.

———. *Holy Scripture: Canon, Authority, Criticism*. Philadelphia: Westminster, 1983.

Barton, John. *People of the Book? The Authority of the Bible in Christianity*. Louisville: Westminster John Knox, 1988.

Bass, Dorothy C. "Women's Studies and Biblical Studies: An Historical Perspective." *JSOT* 22 (1982) 6–12.

Becking, Bob, and Meindert Dijkstra, eds. *On Reading Prophetic Texts: Gender-Specific and Related Studies in Memory of Fokkelien van Dijk-Hemmes*. Biblical Interpretation Series 18. Leiden: Brill, 1996.

Beckwith, Roger. *The Old Testament Canon of the New Testament Church and Its Background in Early Judaism*. Grand Rapids: Eerdmans, 1985.

Bellis, Alice Ogden. "Walter Brueggemann and James Barr: Old Testament Theology and Inclusivity." *RSN* 27 (2001) 233–38.

Bellis, Alice Ogden, and Joel S. Kaminsky, eds. *Jews, Christians, and the Theology of the Hebrew Scriptures.* SBLSymS 8. Atlanta: SBL, 2000.

Berkouwer, G. C. *Man: The Image of God.* Translated by Dirk W. Jellema. Grand Rapids: Eerdmans, 1962.

Binger, Tilde. *Asherah: Goddesses in Ugarit, Israel and the Old Testament.* JSOTSup 232. Copenhangen International Seminar 1. Sheffield: Sheffield Academic, 1997.

Birch, Bruce C. "Old Testament Theology: Its Task and Future." *HBT* 6/1 (1983) iii–viii.

Bird, Phyllis A. "The Authority of the Bible." In *NIB*, 1:33–64. Reprint, chap. 3 in this volume.

———. *The Bible as the Church's Book.* Library of Living Faith 5. Philadelphia: Westminster, 1982.

———. "The Bible in Christian Ethical Deliberation concerning Homosexuality: Old Testament Contributions." In *Homosexuality, Science, and the "Plain Sense" of Scripture*, edited by David L. Balch, 142–76. 2000. Reprinted, Eugene, OR: Wipf & Stock, 2007. Reprint, chap. 4 in this volume.

———. "Biblical Authority in the Light of Feminist Critique." In *Missing Persons and Mistaken Identities: Women and Gender in Ancient Israel*, 248–64. OBT. Minneapolis: Fortress, 1997.

———. "The End of the Male Cult Prostitute." In *Congress Volume: Cambridge 1995*, edited by J. A. Emerton, 37–43. VTSup 66. Leiden: Brill, 1997.

———. "Feminist Old Testament Theology: An Oxymoron?" Paper presented at the 17th Congress of the International Organization for the Study of the Old Testament, Basel, 3 August 2001.

———. "Genesis 1–3 as a Source for a Contemporary Theology of Sexuality." In *Missing Persons and Mistaken Identities: Women and Gender in Ancient Israel*, 155–73. OBT. Minneapolis: Fortress, 1997.

———. "Genesis 3 in Modern Biblical Scholarship." In *Missing Persons and Mistaken Identities: Women and Gender in Ancient Israel*, 174–93. OBT. Minneapolis: Fortress, 1997.

———. "The Harlot as Heroine in Biblical Texts: Narrative Art and Social Presupposition." In *Missing Persons and Mistaken Identities: Women and Gender in Ancient Israel*, 197–218. OBT. Minneapolis: Fortress, 1997.

———. "'Male and Female He Created Them': Gen 1:27b in the Context of the Priestly Creation Account." In *Missing Persons and Mistaken Identities: Women and Gender in Ancient Israel*, 123–54. OBT. Minneapolis: Fortress, 1997.

———. *Missing Persons and Mistaken Identities: Women and Gender in Ancient Israel.* OBT. Minneapolis: Fortress, 1997.

———. "Of Whores and Hounds: A New Interpretation of the Subject of Deuteronomy 23:19." *VT* 65:352–64.

———. "Old Testament Theology and the God of the Fathers: Reflections on Biblical Theology from a North American Feminist Perspective." In *Biblische Theologie: Beiträge des Symposiums "Das Alte Testament und die Kultur der Moderne" anlässlich des 100. Geburtstags Gerhard von Rads (1901–1971) Heidelberg, 18.–21. Oktober 2001*, edited by Bernd Janowski, Michael Welker, and Paul D. Hanson, 69–107. Altes Testament und die Kultur der Moderne 14. Münster: Lit, 2005. Reprint, chap. 1 in this volume.

---. "Poor Man or Poor Woman? Gendering the Poor in Prophetic Texts." In *Missing Persons and Mistaken Identities: Women and Gender in Ancient Israel*, 67–78. OBT. Minneapolis: Fortress, 1997.

---. "Sexual Differentiation and Divine Image in the Genesis Creation Texts." In *Image of God and Gender Models in Judaeo-Christian Tradition*, edited by Kari E. Børresen, 11–34. Oslo: Solum, 1991. Republished under the title *Image of God: Gender Models in Judaeo-Christian Tradition*, 5–28. Minneapolis: Fortress, 1995.

---. "Theological Anthropology in the Hebrew Bible." In *The Blackwell Companion to the Hebrew Bible*, edited by Leo G. Perdue, 258–75. Blackwell Companions to Religion. Oxford: Blackwell, 2001. Reprint, chap. 2 in this volume.

---. "Translating Sexist Language as a Theological and Cultural Problem." In *Missing Persons and Mistaken Identities: Women and Gender in Ancient Israel*, 239–47. OBT. Minneapolis: Fortress, 1997.

Bottéro, Jean, and H. Petschow. "Homosexualität." In *RLA* 4:459–68.

Børresen, Kari Elisabeth, ed. *The Image of God: Gender Models in Judaeo-Christian Tradition*. Minneapolis: Fortress, 1995.

Braulik, Georg et al., eds. *Biblische Theologie und gesellschaftlicher Wandel: für Norbert Lohfink SJ*. Freiburg: Herder, 1993.

Brett, Mark G. "The Future of Old Testament Theology." In *Congress Volume: Oslo 1998*, edited by André Lemaire and M. Saebø, 465–88. VTSup 80. Leiden: Brill, 2000.

Brown, Jerry Wayne. *The Rise of Biblical Criticism in America, 1800–1870: The New England Scholars*. Middletown, CT: Wesleyan University Press, 1969.

Brueggemann, Walter. "Futures in Old Testament Theology." *HBT* 6/1 (1984) 1–11.

---. *Theology of the Old Testament: Testimony, Dispute, Advocacy*. Minneapolis: Fortress, 1997.

Cairns, David. *The Image of God in Man*. London: SCM, 1953.

Camp, Claudia V. "Feminist Theological Hermeneutics: Canon and Christian Identity." In *Searching the Scriptures*. Vol. 1, *A Feminist Introduction*, edited by Elisabeth Schüssler Fiorenza, 154–71. 2 vols. New York: Crossroad, 1993.

---. *Wisdom and the Feminine in the Book of Proverbs*. Bible and Literature Series 11. Sheffield: Almond, 1985.

Campenhausen, Hans von. *The Formation of the Christian Bible*. Translated by J. A. Baker. Philadelphia: Fortress, 1972.

Childs, Brevard S. *Old Testament Theology in a Canonical Context*. Philadelphia: Fortress, 1985.

Clifford, Richard J. "Woman Wisdom in the Book of Proverbs." In *Biblische Theologie und gesellschaftlicher Wandel: für Norbert Lohfink SJ*, 61–72. Freiburg: Herder, 1993.

Collins, Adela Yarbro, ed. *Feminist Perspectives on Biblical Scholarship*. SBLBSNA 10. Chico, CA: Scholars, 1985.

Collins, John J. "Is a Critical Biblical Theology Possible?" In *The Hebrew Bible and Its Interpreters*, edited by William H. Propp et al., 1–17. Biblical and Judaic Studies 1. Winona Lake, IN: Eisenbrauns, 1990.

Collins, Thomas Aquinas, and Raymond E. Brown. "Church Pronouncements." In *The Jerome Biblical Commentary*, edited by Raymond E. Brown et al., 624–32. Englewood Cliffs, NJ: Prentice-Hall, 1968.

Crenshaw, James L. *Prophetic Conflict: Its Effect upon Israelite Religion*. BZAW 124. Berlin: de Gruyter, 1971.

Curtis, Edward M. "Image of God (OT)." In *ABD* 3:389–91.
Davies, Philip R. *Whose Bible Is It Anyway?* JSOTSup 204. Sheffield: Sheffield Academic, 1995.
Day, John. *Molech: A God of Human Sacrifice in the Old Testament*. University of Cambridge Oriental Studies 41. Cambridge: Cambridge University Press, 1989.
Day, Peggy L., ed. *Gender and Difference in Ancient Israel*. Minneapolis: Fortress, 1989.
Dijk-Hemmes, Fokkelien van, and Athalya Brenner. *On Gendering Texts: Female and Male Voices in the Hebrew Bible*. Biblical Interpretation Series 1. Leiden: Brill, 1993.
―――, eds. *Reflections on Theology and Gender*. Kampen: Kok Pharos, 1994.
Dozeman, Thomas B. "Creation and Procreation in the Biblical Teaching on Homosexuality." *USQR* 49 (1995) 169–91.
Dulles, Avery. "Scholasticism and the Church." *ThTo* 38 (1981) 338–43.
―――. "Scripture: Recent Protestant and Catholic Views." *ThTo* 37 (1980) 7–26.
Elliger, Karl. *Leviticus*. Handbuch zum Alten Testament 4. Tübingen: Mohr/Siebeck, 1966.
Flesseman-van Leer, Ellen, ed. *The Bible: Its Authority and Interpretation in the Ecumenical Movement*. Faith and Order Paper 99. Geneva: World Council of Churches, 1980.
Froehlich, Karlfried, trans. and ed. *Biblical Interpretation in the Early Church*. Sources of Early Christian Thought. Philadelphia: Fortress, 1984.
Frymer-Kensky, Tikva. "The Emergence of Jewish Biblical Theologies." In *Jews, Christians, and the Theology of the Hebrew Scriptures*, edited by Alice Ogden Bellis and Joel S. Kaminsky, 109–21. SBLSymS 8. Atlanta: SBL, 2000.
―――. *In the Wake of the Goddesses: Women, Culture, and the Biblical Transformation of Pagan Myth*. New York: Free Press, 1992. **[KC: check Goddesses]**
―――. "Sex and Sexuality." In *ABD* 5:1144–46.
Geisler, Norman L., ed. *Inerrancy*. Grand Rapids: Zondervan, 1979.
Gerrish, B. A. "Biblical Authority and the Continental Reformation." *SJT* 10 (1957) 337–60.
Gerstenberger, Erhard S. *Theologies in the Old Testament*. Translated by John Bowden. Minneapolis: Fortress, 2002.
―――. "tʿb pi. verabscheuen." In *THAT* 2:1051–55.
Gnuse, Robert. *The Authority of the Bible: Theories of Inspiration, Revelation and the Canon of Scripture*. New York: Paulist, 1985.
Goodfriend, Elaine Adler. "Could *keleb* in Deuteronomy 23:19 Actually Refer to a Canine?" In *Pomegranates and Golden Bells: Studies in Biblical, Jewish, and Near Eastern Ritual, Law, and Literature in Honor of Jacob Milgrom*, edited by David Pearson Wright et al., 381–97. Winona Lake, IN: Eisenbrauns, 1995.
―――. "Prostitution (Old Testament)." In *ABD* 5:505–10.
Goshen-Gottstein, Moshe H. "Tanakh Theology: The Religion of the Old Testament and the Place of Jewish Biblical Theology." In *Ancient Israelite Religion: Essays in Honor of Frank Moore Cross*, edited by Patrick D. Miller et al., 617–44. Philadelphia: Fortress, 1987.
Grayson, A. Kirk. "Eunuchs in Power: Their Role in the Assyrian Bureaucracy." In *Vom Alten Orient zum Alten Testament*, edited by Manfried Dietrich and Oswald Loretz, 85–97. AOAT 240. Neukirchen-Vluyn: Neukirchener, 1995.
Greenberg, David F. *The Construction of Homosexuality*. Chicago: University of Chicago Press, 1988.

Greene-McCreight, Kathryn. "The Logic of the Interpretation of Scripture and the Church's Debate over Sexual Ethics." In *Homosexuality, Science, and the "Plain Sense" of Scripture*, edited by David L. Balch, 242–60. 2000. Reprinted, Eugene, OR: Wipf & Stock, 2007.

Greer, Rowan A. "The Christian Bible and Its Interpretation." In *Early Biblical Interpretation* by James L. Kugel and Rowan A. Greer, 107–208. Library of Early Christianity 3. Philadelphia: Westminster, 1986.

Gruber, Mayer I. "Hebrew qĕdēšāh and Her Canaanite and Akkadian Cognates." *UF* 18 (1986) 133–48.

Hadley, Judith M. *The Cult of Asherah in Ancient Israel and Judah: Evidence for a Hebrew Goddess*. University of Cambridge Oriental Publications 57. Cambridge: Cambridge University Press, 2000.

Hall, Douglas John. *Imaging God: Dominion as Stewardship*. 1986. Reprint, Eugene, OR: Wipf & Stock, 2004.

Hanson, Paul et al., eds. *Biblische Theologie: Beiträge des Symposiums "Das Alte Testament und die Kultur der Moderne" anlässlich des 100. Geburtstags Gerhard von Rads (1901–1971) Heidelberg, 18.–21. Oktober 2001*. Alte Testament und und die Kultur der Moderne 14. Münster: Lit, 2005.

Hays, Richard B. "Awaiting the Redemption of Our Bodies: The Witness of Scripture concerning Homosexuality." In *Homosexuality in the Church: Both Sides of the Debate*, edited by Jeffrey S. Siker, 3–17. Louisville: Westminster John Knox, 1994.

Heider, George C. *The Cult of Molek: A Reassessment*. JSOTSup 43. Sheffield: JSOT Press, 1985.

Henshaw, Richard A. *Female and Male: The Cultic Personnel; The Bible and the Rest of the Ancient Near East*. PTMS 31. Allison Park, PA: Pickwick, 1994.

Heschel, Abraham Joshua. "The Concept of Man in Jewish Thought." In *The Concept of Man: A Study in Comparative Philosophy*, edited by Sarvepalli Radhakrishnan and Poola Tirupati Raju, 122–71. London: Allen & Unwin, 1966.

Hiebert, Theodore. "Rethinking Dominion Theology." *Direction* 25/2 (1996) 16–25.

Hodge, Charles. *Systematic Theology*. 3 vols. Grand Rapids: Eerdmans, 1960.

L' Hour, Jean. "Les interdits toʿēbâ dans le Deutéronome." *RB* 71 (1964) 481–503.

Humbert, Paul. "Le substantif toʿēbâ et le verbe tʿb dans l'Ancien Testament." *ZAW* 72 (1960), 217–37.

Jacobsen, Thorkild. *The Treasures of Darkness: A History of Mesopotamian Religion*. New Haven: Yale University Press, 1976.

Janowski, Bernd. "Biblische Theologie: I. Exegetisch." In *RGG*, 1:1544–49.

———. "The One God of the Two Testaments: Basic Questions of a Biblical Theology." *ThTo* 57 (2000), 297–324.

———. "Theologie des Alten Testaments: Plädoyer für eine integrative Perspektive." In *Congress Volume: Basel 2001*, edited by André Lemaire, 241–76. VTSup 92. Leiden: Brill, 2002.

Jodock, Darrell. *The Church's Bible: Its Contemporary Authority*. Minneapolis: Fortress, 1989.

Johnston, Robert K. *Evangelicals at an Impasse: Biblical Authority in Practice*. Atlanta: John Knox, 1979.

Joines, Karen Randolph. *Serpent Symbolism in the Old Testament: A Linguistic, Archaeological, and Literary Study*. Haddonfield, NJ: Haddonfield Home, 1975.

Jónsson, Gunnlaugur A. *The Image of God: Genesis 1:26-28 in a Century of Old Testament Research.* ConBOT 26. Lund: Almquist & Wiksell, 1988.

Joosten, Jan. *People and Land in the Holiness Code: An Exegetical Study of the Ideational Framework of the Law in Leviticus 17-26.* VTSup 67. Leiden: Brill, 1996.

Jost, Renate. *Frauen, Männer und die Himmelskönigin: Exegetische Studien.* Gütersloh: Gütersloher, 1995.

Kalimi, Isaac. "Religionsgeschichte Israels oder Theologie des Alten Testaments? Das jüdische Interesse an der Biblischen Theologie." *Jahrbuch für biblische Theologie* 10 (1995) 45-68.

Keel, Othmar, and Christoph Uehlinger. *Gods, Goddesses, and Images of God in Ancient Israel.* Translated by Thomas H. Trapp. Minneapolis: Fortress, 1998.

Kelsey, David H. *The Uses of Scripture in Recent Theology.* Philadelphia: Fortress, 1975.

Knierim, Rolf P. "The Task of Old Testament Theology." *HBT* 6 (1984) 25-57.

———. "On the Task of Old Testament Theology: A Response to W. Harrelson, S. Towner, and R. E. Murphy." *HBT* 6 (1984) 91-128.

———. *The Task of Old Testament Theology: Substance, Method and Cases; Essays.* Grand Rapids: Eerdmans, 1995.

Kraftchick, Steven J. et al., eds. *Biblical Theology: Problems and Perspectives; In Honor of J. Christiaan Beker.* Nashville: Abingdon, 1995.

Kramer, Samuel Noah. *Sumerian Mythology.* Rev. ed. New York: Harper & Row, 1961.

Kugel, James L. *Early Interpretation: The Common Background of Late Forms.* In *Early Biblical Interpretation*, by James L. Kugel and Rowan A. Greer, 11-106. Library of Early Christianity 3. Philadelphia: Westminster, 1986.

Lambert, W. G. *Babylonian Wisdom Literature.* Oxford: Clarendon, 1960.

Lambert, W. G., and A. R. Millard. *Atra-ḫasīs: The Babylon Story of the Flood, with the Sumerian Flood Story, by M. Civil.* Oxford: Clarendon, 1969.

Leick, Gwendolyn. *Sex and Eroticism in Mesopotamian Literature.* London: Routledge, 1994.

Levenson, Jon. "Why Jews Are not Interested in Biblical Theology." In *Judaic Perspectives on Ancient Israel*, edited by Jacob Neusner et al., 281-307. Philadelphia: Fortress, 1987.

Lindsell, Harold. *The Battle for the Bible.* Grand Rapids: Zondervan, 1976.

Locher, Clemens. *Die Ehre einer Frau in Israel. Exegetische und rechtsvergleichende Studien zum Deuteronomium 22, 13-21.* OBO 70. Göttingen: Vandenhoeck & Ruprecht, 1986.

Lohfink, Norbert. "Poverty in the Laws of the Ancient Near East and of the Bible." *TS* 52 (1991) 34-50.

Long, Burke O. "Letting Rival Gods Be Rivals: Biblical Theology in a Postmodern Age." In *Problems in Biblical Theology: Essays in Honor of Rolf Knierim*, edited by Henry T. C. Sun and Keith L. Eades, 222-33. 1997. Reprinted, Eugene, OR: Wipf & Stock, 2011.

Marsden, George M. *Understanding Fundamentalism and Evangelicalism.* Grand Rapids: Eerdmans, 1991.

Mauser, Ulrich W. "Creation, Sexuality, and Homosexuality in the New Testament." In *Homosexuality and Christian Community*, edited by Choon-Leong Seow, 39-49. Louisville: Westminster John Knox, 1996.

McBride, S. Dean, Jr. "Polity of the Covenant People: The Book of Deuteronomy." *Int* 41 (1987) 229-44.

McDonald, Lee Martin. *The Formation of the Christian Biblical Canon.* Nashville: Abingdon, 1988.
McKim, Donald K. *The Bible in Theology and Preaching.* Nashville: Abingdon, 1994.
Melcher, Sarah J. "The Holiness Code and Human Sexuality." In *Biblical Ethics & Homosexuality: Listening to Scripture,* edited by Robert L. Brawley, 87–102. Louisville: Westminster John Knox, 1996.
Miller, Patrick D. "Things Too Wonderful: Prayers of Women in the Old Testament." In *Biblische Theologie und gesellschaftlicher Wandel: für Norbert Lohfink SJ,* 237–51. Freiburg: Herder, 1993.
Na'aman, Nadab. "The Dedicated Treasures Buildings within the House of YHWH Where Women Weave Coverings for Asherah (2 Kings 23:7)." *BN* 83 (1996) 17–18.
Neil, William. "The Criticism and Theological Use of the Bible, 1700–1950." In *The Cambridge History of the Bible.* Vol. 3, *The West from the Reformation to the Present Day,* edited by S. L. Greenslade, 251–79. Cambridge: Cambridge University Press, 1963.
Newsom, Carol A. "The Moral Sense of Nature: Ethics in the Light of God's Speech to Job." *PSB* 15 (1994) 9–27.
―――. "Woman and the Discourse of Patriarchal Wisdom: A Study of Proverbs 1–9." In *Gender and Difference in Ancient Israel,* edited by Peggy L. Day, 142–60." Minneapolis: Fortress, 1989.
Newsom, Carol A., and Sharon H. Ringe, eds. *The Women's Bible Commentary.* Louisville: Westminster John Knox, 1992.
Nielsen, Kirsten. *Ruth: A Commentary.* OTL. Louisville: Westminster John Knox, 1997.
Nissinen, Martti. *Homoeroticism in the Biblical World: A Historical Perspective.* Translated by Kirsi Stjerna. Minneapolis: Fortress, 1998.
Noll, Mark A. "A Brief History of Inerrancy, Mostly in America." In *The Proceedings of the Conference on Biblical Inerrancy, 1987,* 9–25. Nashville: Broadman, 1987.
―――. "Evangelicals and the Study of the Bible." In *Evangelicalism and Modern America,* edited by George Marsden, 103–121. Grand Rapids: Eerdmans, 1984.
Noth, Martin. *Leviticus.* Translated by J. E. Anderson. OTL. Philadelphia: Westminster, 1965.
O'Connor, Kathleen M. "Wisdom Literature and Experience of the Divine." In *Biblical Theology: Problems and Perspectives: In Honor of J. Christiaan Beker,* edited by Steven J. Kraftchick et al, 183–95, 320–22. Nashville: Abingdon, 1995.
Oden, Robert A., Jr. "Religious Identity and the Sacred Prostitution Accusation." In *The Bible without Theology: The Theological Tradition and Alternatives to It,* 131–53. New Voices in Biblical Studies. San Francisco: Harper & Row, 1987.
Ollenburger, Ben C. "Biblical Theology: Situating the Discipline." In *Understanding the Word: Essays in Honor of Bernard W. Anderson,* edited by James T. Butler et al., 37–62. JSOTSup 37. Sheffield: JSOT Press, 1985.
―――, ed. *Old Testament Theology: Flowering and Future.* Rev. ed. Sources for Biblical and Theological Study 1. Winona Lake, IN: Eisenbrauns, 2004.
Ollenburger, Ben C., et al., eds. *The Flowering of Old Testament Theology: A Reader in Twentieth-Century Old Testament Theology, 1930–1990.* Sources for Biblical and Theological Study 1. Winona Lake, IN: Eisenbrauns, 1992.
Osiek, Carolyn. "The Feminist and the Bible: Hermeneutical Alternatives." In *Feminist Perspectives on Biblical Scholarship,* edited by Adela Yarbro Collins, 93–106. SBLBSNA 10. Chico, CA: Scholars, 1985.

Penchansky, David, and Paul L. Redditt, eds. *Shall Not the Judge of All the Earth Do What Is Right? Studies on the Nature of God in Tribute to James L. Crenshaw*. Winona Lake, IN: Eisenbrauns, 2000.

Perdue, Leo G., ed. *The Blackwell Companion to the Hebrew Bible*. Blackwell Companions to Religion 3. Oxford: Blackwell, 2001.

———. *Wisdom & Creation: The Theology of Wisdom Literature*. Nashville: Abingdon, 1994.

Pressler, Carolyn. *Joshua, Judges, and Ruth*. WBC. Louisville: Westminster John Knox, 2002.

Rad, Gerhard von. *Old Testament Theology*. 2 vols. Translated by D. M. G. Stalker. New York: Harper, 1962-1965.

Reid, J. K. S. *The Authority of Scripture: A Study of Reformation and Post-Reformation Understanding of the Bible*. London: Methuen, 1957.

Rendtorff, Rolf. "Approaches to Old Testament Theology." In *Problems in Biblical Theology: Essays in Honor of Rolf Knierim*, edited by Henry T. C. Sun and Keith L. Eades, 13-26. 1997. Reprinted, Eugene, OR: Wipf & Stock, 2011.

———. "Must 'Biblical Theology' Be Christian Theology?" *BRev* 4 (1988) 40-43.

Renger, Johannes. "Heilige Hochzeit. A. Philologisch." *RLA* 4:251-59.

Reventlow, Henning Graf. "Modern Approaches to Old Testament Theology." In *The Blackwell Companion to the Hebrew Bible*, edited by Leo G. Perdue, 221-40. Blackwell Companions to Religion 3. Oxford: Blackwell, 2001.

Rogers, Jack B., and Donald K. McKim. *The Authority of the Bible: An Historical Approach*. 1979. Reprint, Eugene, OR: Wipf & Stock, 1999.

Russell, Letty M., ed. *Feminist Interpretation of the Bible*. Philadelphia: Westminster, 1985.

———. *Household of Freedom: Authority in Feminist Theology*. The 1986 Annie Kinkead Warfield Lectures. Philadelphia: Westminster, 1987.

Sakenfeld, Katharine Doob. "Feminist Biblical Interpretation." *ThTo* 46 (1989) 154-68.

———. "Feminist Perspectives on Bible and Theology: An Introduction to Selected Issues and Literature." *Int* 42 (1988) 5-18.

———. *The Meaning of Ḥesed in the Hebrew Bible: A New Inquiry*. HSM 17. Missoula: Scholars, 1978.

———. "The Problem of Divine Forgiveness in Numbers 14." *CBQ* 37 (1975) 317-30.

Sanders, James A. *From Sacred Story to Sacred Text: Canon as Paradigm*. 1987. Reprinted, Eugene, OR: Wipf & Stock, 2000.

———. "Hermeneutic in True and False Prophecy." In *Canon and Authority: Essays in Old Testament Religion and Theology*, edited by George W. Coats and Burke O. Long, 21-41. Philadelphia: Fortress, 1977.

———. *Torah and Canon*. Philadelphia: Fortress, 1972.

Saunders, Ernest W. *Searching the Scriptures: A History of the Society of Biblical Literature, 1880-1980*. SBLBSNA 10. Chico, CA: Scholars, 1982.

Schottroff, Luise et al., eds. *Feminist Interpretation: The Bible in Women's Perspective*. Translated by Martin Rumscheidt and Barbara Rumscheidt. Minneapolis: Fortress, 1998.

———. *Feministische Exegese: Forschungserträge zur Bibel aus der Perspektive von Frauen*. Darmstadt: Wissenschaftliche Buchgesellschaft, 1995.

Schottroff, Luise, and Marie-Theres Wacker, eds. *Kompendium Feministische Bibelauslegung*. 2nd ed. Gütersloh: Gütersloher Verlagshaus, 1999.

Schroeder, H. J., trans. *Canons and Decrees of the Council of Trent*. London: Herder, 1941.
Schroer, Silvia. "Die Göttin auf der Stempelsiegeln aus Palästina/Israel." In *Studien zu den Stempelsiegeln aus Palästina/Israel*, edited by Othmar Keel et al., 2:89–207. 4 vols. OBO 88. Göttingen: Vandenhoeck & Ruprecht, 1989. [KC: check book title]
Schüssler Fiorenza, Elisabeth. *Rhetoric and Ethics: The Politics of Biblical Studies*. Minneapolis: Fortress, 1999.
———, ed. *Searching the Scriptures*. Vol. 1, *A Feminist Introduction*. 2 vols. New York: Crossroad, 1993.
Seitz, Christopher. "Sexuality and Scripture's Plain Sense: The Christian Community and the Law of God." In *Homosexuality, Science, and the "Plain Sense" of Scripture*, edited by David L. Balch, 177–96. 2000. Reprinted, Eugene, OR: Wipf & Stock, 2011.
Seow, Choon-Leong. "A Heterotextual Perspective." In *Homosexuality and Christian Community*, edited by Choon-Leong Seow, 14–27. Louisville: Westminster John Knox, 1996.
Sheppard, Gerald T. "Biblical Hermeneutics: The Academic Language of Evangelical Identity." *USQR* 32 (1977) 81–94.
———. "True and False Prophecy within Scripture." In *Canon, Theology, and Old Testament Interpretation: Essays in Honor of Brevard S. Childs*, edited by Gene M. Tucker et al., 262–82. Philadelphia: Fortress, 1988.
———. "The Use of Scripture within the Christian Ethical Debate concerning Same-Sex Oriented Persons." *USQR* 40/1–2 (1985) 13–35.
Shires, Henry M. *Finding the Old Testament in the New*. Philadelphia: Westminster, 1974.
Smith, Mark S. *The Early History of God: Yahweh and the Other Deities in Ancient Israel*. 2nd ed., Grand Rapids: Eerdmans, 2002.
———. *The Origins of Biblical Monotheism: Israel's Polytheistic Background and the Ugaritic Texts*. Oxford: Oxford University Press, 2001.
Smith, Richard F. "Inspiration and Inerrancy." In *The Jerome Biblical Commentary*, edited by Raymond E. Brown et al, 499–514. 2 vols in 1. Englewood Cliffs, NJ: Prentice-Hall, 1968.
Soden, Wolfram von. "Zur Stellung des 'Geweihten' (*qdš*) in Ugarit." *UF* 2 (1970) 329–30.
Stager, Lawrence E. "Why Were Hundreds of Dogs Buried at Ashkelon?" In *Ashkelon Discovered: From Canaanites and Philistines to Romans and Moslems*, 26–42. Washington, DC: Biblical Archaeology Society, 1991.
Sun, Henry T. C., and Keith L. Eades, eds. *Problems in Biblical Theology: Essays in Honor of Rolf Knierim*. 1997. Reprinted, Eugene, OR: Wipf & Stock, 2011.
Sundberg, Albert C. "The Bible Canon and the Christian Doctrine of Inspiration." *Int* 29 (1975) 352–71.
Sweeney, Marvin A. "Tanak versus Old Testament: Concerning the Foundation for a Jewish Theology of the Bible." In *Problems in Biblical Theology: Essays in Honor of Rolf Knierim*, edited by Henry T. C. Sun and Keith L. Eades, 353–72. 1997. Reprinted, Eugene, OR: Wipf & Stock, 2011.
Sykes, J. B., ed. *Concise Oxford Dictionary of Current English*. 6th ed. Oxford: Clarendon, 1976.

Tavard, George H. *Holy Writ or Holy Church: The Crisis of the Protestant Reformation.* New York: Harper & Brothers, 1959.

Tolbert, Mary Ann, ed. *The Bible and Feminist Hermeneutics. Semeia* 28. Chico, CA: Scholars, 1983.

———. "Defining the Problem: The Bible and Feminist Hermeneutics." In *The Bible and Feminist Hermeneutics,* edited by Mary Ann Tolbert, 113–26. *Semeia* 28. Chico, CA: Scholars, 1983.

———. "Protestant Feminists and the Bible: On the Horns of a Dilemma." In *The Pleasure of Her Text: Feminist Readings of Biblical & Historical Texts,* edited by Alice Bach, 5–23. Philadelphia: Trinity, 1990.

Toorn, Karel van der. "Cultic Prostitution." In *ABD* 5:510–13.

———. "Female Prostitution in Payment of Vows in Ancient Israel." *JBL* 108 (1989) 193–205.

Trible, Phyllis. "Depatriarchalizing in Biblical Interpretation." *JAAR* 12 (1973) 30–48.

———. "Feminist Hermeneutics and Biblical Theology." In *The Flowering of Old Testament Theology: A Reader in Twentieth-Century Old Testament Theology, 1930–1990,* edited by Ben C. Ollenburger, 448–64. Sources for Biblical and Theological Study 1. Winona Lake, IN: Eisenbrauns, 1992.

———. "Five Loaves and Two Fishes: Feminist Hermeneutics and Biblical Theology." *TS* 50 (1989) 279–95.

———. *God and the Rhetoric of Sexuality.* OBT 2. Philadelphia: Fortress, 1978.

———. *Texts of Terror: Literary-Feminist Readings of Biblical Narratives.* OBT 13. Philadelphia: Fortress, 1984.

———. "Treasures Old and New: Biblical Theology and the Challenge of Feminism." In *The Open Text: New Directions for Biblical Studies?,* edited by Francis Watson, 32–56. London: SCM, 1993.

Tsevat, Matitiahu. "Theology of the Old Testament—a Jewish View." *HBT* 8 (1986) 33–50.

United Church of Canada, Theology and Faith Committee. *The Authority and Interpretation of Scripture: A Study Document.* Toronto: United Church Publishing House, 1989.

United Methodist Church. *The Book of Discipline of the United Methodist Church.* Nashville: United Methodist Publishing House, 1988.

Wacker, Marie-Theres. "Feministisch-theologische Blicke auf die neuere Monotheismus-Diskussion." In *Der eine Gott und die Göttin: Gottesvorstellungen des biblischen Israel im Horizont feministischer Theologie,* edited by Marie-Theres Wacker and Erich Zenger, 17–48. QD 135. Freiburg: Herder, 1991.

———. "Kosmisches Sakrament oder Verpfändung des Körpers? 'Kult Prostitution' im biblischen Israel und in hinduistischen Indien: Religionsgeschichtliche Überlegungen im Interesse feministischer Theologie." *BN* 61 (1992) 51–75.

Weems, Renita J. *Battered Love: Marriage, Sex, and Violence in the Hebrew Prophets.* OBT. Minneapolis: Fortress, 1995.

Welker, Michael. "Biblische Theologie: II. Fundamentaltheologisch." In *RGG,* 1:1549–53.

Westermann, Claus. *Genesis 1–11: A Commentary.* Translated by John J. Scullion. CC. Minneapolis: Augsburg, 1984.

Whitaker, Richard E. "Creation and Human Sexuality." In *Homosexuality and Christian Community,* edited by Choon-Leong Seow, 3–13. Louisville: Westminster John Knox, 1996.

Wilhelm, Gernot. "Marginalien zu Herodot Klio 199." In *Lingering over Words: Studies in Ancient Near Eastern Literature in Honor of William L. Moran*, edited by Tzvi Abusch et al., 505–24. HSS 37. Atlanta: Scholars, 1990.
Wills, Garry. *Under God: Religion and American Politics*. New York: Simon & Schuster, 1990.
Woodbridge, John D. *Biblical Authority: A Critique of the Rogers/McKim Proposal*. Grand Rapids: Zondervan, 1982.

www.ingramcontent.com/pod-product-compliance
Lightning Source LLC
Chambersburg PA
CBHW020850160426
43192CB00007B/857